The New Manual of WORSHIP

Nancy E. Hall

JUDSON PRESS
PUBLISHERS SINCE 1824
VALLEY FORGE, PA

The New Manual of Worship
© 2018 by Judson Press, Valley Forge, PA 19482-0851. All rights reserved.

Unless otherwise indicated, Bible quotations in this volume are quoted or adapted from the New Revised Standard Version Bible, copyright © 1989, Division of Christian Education of the National Council of the Churches of Christ in the United States of America. Used by permission. All rights reserved.

Other Scriptures are quoted or adapted from the Common English Bible (CEB), © 2011 Common English Bible. Used by permission. All rights reserved. / Contemporary English Version (CEV), © 1991, 1992, 1995 by American Bible Society. Used by permission. / The Holy Bible, English Standard Version (ESV), © 2001 by Crossway Bibles, a publishing ministry of Good News Publishers. / Good News Bible (GNT), the Bible in Today's English Version. Copyright © American Bible Society, 1976. Used by permission. / The Holy Bible, King James Version (KJV). / The Living Bible (TLB), The Living Bible copyright © 1971 by Tyndale House Foundation. Used by permission of Tyndale House Publishers Inc., Carol Stream, Illinois 60188. All rights reserved. / The Message. Copyright © 1993, 1994, 1995. Used by permission of NavPress Publishing Group. / The Holy Bible, New International Version®, NIV®, copyright © 1973, 1978, 1984, 2011 by Biblica Inc. Used by permission. All rights reserved worldwide. / The Voice Bible, Copyright © 2012 Thomas Nelson, Inc. The Voice™ translation © 2012 Ecclesia Bible Society. All rights reserved.

Bible passages that have been adapted for liturgical use may differ from the sources listed.

The Lord's Prayer from A *New Zealand Prayer Book – He Karakia Mihinare o Aotearoa* used by permission of the Anglican Church in Aotearoa, New Zealand, and Polynesia, Michael Hughes, General Secretary.

Interior design by Crystal Devine.
Cover design by Danny Ellison.

Library of Congress Cataloging-in-Publication data

Names: Hall, Nancy E. (Nancy Elizabeth), 1951- author. | Skoglund, John E.
    Manual of worship.
Title: The new manual of worship / Nancy E. Hall.
Description: first [edition]. | Valley Forge : Judson Press, 2018. | Previous
    two editions: A manual of worship / John E. Skoglund. Nancy E. Hall
    co-authored 2nd edition.
Identifiers: LCCN 2017025706 (print) | LCCN 2017032378 (ebook) | ISBN
    9780817081836 (ebook) | ISBN 9780817017927 (pbk. : alk. paper)
Subjects: LCSH: Public worship--Handbooks, manuals, etc. | Free
    churches--Liturgy--Texts. | Worship programs.
Classification: LCC BV25 (ebook) | LCC BV25 .H35 2018 (print) | DDC
    264/.06--dc23
LC record available at https://lccn.loc.gov/2017025706

Printed in the U.S.A.
First printing, 2018.

To
John E. Skoglund and Robert H. Mitchell,
beloved mentors in worship and the arts,
and to my congregation,
First Baptist Church of Berkeley

Contents

Preface

IN 1965 JUDSON PRESS published John E. Skoglund's *Worship in the Free Churches*; as an American Baptist, Skoglund was one of his denomination's few scholars and practitioners researching, reflecting, teaching, and writing on the topic. Shortly after this significant work became available, Judson Press returned to Skoglund and asked if he could next prepare a "manual of worship" as a practical aid to Baptist and other free church pastors and worship planners. It would include full worship services, liturgical materials (prayers, responsive readings, litanies), and other resources, not only for regular Sunday worship but also for such special occasions as baptisms, weddings, and funerals. Worship materials for the seasons of the Christian year and other times and seasons in church life would be included as well.

That 1968 manual became an invaluable tool for ministers, students, and congregations. As a seminarian in the late 1970s, I not only used *A Manual of Worship* in both class and ministry assignments but had the privilege of studying with Dr. Skoglund at American Baptist Seminary of the West. Since I had little prior experience of Baptists or other free church traditions, his classes and the manual helped build a bridge between my Lutheran upbringing and the worship practices of my new denominational family. At a deeper level, I came to cherish the freedom to draw upon the best of both traditions.

In addition to studying with Dr. Skoglund, I benefited from the teaching and mentorship of Robert H. Mitchell, professor of worship and the arts. These two men possessed admirable patience toward a young woman who was full of enthusiasm and love for leading worship and music (the *how*), but needed theological knowledge and understanding (the *why*). I was therefore blessed to receive a thorough grounding in not only the arts of worship and music planning, but the history and theology of Christian worship and sacred song, from two generous teachers filled with passion for the worship of God.

About a decade after these experiences, the seminary called upon me to begin teaching courses in worship; not long after, Dr. Skoglund returned to Berkeley after teaching abroad, and in retirement served ABSW in a number of roles. For several years we co-taught the course "Worship in the Free Churches." It was during this time that Judson Press agreed that a new edition of *A Manual of Worship* was in order, and I was honored and delighted when Dr. Skoglund asked me to join him in a full revision. *A Manual of Worship: New Edition* appeared in 1993, twenty-five years after the original volume.

Another twenty-five years have swiftly passed. I've continued to teach courses in ministry, worship, and music at my alma mater, regularly assigning the 1993 edition as a textbook. Now I am once again privileged to bring this book into a new era. John E. Skoglund passed away in

2005, still vitally engaged with scholarship and praxis at ninety-three. For this third edition, the work of a full up-dating and re-envisioning is mine, but John is a welcome and essential presence throughout these pages still.

So I echo my teacher, mentor, and friend in saying: it is my hope that this volume will help to enrich the worship life of congregations, and will serve as a resource for pas-tors, churches, and students of worship for years to come.

NANCY E. HALL

Acknowledgments

A BOOK LIKE THIS ONE, drawing on centuries of Christian worship, naturally owes gratitude to many people, but I wish to offer thanks to those who have had a direct role in making this work possible.

I have already spoken of John E. Skoglund's pioneering research and writings about worship in the free church traditions. He was not only a gifted scholar and professor but also a dedicated missionary, pastor, theologian, and ecumenical leader. I have also mentioned Robert H. Mitchell, whose deepest commitment was to congregational song as the highest expression of praise to God—and indeed, to the understanding that all other worship music, though blest and important, is secondary to what comes from the lips and hearts of the people. It is the influence of these two mentors, in particular, that continues to guide my teaching and my ministry.

Many of my former students at American Baptist Seminary of the West, as well as a number of current ministry colleagues, have contributed materials to this volume. These prayers and other worship materials enhance this third edition immensely; my thanks to the authors for their creativity and love of liturgy.

Thank you to the many hymn writers whose texts I've included in this book. Special thanks to Hope Publishing Company and GIA Publications, Inc., for permission to reprint many of these texts. New words and music for congregational singing are being written every day, and I'm blessed beyond measure that hymnody continues to flourish across our continent and around the world. No one does more toward preserving and championing congregational song than The Hymn Society in the United States and Canada. You, cherished friends and colleagues, are my tribe.

To the team at Judson Press, particularly my editor, Rebecca Irwin-Diehl, and Lisa Blair, I am grateful for your encouragement, expertise, and patience toward bringing this third edition of *The Manual of Worship* into being. Thanks also to Brad Berglund, who graciously consented to my reprinting a number of prayers from his book, *Reinventing Worship*.

My beloved congregation, First Baptist Church of Berkeley, has been the source and seedbed for my worship and music ministry since 1984. Their love of liturgy and music, their open-hearted theology, adventurous spirit, and welcome to all have been a continuing joy and sustenance in my life and work all these years. It's been an honor to serve as your minister of music, and now, since 2009, as your pastor.

Finally, few people are fortunate enough to have an in-house editor and tireless supporter such as my spouse, Mark Theodoropoulos. Thank you. Your keen eye and loving counsel are present in every page of this book.

NANCY E. HALL

Introduction

CHRISTIAN PROTESTANT worship practices on the North American continent are ever-evolving, a constant work in progress. Sometimes that evolution has unfolded slowly, over decades or centuries, but in the twenty-first century the pace of change feels breathtaking. Perhaps it seemed so in earlier times too. Yet no one can deny that advances in the speed and nature of communications, and in how we access information, have greatly affected the majority of churches across the land, certainly since the 1993 edition of this book.

For those of us whose congregations faithfully gather once a week as part of Christ's body, our order of worship might still closely resemble what it once was; but it's more likely that the way we worship has undergone a series of changes over the decades. These have arisen from an increase or decrease in membership; shifting demographics in neighborhoods, towns, and cities; changes in the physical place of worship; new leadership and ideas from ministers and lay members; influences and trends in music, language, preaching, and theological convictions; and more.

What's distinctive about evolving worship and liturgy in Christian Protestant *free churches,* though, is that in most cases the changes are being proposed, considered, and implemented at the congregational level. A hallmark of free church traditions is the congregation's authority. Guided by the Holy Spirit, we order our life and worship as we see fit, for our specific time, place, and circumstances.

Nevertheless, basic and historic patterns of worship will be clearly evident in most churches' Sabbath day services. Even if the liturgy is simple in the extreme, prayer, singing, and proclamation of the word are sure to be found. These are expressed in countless ways, through the grace and power of the Holy Spirit.

Free Church Worship

"Free church" may raise a question mark for the reader; it's not a term we tend to use much today. A more descriptive term might be "non-liturgical church," but that's not entirely accurate either, for virtually every church has a liturgy of some kind. In the 1993 edition of this book, John E. Skoglund wrote:

> When the term *free church* is used in relation to worship, it means a church that does not have prescribed and required forms of worship. Some churches designated as free churches have liturgies that have been developed by the official body to which these congregations belong, but each remains free to use these worship forms, modify them, or ignore them. Included among the free churches are Adventists, Baptists, Congregationalists, Disciples of Christ, Mennonites, Methodists, Pentecostalists, Presbyterians and other Reformed groups, and many smaller Christian bodies.

Even though their worship is not bound by prescribed words and actions, the free churches claim that their worship embodies the same essential elements as the worship of the "liturgical" churches. For the free churches, as in all churches from apostolic times to the present, worship takes place primarily when a group of believers gather about the Lord's table to sing and pray, to hear the scriptures read and preached, to break bread and drink wine in remembrance of Christ's death until he comes, and to offer praise and thanksgiving.

Thus worship in the free churches has much in common with our sister and brother Christians in the Catholic, Orthodox, Episcopalian, Lutheran, African Methodist Episcopal churches, and other liturgical traditions; for all of us, worship is a *dialogue* between God and God's people.

But there are also significant divergences; the following are some of the distinctive characteristics of free church worship.

1. *Congregational responsibility for worship.* While it may accept recommendations regarding worship from a denominational body, the congregation itself has primary responsibility for its worship life. The members designate a responsible group—such as deacons or elders—to develop worship policy and practice. Carrying these out is generally left to the ministerial staff, often working with a lay worship committee.

Although each congregation is free to order and plan its worship as it sees fit, most churches build their services as a dialogue with God, and a response to God's gracious self-giving, by offering praise, thanksgiving, prayer for self and others, dedication of gifts, and commitment to God's service. We recognize that God has been made known in Jesus Christ, the Word, whose acts are brought to remembrance in the Gospel readings and in the interpretation of these readings through preaching. The Hebrew Scriptures, the Psalms, and the Epistles may be read and interpreted as well. All these elements, along with regular sharing of the bread and cup, provide the pattern and structure of Christian worship.

Congregational hymns and songs, choral anthems, and instrumental and vocal solos serve to enrich the service. Traditional and contemporary music bring the congregation into contact with the musical forms of the past as well as the musical expressions of the present.

2. *Lay leadership in worship.* Though the pastor usually presides over the service, members of the congregation may participate in reading scripture, offering prayers, leading litanies, and singing in a choir or ensemble. In some churches lay persons are encouraged to preach and administer Communion. The whole congregation joins in the singing of hymns and songs, in unison and responsive scripture readings, prayers, and litanies, and—in some congregations—simultaneous dialogue with the pastor during the sermon.

3. *Extemporaneous prayer.* Although many congregations use written prayers, free or extemporaneous prayer is also common. In some churches the only written or memorized prayer used in public worship is the Lord's Prayer; all other public prayers are created as they are spoken, under the guidance of the Holy Spirit. Nevertheless, careful preparation should still be made as to the topics covered and even the words to be used. Such is the case in the pastoral or altar

prayer, summing up the prayers of the people. While it is primarily for the voicing of petitions and intercessions, this prayer may also include elements of confession, thanksgiving, and praise. Lay persons, as well, can be called upon to offer prayer and to present the specific joys and concerns of the congregation. The prayers included in a manual of worship such as this one can be used in public worship, but they can also be a starting point for developing and enriching the art of extemporaneous prayer.

4. *Sacraments*. Baptism and the Lord's Supper are symbolic reenactments instituted by Christ. Free churches usually prefer to use the word *ordinance* instead of "sacrament" when referring to baptism and communion. Ordinances are practiced by the command of Jesus Christ (Matthew 26:26-30; 28:19). The preaching of the word is given high honor and place in worship, but not the status of a sacrament; marriage, memorial, and the laying on of hands for the sick are also important services of the church, though not considered sacraments. Most free churches observe the Lord's Supper monthly or quarterly, although some commune weekly, either as part of their tradition or because the congregation desires to share the bread and cup on every Sabbath day.

5. *Overall, a less elaborate order of worship.* Free church worship is genuine and heartfelt; at the same time it is also steeped in the history and tradition of several centuries. Ever since the time of the European reformations, the practice in many free church bodies has been to present a simpler form of worship than that of the Roman Catholic, Episcopal/Anglican, or Eastern Orthodox liturgies.

The free church pioneers did away with the elaborate rituals and ceremonies of the established churches of the time, and replaced them with services of Bible reading, preaching, psalm singing, prayer, and comparatively infrequent observance of the Lord's Supper. They built unadorned chapels and meeting houses for their congregational gatherings. While most free churches in more recent times gather in buildings less severely minimal, there still remains a strong theme of simplicity.

New in This Edition

Just as in previous editions, *The New Manual of Worship* provides materials for pastors, worship planners, and congregations to use when they are designing weekly services or other worship occasions in church life.

This edition represents a thorough revision and re-envisioning of the volume published in 1993. As before, care continues to be taken that the language used is gender inclusive for humanity and gender neutral for God. Although the majority of scriptural materials are taken or adapted from the New Revised Standard Version, a wider variety of other biblical translations and paraphrases have been included here, many of which were not available in 1993. Language is also consciously corporate in most cases, recognizing that when the family, the Body of Christ, gathers, it is an act of *communal* worship and dialogue with the Creator. "We," "us," and "ours" are important words for binding hearts as one people, in service and love toward God, one another, and the world.

In Part 1, the two examples of service orders are significantly revised and simplified. This is in recognition of how many congregations—though not all, of course—have developed weekly services that strive to be less formal and more understandable to members and guests alike as to "why we do what we do." The services in Part 1 are divided into fewer sections, with clear designations about what each part of worship represents.

In most instances, the language—whether spoken by clergy or congregation—is designed to be vivid and evocative, but it is also written with an ear toward current forms of speech and expression. The intent has been to create a sense of welcome and invitation throughout the service, as opposed to formality or rigidity. As in previous editions there is an emphasis on the Bible as the source for many of the readings. Responsive readings for leader and congregation are plentiful, both from scripture and other resources. Note that boldface type within the text of worship materials indicates congregational response; the notation "(*All:*)" invites the leader to join with the congregation in the final response.

A prominent feature beginning with Part 2 and continuing throughout is the inclusion of hymn and song suggestions. These lists represent a sample of congregational music that emphasizes and uplifts each part of Sabbath worship. Many of the hymns listed have been written in recent decades, some in just the last few years. These texts represent the thoughtful poetic work of living hymnists who strive to create words that reflect our common experiences as community and as globally minded people—the joy, lament, hope, and commitment we share toward doing justice and walking in godly pathways.

Reference is frequently made to www.hymnary.org. If this website is new to you, be prepared for an amazing and comprehensive resource for finding and using congregational music, by title, topic, scripture reference, tune, meter, and many other categories.

Part 3, "Scriptures, Prayers, and Readings for the Christian Year," has been significantly expanded, with several new sections and fresh worship materials throughout. Although this edition does not include a three-year set of lectionary readings, Part 3 relates well to the seasons and scripture readings found in the Revised Common Lectionary (RCL) used by many Protestant churches. An excellent source for accessing the complete RCL can be found at lectionary.library.vanderbilt.edu. Another superb resource for weekly worship planning is www.textweek.com. There you will find an abundance of links to every facet of creating worship services and preparing sermons centered on the RCL readings, including biblical research, commentary, liturgical materials, graphics, music, art, drama, children's worship, and more.

A number of new occasions and themes for worship are found in Part 4, such as Martin Luther King Jr. Day, African American History Month, Annual Meeting Sunday, Earth Day / Celebrating the Environment, Interfaith Worship, In Times of Crisis or Disaster, and others. In pastoral and community ministry we are confronted with an ever-increasing need to address events occurring in our cities, nation, and world. Some of these are joyous, some somber. Because of the explosion in new ways of communication in the last twenty-five years, this edition seeks to reflect the reality that congregations in worship are less isolated than ever before from what happens beyond their walls. What's important and relevant in the lives of our people—while not supplanting the foundations of Christian worship—needs to be included in our weekly and special times of gathering together as the Body of Christ.

Materials in Parts 5, 6, and 7—concerning life transitions, special occasions, and blessings—are updated, with several new services added. Also new are listings of additional books, websites, and other useful resources provided at the end of most chapters.

The final chapter, Part 8, is a brief consideration of the art of worship planning: how we can craft and carry out worship that is thoughtful, creative, and holistic. Finding the central theme for an arc or trajectory of worship, from beginning to end, is suggested as a starting point for creating services that can deepen, enrich, and expand the congregation's life together.

Who Is This Book For?

If you are called to help revise, renew, or revitalize your congregation's worship; or if you are faced for the first time with creating a service for an occasion for which you have no models; in short, if you seek resources to help make worship alive with congregational participation, and authentic without divorcing it from historical roots, this book has been written for you.

Above all, my hope is that this book helps us stay focused on why we gather as the Body of Christ. Mark Clinger, pastor of First Baptist Church, Madison, Wisconsin, writes:

Worship matters. Worship is one of the unique practices distinguishing a faith community from any other organization, institution, or corporation. Here we intentionally focus on God. Here we regain our bearings on life. Here we discover the unique person God means each of us to be. We may weep, tremble, rejoice, gain fresh resolve, hope again, lean our heads back in gratitude, and turn our lives toward tomorrow. Each of these experiences is so much greater than merely being entertained.

This speaks to the heart of what we must not allow to fade from our worship: the breadth and depth of our human condition and experience. Along with this, may our Sabbath time together bless us with glimpses of awe and glory such as the account found in 2 Chronicles 5:11-14:

All the priests who were present had sanctified themselves, regardless of their divisions. All the Levitical musicians were dressed in fine linen and stood east of the altar with cymbals, harps, and zithers, along with one hundred twenty priests blowing trumpets. The trumpeters and singers joined together to praise and thank the Lord as one. All together they began the song of praise:
Yes, God is good!
Yes, God's faithful love lasts forever!
Then a cloud filled the temple. The priests were unable to carry out their duties on account of the cloud, because the Lord's glory filled God's temple. (CEV, adapted)

PART 1

Worship Services for the Sabbath Day

If we keep God as the center of our worship life and worship-full lives, then we will find countless possibilities, endless resources, innumerable ways to encounter and express God's infinite presence.

—Marva J. Dawn, *A Royal "Waste" of Time*

IRST, WHY REFER to it as "the Sabbath day," when so few Protestant churches use the term these days? Since this manual is meant to be shared with ministers and congregations of many branches in the stream of Christian fellowship, we wish to recognize and honor those sisters and brothers who worship on Saturday as the Sabbath—or any other day. Use of the word *sabbath* also refers us to the source in Exodus 20:8-10:

Remember the sabbath day, and keep it holy.
Six days you shall labor and do all your work.
But the seventh day is a sabbath to the Lord your God;
you shall not do any work.

Second, this book covers a wide variety of worship occasions, as will be seen in upcoming chapters; Part 1 focuses on the main weekly occasion when the church community gathers, anticipating the ongoing work of the people in a familiar form.

These services and materials are intended simply as guides. They have been developed in accordance with historic forms of worship in the free churches, but are by no means comprehensive. The goal for the services shown here is to present two basic orders of worship that congregations can change, expand, or further simplify, according to their needs and desires. That no two congregations worship exactly alike is a wonderful fact of our Christian life—especially so in the free church tradition. Some share in Communion, the Lord's Supper, every week; others include the Table once a month or less frequently. Some churches' worship services are elaborate, others spare; some the height of formality, others casual and improvised; much depends on the congregation's customs as they have developed over the years.

What's shown in Part 1 are examples that await the work of a worship committee, ministry staff, and congregation: adding their own themes, hymns and songs, scripture lessons, and spoken materials each week, in order that the congregation's sacred time together be vital, lively, creative, and affirming of God's gifts to the people, the church, and the world. Further possibilities for the various elements of the services are given in Part 2, along with suggested additional resources to consult, all of which expand the options and opportunities for making worship fresh and vibrant—anticipated by all of God's people as the high point of their week.

Patterns of Worship: Style and Structure

The majority of established congregations have been practicing their form of Sabbath worship for decades or longer. For many, the terms "high church" and "low church" are familiar markers along the continuum from the elaborate to the simple, and from formal to casual. But these terms can be off-putting, to say the least. Churches seeking to identify their customary style of worship have sometimes used words such as "classic," "historic," or "contemporary"; but whatever the terms, a church seeking significant change to its established order of worship is much more likely to start a second service in a different worship style than to attempt substantial renovations to its longstanding practice.

The 1968 and 1993 editions of *A Manual of Worship* included a Service for the Lord's Day of a type that now seems to be practiced by only a very few US churches of the non-liturgical tradition; it therefore no longer appears here. Even in Catholic, Episcopalian, Lutheran, and other historically liturgical denominations, some congregations have eliminated or simplified parts or moments in worship regarded as too elaborate for twenty-first-century churchgoers. Such changes, for good or ill, can be (and have been) endlessly debated.

Rather than choosing sides in these debates, this manual proposes a middle way. Can we continue to treasure and employ historic practices in worship, recognizing these not only as sacred tradition but also as a vital, life-giving art form? At the same time, can we, as worship planners, musicians, pastors, and congregations, stay alert and aware of how crucial it is that all who participate understand *why* we do what we do, as opposed to the default "we've always done it this way"? And can we strive to be open to changes and innovations that are not mere trends or gimmicks—that deepen, broaden, and engage our people, while taking into account their diversity, and the diversity of words, music, and ceremonies that speak to them? It is essential that as ministers and worship planners we not only cultivate openness ourselves, but find ways to nurture it in our people, as together we grow in our faith and our fellowship.

In a lifetime of worship, both in liturgical and non-liturgical settings, this author has seen convincing evidence of the spiritual and emotional benefits that flow from attendance at weekly worship, for those who embrace it as a distinct and set-apart time to experience the holy. Ritual—if we in the free churches are willing to use the term in spite of historical reservations—can be a lifeline; indeed, regular participation in a worshiping community can quite literally be a lifesaver. It behooves us, then, to plan our worship with care, taking a holistic view both of our current church family as it is here and now, and of our church family's history.

Granted, this is no easy task. Consider the service outlines, worship materials, and other resources in Part 1 as only a guide. Let these start the conversation and fire the imagination for creating worship that inspires our people; worship that offers thoughtfully planned experiences for uniting with God and with each other; that through words and music, expressing both joy and lament, through both inner stillness and outward praise, employing heart, mind, and spirit to the fullest, we honor the Sabbath day and keep it holy.

Turning from the style to the structure of worship, the focus should be upon *dialogue* and *prayer*. As John Skoglund wrote in the 1993 edition,

> In Christian worship we respond from the depths of our being to God's mighty acts, particularly to the act of love, forgiveness, and reconciliation in Jesus Christ. Thus worship is a dialogue between God and God's people. God, who has been made known in Jesus Christ and whose acts are brought to remembrance in the reading of the scriptures, in the preaching, and in the administration of the sacraments, comes to the faithful believer in worship as a living presence by the power of the Holy Spirit. The worshiper in turn responds to God's gracious self-giving by offering adoration, praise, thanksgiving, confession of sin, petition for God's presence, dedication of gifts and self to God's service, and prayer for others. It is this self-giving of God and the human response through prayer and action that provides the pattern of Christian worship.
>
> These responsive elements of worship can readily be recognized as the various types of prayer. In the service of worship they need not be put together in one long pastoral prayer, but can become the responsive parts of the total worship service.

The worship service, therefore, becomes common prayer, both a dialogue between God and God's people, and a dialogue between the worship leaders and the congregation. In this light we now recommend a simpler structure for worship than that in previous editions, while keeping intact the overall historic design:

We Open Our Hearts for Worship	Words of Welcome / Call to Worship Invocation / Prayer of God's Presence [Prayer of Confession and Words of Assurance]
We Hear and Proclaim God's Story	Scripture Lessons Prayer for Illumination Sermon / Message
We Offer Our Joys, Laments, and Thanks	Invitation to Prayer Prayers of the People / Pastoral Prayer Invitation to Offering Prayer of Dedication [Invitation to Communion and Words of Institution] [Sharing Bread and Cup] [Prayer of Thanksgiving]
We Go Out Praising God	Blessing/Benediction Passing the Peace

What unifies the above worship order, and, indeed, the historic order of Christian worship on the whole? It's all about prayer. Prayer is how we communicate with our Creator; that dialogue takes many forms. We express our adoration toward God the Eternal. We call upon God to bring a visible presence into our midst. We take a moment to be mindful of our sins and shortcomings. We ask that the word of God become a living light to our minds and hearts. We lift up our appeals to the Holy One on behalf of ourselves and others. We dedicate the gifts of our substance and our selves to God's good work. We recommit ourselves to living in the light of God and receive a final blessing before resuming our lives outside the sanctuary of worship.

Our Sabbath worship, then, is woven together with prayer. Many of us associate prayer only with quiet, stillness, and bowed heads. Surely this is but one manner in which we approach God with our joys and sorrows; the ways to communicate with God are boundless. For instance, many Korean congregations pray in what is called *Tongsung Kido*, "praying aloud"; the power and vitality of all voices raised in a tumult of individual prayers is awesome to experience. And of course, prayer does not have to take place only in a communal setting. We pray throughout the week—anywhere and at any time it occurs to us to speak with God, whether in praise, supplication, thanksgiving, or even anger.

Sabbath worship that is consciously planned and woven together with prayer encourages our congregations to recognize that there is no single "approved" way to talk with God. Emphasizing that worship is dialogue and prayer supports our people in opening up to the Holy One more often in daily life, at all times and in all places.

In summary, churches that are not clearly bound by a Sabbath liturgy specific to their denomination are free to order their worship life as they see fit. But as the Body of Christ and as people who love and desire to serve God, let us be *mindful* of the way we worship. The Service of Word and Table is an ongoing dialogue between God and God's people. As it has for centuries, it brings form and harmony to the Sabbath day, blessing and undergirding the lives of our sisters and brothers as they go out to face a complex and challenging world.

WORSHIP ON THE SABBATH DAY – I

A sample service, with optional sharing of the Lord's Supper

We Open Our Hearts for Worship

Music for Gathering

Words of Welcome / Call to Worship

Praise God! Blessed be the name of God from this time on and forevermore. From the rising of the sun to its setting the name of the Holy One is to be praised.
This is the day that God has made; let us rejoice and be glad in it.   —Psalm 113:1-3; Psalm 118:24

Hymn or Song of Praise

Invocation / Prayer of God's Presence

Gracious God, Creator and Ruler of the world, we come today with humility and gratitude as we gather in your presence. Inspire, refresh, and revive us, that we may truly worship you with songs and prayers; with words and deeds. In Christ's name, we pray. **Amen.**

[Prayer of Confession and Words of Assurance, if included]

People: **If we say that we have no sin, we deceive ourselves, and the truth is not in us; but if we confess our sins, God**

is faithful and just to forgive us, and cleanse us from all wrongdoing. (*Offer silent prayers of confession*)

Leader: Now the message that we have heard from Jesus Christ and announce is this: God is light, and there are no shadows in the realm of God. If we live in the light—just as God is in the light—then we have fellowship with one another, and the lifeblood of Christ washes us clean from every sin. —From 1 John 1

Psalm Reading of the Day

We Hear and Proclaim God's Story

Scripture Lessons

Hebrew Scripture, Epistle, or Gospel can be read, depending on which text or texts the preacher will address.

Hymn or Song (relating to the lessons)

Prayer for Illumination

(*All:*) **O God, may the word that is read and spoken become through us a liberating word to all who are in bondage and who long for freedom. Open our hearts to hear your call for justice and to answer it with our prayers and our actions. Amen.**

Sermon/Message

Hymn or Song (reflecting upon and emphasizing the preached word)

We Offer Our Joys, Laments, and Thanks

Invitation to Prayer

God is our light and our salvation; whom shall we fear? God is the strength of our lives; of whom shall we be afraid? The Eternal One shelters us in the day of trouble, keeping us safe and secure. Hear us, O God, when we call to you. Show us your loving mercy and respond to our prayers.   —Based on Psalm 27

Sharing of Joys and Concerns

Hymn or Song of Prayer

Prayers of the People / Pastoral Prayer (for ourselves and for others, in praise and lament)

Merciful God, who has promised that through Christ Jesus nothing can separate us from your love, be with us today as we come to you with our needs and desires. If we are in mourning, comfort us. If we are sick, restore us to health; if we are despairing, encourage us; if are overwhelmed, give us strength and calm. If we are in the midst of joy and celebration, rejoice with us and remind us to have hearts of gratitude. We bring before you today, as well, those whom we name according to their particular needs *(specific names and requests may be inserted here)*. May the full measure of your love and grace be evident to them, along with our outreach to them through prayer. May each and all of us be uplifted now by the power of your Holy Spirit as ministers and ambassadors of Jesus Christ, as the hands and feet and hearts of compassion and love in our community and in the world. Amen.

[*The Lord's Prayer*]

And now, to gather all our requests, let us pray the prayer that Jesus has taught us:
Our Father, who art in heaven . . .

Invitation to Offering

From the heart bring forth incense of praise, from the store of a good conscience bring forth the sacrifice of faith, and whatsoever you bring forth kindle it with love. These are the most acceptable offerings to God: mercy, humility, confession, peace, love. It is you that God seeks more than any gift. —Augustine of Hippo (354–430)

Receiving of Offerings, Pledges, and Tithes (with a musical offertory)

Hymn or Song of Dedication (or Doxology)

Prayer of Dedication

(*All:*) **As a sign of our thankfulness we bring these gifts to you. Use them for the renewal of your creation, and use us as your ministers of compassion and grace. Through Christ, we pray. Amen.**

Gathering at Christ's Table
(when the Lord's Supper is included)

Invitation to Communion

O taste and see the goodness of God; happy are those who
  dwell in the Holy One.
Hold God in awe, you faithful ones, for those who worship
  God will want for nothing.   —Psalm 34:8-9

Words of Institution

Hear these words as written by Paul the apostle: "For I
received from the Lord what I also handed on to you, that
Jesus on the night when he was betrayed took a loaf of
bread, and when he had given thanks, he broke it and said,
'This is my body that is given for you. Do this in remembrance of me.' In the same way he took the cup also, after
supper, saying, 'This cup is the new covenant in my blood.
As often as you drink this, do it in remembrance of me.'
For whenever you eat this bread and drink the cup, you
proclaim the Lord's death until he comes again."

                                      —1 Corinthians 11:23-26

Prayer of Thanksgiving for the Meal
(before or after the elements are shared)

As each of us is able, we offer thanks to you, O God, for
  Jesus Christ. We thank you for his life and ministry, for
  his sacrificial death on the cross, and for his resurrection
  and the promise he gives to all who trust in him, that
  they too shall share in new life.

To Christ be honor and glory, now and forever.

Through the breaking and eating of the bread and the drinking of the cup help us to remember Jesus Christ, his words and his works. Consecrate by your Spirit these symbols, that they may become a vital encounter with the living Christ.

Accept our offering of praise and thanksgiving, O God, and receive us as we dedicate ourselves anew to you. Amen.

Sharing Bread and Cup

We Go Out Praising God

Hymn or Song of Invitation, Commitment, or Blessing

(Those who wish to join with the congregation may come forward and be greeted by the pastor.)

Blessing/Benediction

Go forth in joy. Love and serve one another. Be a faithful witness to God in the world and live in such a way that the gracious Spirit of Christ may be with you in all that you do and say. **Amen.**

Passing the Peace

May the peace of Christ be with you always.
And also with you.
Please share signs of love and peace with your church family.

Music for Departing

WORSHIP ON THE SABBATH DAY – II
PRAISE AND PRAYER

A sample service, with optional sharing of the Lord's Supper

This service is designed so that a printed order of worship may be used or not. It's a less detailed style of liturgy and one that many congregations use—a worship structure that highlights prayer, through sung and spoken word, as a dialogue with God.

Gathering

Songs and Hymns of Praise

A period of ten to fifteen minutes of congregational singing, led by church musicians, provides a welcome and beginning to the Sabbath worship.

Greeting

The pastor or worship leader offers a greeting in the name of God to those present.

This is the day that God has made. Let us rejoice and be glad! We have come before the Holy One with singing and are ready to receive the Holy Spirit in our hearts and in this place of worship. Please pray with me:

Eternal One, we come before you this day as part of the human family. Inspire us, O God; open our hearts. We come in our diversity to catch your vision of unity. Inspire us, O God; open our eyes. We come to hear your challenging word of truth. Inspire us, O God, open our ears. We come to thank you for your gifts of beauty, joy, and hope. O God of love, vision, and truth, we praise your blessed name. **Amen.**

The Work and Witness of Our Church Family

At this point, announcements may be made concerning church life. This may also be a good time for a testimony from a member or guest, or for a special presentation.

Offerings

Song or Hymn of Prayer

In preparation for a time of congregational prayer, a quieter and more reflective piece of music may be shared by the musicians or sung by the congregation.

Sharing of Joys and Concerns, Pastoral Prayer

Those prayer requests known to the pastor and church leaders may be shared with the congregation. If the gathering is small and can accommodate spoken prayer requests from the people, this is the time for such sharing.

Offering

The people prepare to present their offerings. The collection of gifts is preceded by an invitation to give of our money and our selves.

How does God's love abide in anyone who has the world's goods and sees a brother or sister in need and yet refuses help? Let us love, not in word or speech, but in truth and action.   —1 John 3:17-18

As the offerings are brought forward, a song or hymn of dedication may be sung, or a doxology. A lay person or minister leads the dedication prayer.

Loving God, giver of every good and perfect gift, in gratitude we give these offerings to you and with them, we consecrate ourselves to your service. Use us and that which we have given for your work in the world, that both gift and giver may be a blessing to those who receive. **Amen.**

[*The Lord's Supper may be included here*]

Sharing God's Word

Preparing to Hear the Word

A time of congregational singing invigorates the people for the scripture reading(s) ahead.

Reading of Scripture Lesson(s)

A lay person, one of the ministry staff, or the preacher reads the Bible passages on which the message will be based.

Prayer of the Preacher and Congregation

Preacher: May the words of my mouth,
Congregation: **and the meditations of our hearts be acceptable to you, our strength and our redeemer. Amen.**

Sermon/Message

Departing to Serve

Song or Hymn of Invitation and Blessing

The preacher invites those who wish to make a decision to accept Christ into their hearts (or to seek church membership, or for a special prayer or blessing) to come forward. The people rise and affirm the proclamation of God's word with a final song or set of songs.

Blessing

A blessing is given that sends the congregation out to love and serve God, and closes the service of worship.

The grace of the Lord Jesus Christ, and the love of God, and the communion of the Holy Spirit be with you all. **Amen.**

The people may also be invited to pass the peace of Christ or greet their neighbors.

Closing instrumental or vocal pieces by the musicians

Resources for Part 1

Calvin Institute of Christian Worship: www.worship.calvin.edu/

Christian Resource Institute: www.crivoice.org/lowhighchurch.html

Dawn, Marva J. *Keeping the Sabbath Wholly*. Grand Rapids, MI: Eerdmans, 1989.

———. *A Royal "Waste" of Time: The Splendor of Worshiping God and Being Church of the World*. Grand Rapids, MI: Eerdmans, 1999.

www.engageworship.org

www.ministrymatters.com/worship/

United Church of Christ: www.ucc.org/worship_worship-ways

White, James F. *Introduction to Christian Worship*. 3rd ed. Nashville: Abingdon, 2001.

Willimon, William H. *Word, Water, Wine and Bread: How Worship Has Changed Over the Years*. Valley Forge, PA: Judson Press, 1980.

PART 2

Further Resources for Sabbath Worship

*Worship forms us to live as disciples of
Jesus Christ, here and now.
In worship, God calls us into disciple-forming dialogue,
a living and continuing conversation.
In worship we experience God's welcome, grace, and love.*

—John G. Stevens and Michael Waschevski,
Rhythms of Worship

THESE RESOURCES FOLLOW the basic outline found in Part 1, "Worship Services for the Sabbath Day." This part gives worship planners a variety of possibilities for liturgical materials in weekly worship. Some prayers are for a single voice; others are shown as responsive readings for leader and congregation. Lists of suggested hymns and songs are found at the end of each section. Additional materials (versions of the Lord's Prayer, doxologies, and psalms for use in Sabbath worship) are included at the end of Part 2.

MINISTRY OF THE WORD

We Open Our Hearts for Worship

Call to Worship

The purpose of a call to worship is to draw together the hearts, minds, and spirits of the congregation to this time and place, when we gather to worship God as a community. It is not necessarily a prayer but a spoken signal—warm, positive, and uplifting—as we seek to create an atmosphere of trust and anticipation for all present. Prior to the call to worship, brief words of welcome to the congregation may be shared.

Scriptures

Give thanks and call upon God's name, make known God's deeds among the peoples. Sing praises, tell of all God's wonderful works. Blessed are you, Holy One, forever and ever. Yours are the greatness, the power, the glory, the victory, and the majesty, for all that is in the heavens and on the earth is yours; you are exalted above all.

—1 Chronicles 16:8-9; 29:10-11

O magnify the Lord with me,
    and let us praise God's name together.
Hallelujah! For our God the Almighty One reigns.
    Let us rejoice and give to God the glory.

—Psalm 34:3; Revelation 19:6-7

It is good to give thanks to God,
    to sing praises to your name, O Most High;
to declare your steadfast love in the morning,
    and your faithfulness by night,
to the music of the lute and the harp,
    to the melody of the lyre.
For you, O God, have made me glad by your work;
    at the works of your hands I sing for joy.   —Psalm 92:1-4

Sing to God a new song; sing to God, all the earth.
Sing and bless God's name;
    tell of salvation from day to day.
Declare God's glory among the nations,
    and God's marvelous works among all the peoples.
For great is the Holy One, and greatly to be praised.

                                                    —Psalm 96:1-4

Praise God in this holy house of worship,
    and under the open skies;
Praise God for acts of power and for magnificent greatness;
Praise with a blast on the trumpet,
    praise by strumming soft strings;
Praise God with castanets and dance, with banjo and flute;
Praise with cymbals and a big bass drum,
    with fiddles and mandolin.
Let every living, breathing creature praise God! Hallelujah!
                        —Psalm 150 (*The Message*, adapted)

You are worthy, our God, to receive glory and honor and
power, for you created all things, and by your will they
existed and were created. Blessing and glory and wisdom

and thanksgiving and honor and power and might be to our God forever and ever!   —Revelation 4:11; 7:12

We praise you, O God; we acknowledge you to be the ruler over all. All the earth worships you, the Eternal One, everlasting. Holy, holy, holy, God of hosts, heaven and earth are full of the majesty of your glory. Praise to you, O God most high.   —From the *Te Deum*

Great are you, O God, and greatly to be praised. Vast is your love as shown in Christ Jesus. We will praise your name without ceasing, for you have made us for yourself, and our hearts find no rest until they rest in you. Come, let us worship!

Glory be to you, Creator God, giver of life and love, who sent Christ into the world to declare your good news of liberation.
Glory be to you, O Christ, who has brought life and freedom to light through the good news of the gospel.
Glory be to you, Three in One, One in Three, Creator, Christ, and Holy Spirit!
We praise you; we bless you; we thank you. Come, let us worship!

Prayers and Readings

Holy One, we come before you this day
  as part of the human family.
Inspire us, O God; open our hearts.
We come in our diversity to catch your vision of unity.
Inspire us, O God; open our eyes.

We come to hear your challenging word of truth.
Inspire us, O God, open our ears.
We come to thank you for your gifts of beauty, joy, and hope.
**O God of love, vision, and truth, we praise your blessed
name.**

This is the day the Lord has made, Hallelujah!
God has blessed us with a new day!
**We are warmed by God's presence in the sun
and surrounded by God's presence in the wind.**
We are blessed to come into the Holy One's house to wor-
ship and pray.
**We come together to give thanks and to praise Jesus Christ
our Lord!**
Let us gather in humble submission to receive the Holy
Spirit and the Word of God.
(All:) **This is the day the Lord has made.**
Let us rejoice and be glad in it!   —Valerie Miles-Tribble

This is the day of the Lord, the always and not yet sound-
ing of trumpet, our reason to call a solemn assembly.
We have been given this time and not some other.
We have been given this day and not some other.
We have been given this moment, and it is an acceptable
time to the Lord.   —Tripp Hudgins

Our hearts are open to the One,
to the One who breathes life into all that lives.
Our hearts are open to the One,
the Maker of meaning, the inspiration of the human heart.
Our hearts are open to the Infinite One,
creator of beginnings, ever-present, everywhere.

Our hearts are open to the Compassionate One,
the One who empowers us to bear one another's burdens.
We are emboldened to rise up in the Spirit of this One,
the gracious One who causes our fears to subside.
We are immersed in the presence of this One,
for in the One God is our joy and our peace.

—Michael Burch

Gather us in and hold us forever,
 gather us in and make us your own;
Gather us in—all peoples together,
 fire of love in our flesh and our bone.   —Marty Haugen

SUGGESTED HYMNS AND SONGS
For Call to Worship
(see hymnary.org or other sources as noted)

Called to Gather as God's People (Carl P. Daw Jr.)
Come into God's Presence Singing Alleluia (Anonymous)
Come We That Love the Lord/Marching to Zion (Isaac Watts)
Gather Us In/Here in This Place (Marty Haugen)
God Welcomes All (John L. Bell)
How Great Thou Art (Stuart K. Hine)
In This Very Room (Ron and Carol Harris)
Listen for the Call of God (Mary Louise Bringle)
O God of Vision (Jane Parker Huber)
O Lord, Our Lord, How Majestic Is Your Name (Michael W. Smith)
The God of Abraham Praise (Moses Maimonides)
This Is the Day (para. Les Garrett)
Uyai Mose/Come All You People (Alexander Gondo)

Invocation / Prayer of God's Presence

This first prayer of the service intentionally asks that God be present for our time of worship. Although God is always with us, the prayer reminds us that we not only direct our worship to God, but join in worship with God in our midst.

Holy Spirit, making life alive, moving in all things,
   root of all created being,
cleansing the cosmos of every impurity,
   erasing guilt, anointing wounds.
You are lustrous and praiseworthy life,
   you waken and reawaken everything that is. **Amen.**

—Hildegard of Bingen (1098–1179)

Teach us, O Merciful One, to have generous hearts, offering all we are in the name of Love. Help us to live in the eternal moment, awaiting your perfect timing in all things. In you alone is our trust, O Holy One, walking your Way is the truth that sets us free. Open our minds and hearts that we might welcome you in our midst. And may we live this day conversing with you, O Loving Companion Presence! **Amen.** —Jennifer W. Davidson, based on Psalm 106

Eternal God, we gather in your presence and reach out to you in prayer. We thank you for your constant love and boundless wisdom. We praise you for the glory of creation and the joy of our faith. Be with us now in this hour of worship, for it is in answer to your call that we gather. **Amen.**

Loving and gracious God, we praise you and thank you for the guidance that you give us from day to day in your Word and in your Spirit. Thank you for choosing to dwell among us and for calling us to be your faithful people. Bless this time of worship and prayer, that we may grow closer together as your children. **Amen.** —Sharon Allen

Gracious God, Creator and Ruler of the world, we come today with humility and gratitude as we gather in your presence. Inspire, refresh, and revive us, that we may truly worship you with songs and prayers; with words and deeds. In Christ's name, we pray. **Amen.**

Holy One, who gave the sun to illumine the day and the moon and stars to shine by night, enlighten us in this hour of worship that we may become children of light. May the radiance you give us so shine before others that they, too, will know your glory and be drawn to praise you. Through Christ, who is the light of the world, we pray. **Amen.**

This is the time and this is the place. We wait for you, God:
To change our minds, to remold our lives,
   to fill us with hope.
Here and now, come to us, O Holy One. Amen.

O God, who is the light of the minds that know you, the life of the souls that love you, and the strength of the thoughts that seek you;
Help us to know you so that we may truly love you, and so to love you that we may truly serve you, whose service is perfect freedom; through Jesus Christ, we pray. Amen.
—Gelasian Sacramentary

As we gather together this morning:
**May we release our expectations, resentments,
and concerns.**
May we make ourselves available to your ineffable presence, O God, as we settle into our worship today.
**Let us relax our bodies, breathe a bit more deeply
and receive the blessing that each of us offers the others.
Amen.**
—Sharon P. Burch

Come and find the quiet center
in the crowded life we lead,
find the room for hope to enter,
find the frame where we are freed:
clear the chaos and the clutter,
clear our eyes, that we can see
all the things that really matter,
be at peace, and simply be.

—Shirley Erena Murray

SUGGESTED HYMNS AND SONGS
For Invocation / Prayer of God's Presence
(see hymnary.org or other sources as noted)

Be Thou My Vision (Ancient Irish poem)
Come and Find the Quiet Center (Shirley Erena Murray)
I Love You, Lord (Laurie Klein)
Lead Me, Guide Me (Doris Akers)
Lord, Let My Heart Be Good Soil (Handt Hanson)
Open My Eyes, That I May See (Clara H. Scott)
Open the Eyes of My Heart, Lord (Paul Baloche)
Santo, Santo, Santo/Holy, Holy, Holy (Argentine folk song)
Spirit, Divine, Attend Our Prayers (Andrew Reed)
We Are Standing on Holy Ground (Geron Davis)

Prayer of Confession and Words of Assurance and Renewal

Sabbath worship in churches without a fixed liturgy does not typically include a time of confession. Worship planners and leaders may want to consider, however, that "confession is good for the soul" and incorporate such prayer more often. The season of Lent is a particularly appropriate time for prayers of confession. Provided here are several confessions, followed by words of forgiveness and assurance. Just as we are called to confess our failings, so too are we granted the promise that God loves us as whole people: human, fallible, and capable of growing in goodness.

Scriptures

God, listen! Listen to my prayer,
  listen to the pain in my cries.
Don't turn your back on me
  just when I need you so desperately.
Pay attention! This is a cry for *help*!
  And hurry—this can't wait!
God is sheer mercy and grace;
  not easily angered, rich in love.
The Holy One doesn't endlessly nag and scold,
  nor hold grudges forever,
nor treat us as our sins deserve,
  nor pay us back in full for our wrongs.

—Psalm 102:1-2; 103:8-10 (*The Message*)

We cry out to you from the depths—
  O God, listen to our voice!

Let your ears pay close attention to our request for mercy!
If you kept track of sins, who would stand a chance?
But forgiveness is with you—that's why you are honored.
We hope, God. Our whole being hopes,
    and waits for your promise.
Our whole being waits for you—
    more than the night watch waits for morning.
Israel, wait for the Holy One,
    because faithful love and redemption is with our God!
You are the one, gracious God,
    who will redeem Israel from all its sin.

—Psalm 130:1-8 (CEV)

Let us test and examine our ways, and return to God. Let us lift up to heaven our hearts as well as our hands. We have done wrong and rebelled against the Holy One. (*Offer silent prayers of confession*)
The steadfast love and mercy of God never cease; they are new every morning; for great is God's faithfulness. The Holy One is all we need, therefore we live in hope. Amen.

—Lamentations 3:40-42, 22-24, adapted

So if anyone is in Christ, there is a new creation: everything old has passed away; see, everything has become new! All this is from God, who reconciled with us through Christ.

—2 Corinthians 5:17-18

Let us come before God with our confessions:
If we say that we have no sin, we deceive ourselves, and the truth is not in us; but if we confess our sins, God is faithful and just to forgive us, and cleanses us from all wrongdoing.
(*Offer silent prayers of confession*)

Now the message that we have heard from Jesus Christ and announce is this: God is light, and there are no shadows in the realm of God. If we live in the light—just as God is in the light—then we have fellowship with one another, and the lifeblood of Christ washes us clean from every sin.

—From 1 John 1

Prayers and Readings

Let us confess our sins.
Most merciful God, we confess that we have sinned against you in thought, word, and deed, by what we have done, and by what we have left undone. We have not loved you with our whole heart; we have not loved our neighbors as ourselves. We are truly sorry, and we earnestly repent. For the sake of your Son Jesus Christ, have mercy on us and forgive us; that we may delight in your will, and walk in your ways, to the glory of your name, we pray.
The almighty and merciful God grant you forgiveness of all your sins, true repentance, and the grace and comfort of the Holy Spirit. **Amen.**

—Based on *The Book of Common Prayer*

(*In unison*) **Almighty God, unto whom all hearts are open, all desires known, and from whom no secrets are hid; cleanse the thoughts of our hearts by the inspiration of your Holy Spirit, that we may perfectly love you, and worthily magnify your holy name, through Jesus Christ, we pray. Amen.**

—Based on *The Book of Common Prayer*

Touch me, Lord Jesus, with thy hand of mercy,
Make each throbbing heartbeat feel thy power divine.
Take my will forever, I will doubt you never,
Cleanse me, dear Savior, make me wholly thine.

—Lucie E. Campbell (1885–1963)

Dear God, embracing humankind,
    forgive our foolish ways;
reclothe us in our rightful mind,
    in purer lives your service find,
    in deeper reverence, praise.
Drop your still dews of quietness,
    till all our strivings cease;
take from our souls the strain and stress,
    and let our ordered lives confess
    the beauty of your peace.

—John Greenleaf Whittier, 1872; adapted

This is a day of new beginnings,
    time to remember and move on,
time to believe what love is bringing,
    laying to rest the pain that's gone.
For by the life and death of Jesus,
    love's mighty Spirit, now as then,
can make for us a world of difference,
    as faith and hope are born again.

—Brian A. Wren

SUGGESTED HYMNS AND SONGS

For Prayer of Confession and Words of Assurance
(see hymnary.org or other sources as noted)

Change My Heart, O God/Cámbiame, Señor (Eddie
   Espinosa)

Come As You Are, That's How I Want You (Deidre Browne)

Dear God, Embracing Humankind (John Greenleaf
   Whittier)

Give Me a Clean Heart (Margaret Pleasant Douroux)

God Is a Wonder to My Soul (Robert J. Fryson)

God Is Forgiveness (Taizé Community)

God! When Human Bonds Are Broken (Fred Kaan)

Humble Thyself (Bob Hudson)

I'm So Glad Jesus Lifted Me (African American spiritual)

Softly and Tenderly Jesus Is Calling (Will L. Thompson)

There Is a Balm in Gilead (African American spiritual)

This Is a Day of New Beginnings (Brian A. Wren)

Touch Me, Lord Jesus (Lucie Campbell)

When We Are Called to Sing (Mary Nelson Keithahn)

We Hear and Proclaim God's Story

Prayer for Illumination

*Many of us are familiar with the words from Psalm 19:14
("Let the words of my mouth and the meditation of my
heart . . .") as prayed by the preacher just before a sermon.
When the word is to be interpreted and proclaimed, both
the preacher and the congregation should seek the light
and clarity given by calling upon the Holy Spirit. Consider
sharing the prayer for illumination prior to the sermon text*

*being read, so that both the scripture passage and its proc-
lamation may be blessed.*

Scriptures

May the words of my mouth and the meditations of our
hearts be acceptable to you, our rock and our redeemer.
Amen.

or

May the words of my mouth,

**and the meditations of our hearts be acceptable to you, our
strength and our redeemer. Amen.**   —Psalm 19:14

I pray that the glorious God of our Savior, Jesus Christ,
give us a spirit of wisdom and revelation. With the eyes
of our hearts enlightened, may we embrace that hope to
which God has called us; our rich inheritance among the
saints and the immeasurable greatness of holy power for
those who trust and follow Christ.

—Based on Ephesians 1:17-19

Prayers and Readings

Since we do not live by bread alone, but by every word that
comes from your mouth, make us hunger for this heavenly
food, that it may nourish us today in the ways of eternal
life; through Jesus Christ, the bread of heaven. **Amen.**

Guide the thinking and speaking of your servant this hour
so that your people in their living will become more like
the Eternal Christ of the ages. In his name, we pray. **Amen.**

—J. Alfred Smith Sr.

(*In unison*) O God, may the word that is read and spoken become through us a liberating word to all who are in bondage and who long for freedom. Open our hearts to hear your call for justice and to answer it with our prayers and our actions. **Amen.**

Prayer before the Reading of Scripture

Blessed Lord, who caused all holy scriptures to be written for our learning: Grant us so to hear them, read, mark, learn, and inwardly digest them, that we may embrace and ever hold fast the blessed hope of everlasting life, which you have given us in our Savior Jesus Christ; who lives and reigns with you and the Holy Spirit, one God, forever and ever. **Amen.**   —*The Book of Common Prayer*

No creature has meaning without the Word of God.
God's Word is in all creation, visible and invisible.
The Word is living, being, spirit, all verdant, all creativity.
This Word flashes out in every creature.
This is how the spirit is in the flesh—
the Word is indivisible from God.

                                    —Hildegard of Bingen (1098–1179)

May we hear with understanding, by your Spirit taught
    and led.
May the springs of all our being by your living Word be
    fed.   —Margaret Clarkson

SUGGESTED HYMNS AND SONGS
For Prayer for Illumination
(see hymnary.org or other sources as noted)

Come Light, Light of God (The Sisters of the Community
    of Grandchamp, Switzerland)
In My Life, Lord, Be Glorified (Bob Kilpatrick)
Light of the World (Daniel C. Damon, *Garden of Joy*,
    Hope Publishing Company and Hope Hymns Online)
Lord, Let My Heart Be Good Soil (Hans Handt)
Lord, Speak to Me (Frances R. Havergal)
Lord, We Hear Your Word with Gladness (Margaret
    Clarkson)
Open My Eyes That I May See (Clara Scott)
Spirit of the Living God (Daniel Iverson)
Thy Word Is a Lamp Unto My Feet (Michael W. Smith)
Wonderful Words of Life (Philip P. Bliss)

MINISTRY OF THE TABLE

We Offer Our Joys, Laments, and Thanks

The two classic sections of the Sabbath service are Word
and Table. Many congregations in the free church tradition
share bread and cup less often than weekly. Whether the
Lord's Supper is shared or not, this part of worship is the
time for lifting up our specific prayers, for our offerings of
gratitude to God, and for a blessing as we leave worship
and return to the world.

In this time of community prayer we specifically focus on personal needs (petitions) and our requests for others (intercessions), as well as on celebrations (praises) and sorrows (laments). The opportunity for lament, in particular, is crucial for the health of individuals and for the gathered community. All these expressions that we lift up to God are the Prayers of the People.

Every congregation develops its own way of sharing and articulating the blessings and burdens brought to worship that dwell in each person's heart and mind. Prayer requests may be made within worship (written or spoken) or may be prepared ahead of time. The prayers shared below are meant to serve as models and guides for this significant and vital time in the service when we pray for ourselves and for others, for our community and for our world. The culminating prayer in this part of worship is usually known as the Pastoral Prayer or the Altar Prayer.

Invitation to Prayer

Teach us your ways, O God; make them known to us. Guide us in living according to your truths, for you are the Holy One, the Saving One. We place our trust in you.

—Based on Psalm 25:4-5

God is our light and our salvation; whom shall we fear? God is the strength of our lives; of whom shall we be afraid? The Eternal One shelters us in the day of trouble, keeping us safe and secure. Hear us, O God, when we call to you. Show us your loving mercy and respond to our prayers.

—Based on Psalm 27

Cast your cares on God and you will be sustained. The Holy One upholds us and will not let the faithful fall. With great and holy mercy that rises far above the heavens, let none be ashamed to wait upon the Eternal God.

—Based on Psalm 55

For God, the Holy One of Israel, has said: "In returning and rest you shall be saved; in quietness and in trust shall be your strength."

—Isaiah 30:15

Return to your God, for the Holy One is gracious and merciful, slow to anger, and abounding in steadfast love.

—Joel 2:13

Jesus said, "Come to me, all of you who are tired from carrying heavy burdens, and I will give you rest. Take my yoke and put it on and learn from me, because I am gentle and humble of spirit; and you will find rest. For the yoke I give you is easy, and the burden I put on you is light."

—Matthew 11:28-30

Ask, and it will be given you; seek and you will find; knock, and the door will be opened to you. For everyone who asks will be heard, and those who seek will find, and all who knock will find an open door.

—Matthew 7:7-8

Don't worry about anything, but with a thankful heart in all your prayers ask God for what you need. And the peace of God, which is far beyond human understanding, will keep your hearts and minds centered on Christ Jesus.

—Philippians 4:6-7

There is a place of full release, near to the heart of God,
a place where all is joy and peace, near to the heart of God.
O Jesus, blest Redeemer, sent from the heart of God,
hold us, who wait before you, near to the heart of God.

—Cleland B. McAfee

Prayers of the People — for ourselves and for others, in praise and lament

Pastoral Prayer / Altar Prayer

The psalmist cries: "How long, O Lord? Will you forget me forever? How long will you hide your face from me? How long must I bear pain in my soul, and have sorrow in my heart all day long? How long shall my enemy be exalted over me? Consider and answer me, my God! Give light to my eyes, or I will sleep the sleep of death, and my enemy will say, 'I have prevailed,' my foes will rejoice because I am shaken. But I trusted in your steadfast love; my heart shall rejoice in your salvation. I will sing to the Eternal One, who has dealt bountifully with me." May we, like the psalmist, proclaim you as our shelter and our redeemer, giving praise for the unconditional love from you that we receive and cherish. Through the peace of Jesus Christ and the power of your Holy Spirit, we pray. **Amen.**

Not unto us, O Lord, but unto your name be the glory. From the rising of the sun unto the going down of the same, may your name be praised from the east to the west, from the north to the south. Incomprehensible is your love. When life deals us heavy blows, you pick us up out of the dust. When sorrow leaves the salt stains of dried tears on our faces, you lift us from the ashes of grief. When mountains of trouble intimidate us and when the hills of opposition threaten us, you make mountains skip like rams and you make the hills free like lambs! Glory, honor, and power belong to you, alone, O Incomparable One. Though our sins are red like crimson, you have promised those of us who ask for forgiveness that our sins will become as wool. For the pardon and peace that come to us in Jesus Christ, we shout glad hallelujahs. May all who have needs find their fulfillment in you. In Jesus' name we pray. **Amen.**

—J. Alfred Smith Sr.

God of all peoples, we cannot fully comprehend the struggles of other nations, but we see the disparities of resources and power and the effects of violence and injustice. We hear of dictators and disasters and we pray for peoples whose lives are at their mercies. As a community, we name the global concerns that need your care . . . (*Individual prayer concerns are shared aloud at each pause*)

God of liberty and justice, we pray today for our own country that so desperately needs more respectful systems for relating to one another and more equitable structures for providing for basic needs and opportunities for all who live in our land. As a community, we name our country's concerns that need your justice and mercy . . .

God of healing and hope, we pray this morning for our congregation, lifting up its ministries that seek to meet the needs of our community and lifting up its members who make up the Body of Christ. As a community, we name the ministries of our congregation and the members of our community who need your provision . . .

God of comfort and wisdom, we pray this morning for ourselves and our loved ones. We ask strength for the journey, your healing touch, wisdom, and guidance for the week ahead. As a community, we name our loved ones needing your care . . .

and we call out our own names, recognizing our dependence on you . . .

Most Holy God—we are grateful that you hear our prayers. **Amen.** —Allison J. Tanner

Dear Lord, you are the most essential and important part of our lives. Thank you for waking us and bringing us to church. Thank you for this body of believers and for the visitors here today. Thank you for the good news! May we live to serve you, always.

Some of us, Lord, are dealing with bad news and are struggling right now. Please remember:

those dealing with health issues,

those dealing with grief and the loss of a loved one,

those dealing with issues at school and at work,

those searching for a job,

those dealing with family and relationship issues,

those dealing with financial issues,

those who are in leadership, both in the church and in our nation.

We know you can do anything, Lord. You supply all our needs and there's no problem too big for you. In times of trouble, you always comfort our souls. Help us to look beyond our problems and trust in you. Help us to do what is right. Touch us with your unconditional love.

You are so amazing, Lord! May your love, grace, and mercy sustain us, always. We pray now in Jesus' name. Amen! —Paul J. Keener

Dear God, it has been a hard week. We come to you in need of comfort and encouragement. Sometimes it feels as if no one understands the pain and frustration; no one, that is, but you, Holy One. Please take our disappointment and distress, giving us the hope and encouragement that we seek. Send us into the world this week with renewed strength, and the reassurance that we are not alone in our daily trials, because you are with us now and forever. Amen.

—Michelle M. Holmes

God of still waiting, God of deep longing,
    God of the heart's true rest:
hold us in fathomless peace, guard us with unwaning love.

—Carl P. Daw Jr.

SUGGESTED HYMNS AND SONGS
For the Time of Prayer
(see hymnary.org or other sources as noted)

Bless the Lord, My Soul (Taizé Community)
Cast Thy Burden Upon the Lord (from *Elijah*)
Come and Fill Our Hearts with Your Peace/Confitemini
    Domino (Taizé Community)
Give Me Jesus (African American spiritual)
God of Still Waiting (Carl P. Daw Jr.)
Golden Breaks the Dawn (Tzu-chen Chao)
I Need Thee Every Hour (Annie S. Hawks)
Lord, Listen to Your Children Praying (Ken Medema)
Near to the Heart of God (Cleland B. McAfee)
O Lord, Hear My Prayer (Taizé Community)
On Eagle's Wings/You Who Dwell in the Shelter of the
    Lord (Michael Joncas)

Somebody Prayed for Me (Dorothy Norwood, Alvin
   Darling)
Spirit of God, Descend Upon My Heart (George Croly)
Steal Away (African American spiritual)
What a Friend We Have in Jesus (Joseph M. Scriven)

The Lord's Prayer

*The prayer Jesus taught may be shared at various points
in worship, such as the close of the Pastoral Prayer, during
the dedication of offerings, or as part of the Lord's Supper.
Several versions of the Lord's Prayer can be found in the
Additional Worship Materials at the end of Part 2.*

Invitation to Offering

*For those congregations that receive their offerings early
in the worship service, it's worth considering this question:
when are we as worshipers most ready to be in a true attitude of thanks? Giving to God and to the church our
offerings, pledges, and tithes is a significant part of the Sabbath and of our week. Historically and liturgically, the offering belongs in this second half of the service, along with
the Prayers of the People and the Lord's Supper (when
included).*

*During the first part of worship, we lift our praises to
God and experience the gift of God's word through scripture and proclamation. We then have the opportunity to
respond by presenting the Holy One with gifts that symbolize the work of our hands, as well as show gratitude for
our lives and for our church. The time of offering is also
the opportunity for us to rededicate ourselves to Christ and*

to God's service. When the Lord's Supper is to be shared, we include a dedication for the bread and cup.

Scriptures

Praise our splendid and mighty God, all people on earth. The Holy One is to be honored above all gods and by all nations. Praise God's glorious name; bring an offering and come into the holy temple.   —From Psalm 96

Jesus said, "Do not store up for yourselves treasures on earth, where moth and rust consume and where thieves break in and steal; but store up for yourselves treasures in heaven. For where your treasure is, there will your heart be also."   —Matthew 6:19-21

They voluntarily gave according to their means, and even beyond their means, . . . but first they gave themselves to God.   —2 Corinthians 8:3-5

How does God's love abide in anyone who has the world's goods and sees a brother or sister in need and yet refuses help? Let us love, not in word or speech, but in truth and action.   —1 John 3:17-18

Prayers and Readings

From the heart bring forth incense of praise, from the store of a good conscience bring forth the sacrifice of faith, and whatsoever you bring forth kindle it with love. These are the most acceptable offerings to God: mercy, humility, confession, peace, love. It is you that God seeks more than any gift.   —Augustine of Hippo (354–430)

Teach us, God, to serve you as you deserve: to give and not to count the cost; to labor and not ask for reward, save in the knowledge that we do your will.

—Ignatius of Loyola (1491–1556)

The psalmist wrote: "Happy are those who keep God's decrees, who seek the Holy One with their whole heart; who walk in holy ways." Part of that walk is a commitment to support God's work in the world. Therefore let us offer our resources of time, talent, and treasure to the Holy One by bringing our gifts this morning.   —Sharon Allen

Doxologies—see Additional Worship Materials at the end of Part 2

Prayer of Dedication

God grant us grace and bless us; let God's face shine on us so that the ways of the Holy One become known on earth, and God's salvation becomes known among all the nations.
Let the people praise you, O God!
  Let all the people praise you!
Let us celebrate and shout with joy because you judge the nations fairly and guide all nations on the earth.
Let the people praise you, O God!
  Let all the people praise you!
The earth has yielded its harvest. God blesses us!
May God continue to bless us;
  let all ends of the earth give honor and praise!

—Psalm 67

God, whose we are and whom we serve, help us to glorify you this day, in all the thoughts of our hearts, in all the words of our lips, and in all the work of our hands, as is fitting those who are your servants. Through Jesus Christ, who gave everything for us, we pray. **Amen.**

Loving God, giver of every good and perfect gift, in gratitude we give these offerings to you, and with them we consecrate ourselves to your service. Use us and that which we have given for your work in the world, that both gift and giver may be a blessing to those who receive. **Amen.**

Creator God, by whose will the world came into being and who has given to us life and substance: with grateful hearts we praise you for your goodness and thank you for your blessings.
(*In unison*) **As a sign of our thankfulness we bring these gifts to you. Use them for the renewal of your creation, and use us as your ministers of compassion and grace. Through Christ, we pray. Amen.**

Prayer of Dedication — when the Lord's Supper is included in worship

We offer to you, O God, this bread and cup, to be set apart for the remembrance of the passion of Jesus Christ, our Savior. We present to you these gifts, thanking you for the skill to do our daily work. We also offer ourselves, asking you to strengthen us, that all our work may be to your service, all our meals a thankful remembrance of your blessings to us. May we be a living sacrifice, holy and acceptable to you; through Jesus Christ. **Amen.**

We bring these gifts to you, our God, and with them we bring ourselves. Be pleased to accept all that we have brought. May our offerings of money be used in the proclamation of the Good News in this place and beyond.

May the bread and cup be a reminder that Christ lives and abides with us as our constant companion and friend. May we gladly offer ourselves now as signs of Christ's love and peace in our midst. Amen.

For all the riches you bestow, for all the good you supply, for all the guidance you offer day by day, we give thanks, gracious God. All that we give we owe to you, and life itself is a gift from your hand.

We dedicate our offerings, this bread and cup, and our lives to your honor and glory, God. Amen.

For the harvests of the Spirit, thanks be to God.
For the good we all inherit, thanks be to God.
For the wonders that astound us,
   for the truths that still confound us,
most of all, that love has found us, thanks be to God.

—Fred Pratt Green

SUGGESTED HYMNS AND SONGS
For Invitation to Offering or Prayer of Dedication
(see hymnary.org or other sources as noted)

Can We Calculate Our Giving (Danny A. Belrose, *Community of Christ Sings*, Herald Publishing House)
For the Fruit of All Creation (Fred Pratt Green)
For the Life That You Have Given (Carl P. Daw Jr.)
Give Thanks (Henry Smith)

God, Whose Giving Knows No Ending (Robert L. Edwards)

I'm Gonna Live So God Can Use Me (African American spiritual)

Take, O Take Me as I Am (John L. Bell)

Take My Life and Let It Be (Frances Ridley Havergal)

Thank You Lord, I Just Want to Thank You Lord (Traditional African American song)

Ubi Cáritas / Live in Charity / Donde hay amor (Taizé Community)

We Give Thee But Thine Own (William Walsham How)

Gathering at Christ's Table—Invitation to Communion—Words of Institution

Whether we call it the Lord's Supper, Communion, or Eucharist, when the family gathers to share the bread and cup it is a hallowed moment in worship. There are many ways to bless and distribute the elements in our free church traditions. A small congregation may gather around the table. A large congregation may receive bread and cup by passing it among those sitting in the pews. We may sit, stand, or kneel; come to the front of the sanctuary or commune in place. The Lord's Supper is a time of remembrance for all that Jesus sacrificed on our behalf. It is also a time of celebration for our present and future life together as God's family, through Christ.

Scriptures

O taste and see the goodness of God; happy are those who dwell in the Holy One.

Hold God in awe, you faithful ones, for those who worship God will want for nothing. —Psalm 34:8-9

What shall we return to God for all God's bounty to us?
We will lift up the cup of salvation and call upon the name of God. We will pay our vows to God in the presence of all the people.
—Psalm 116:12-14

When Jesus was at the table with the two men of Emmaus, he took bread, blessed and broke it, and gave it to them. Then their eyes were opened, and they recognized him; and he vanished from their sight. They said to each other, "Were not our hearts burning within us while he was talking to us on the road, while he was opening the scriptures to us?"
—Luke 24:30-32

Jesus said, "I am the bread of life. Whoever comes to me will never be hungry, and whoever trusts in me will never thirst."
—John 6:35

The cup of blessing that we bless, is it not a sharing in the blood of Christ?
Because there is one bread, we who are many are one body, for we all partake of the one bread.   —1 Corinthians 10:16-17

Words of Institution

While they were eating, Jesus took a loaf of bread, and after blessing it he broke it, gave it to them, and said, "Take; this is my body." Then he took a cup, and after giving thanks he gave it to them, and all of them drank from it. He said, "This is my blood of the covenant, which is poured out for many. Truly I tell you, I will never again drink of the fruit of the vine until that day when I drink it new in the kingdom of God."
—Mark 14:22-25

When the hour for the Passover meal came, Jesus took his place at the table, and the apostles with him. He said to them, "I have eagerly desired to eat this Passover with you before I suffer; for I tell you, I will not eat it again until it is fulfilled in the kingdom of God." Then he took a cup, and after giving thanks he said, "Take this and divide it among yourselves; for I tell you that from now on I will not drink of the fruit of the vine until the kingdom of God comes." Then he took a loaf of bread, and when he had given thanks, he broke it and gave it to them, saying, "This is my body, which is given for you. Do this in remembrance of me." And he did the same with the cup after supper, saying, "This cup that is poured out for you is the new covenant in my blood." —Luke 22:14-20

Hear these words as written by the apostle Paul: "For I received from the Lord what I also handed on to you, that Jesus on the night when he was betrayed took a loaf of bread, and when he had given thanks, he broke it and said, 'This is my body that is given for you. Do this in remembrance of me.' In the same way he took the cup also, after supper, saying, 'This cup is the new covenant in my blood. As often as you drink this, do it in remembrance of me.' For whenever you eat this bread and drink the cup, you proclaim the Lord's death until he comes again." —1 Corinthians 11:23-26

Jesus said, "This is my body, which is given for you. Do this in remembrance of me."
Jesus said, "Drink from it, all of you; for this is my blood of the covenant, which is poured out for many for the forgiveness of sins." —Luke 22:19; Matthew 26:27-28

Prayers

The Gospel tells us that as the risen Christ sat at table with two of his followers he was made known to them in the breaking of bread. At this table we invite all who are in fellowship with Christ and with one another to partake of this holy Supper. Let us pray together:

Our God, we who are at this table trust that through the eating of the bread and drinking of the cup we shall come to a thankful remembrance of Jesus Christ, and that, by your Holy Spirit, Christ will come to dwell within and among us. Amen.

Come, my way, my truth, my life:
   such a way, as gives us breath;
such a truth, as ends all strife;
   such a life as conquers death.
Come, my light, my feast, my strength:
   such a light as shows a feast;
such a feast as mends in length;
   such a strength as makes his guest.
Come, my joy, my love, my heart:
   such a joy as none can move;
such a love as none can part;
   such a heart as joys in love.   —George Herbert (1593–1632)

Loving God, we see before us this common food, simple bread and juice. But through his life and death and resurrection, Jesus Christ has made these common elements exceptional and holy for us. Today we gather at the table to celebrate all that Christ has done, for the world and for each of us. His work and his mission continue and we are called to carry it forward.

As we receive the bread and cup may we be empowered with grace and compassion to do your will, O God, for the good of all people. May we live out the Good News of your love and the joy of our faith. Amen.

The rice of life from heaven
 came to bring true life from God above.
Receive this gift; God's mercy claim;
 in joy and pain give thanks for love.

True rice the hungry world has fed,
 the rice required for life below.
Provide this gift; God's mercy spread;
 in weakness God's compassion show.

The rice of God for all is meant;
 no one who comes is turned away.
Believe in Christ whom God has sent;
 in humble trust God's will obey.

The living rice, for all a sign,
 came down eternal life to give.
Abide in Christ, the living vine;
 in Christ, with people die and live.

—J. Andrew Fowler, © 1990 Christian Conference of Asia
(administered by GIA Publications, Inc.)
Sing to the tune BÍ–NÎU or TALLIS' CANON

SUGGESTED HYMNS AND SONGS
For Invitation to Communion and Thanksgiving for the Meal
(see hymnary.org or other sources as noted)

All Who Hunger, Gather Gladly (Sylvia G. Dunstan)
Come to the Table of Grace (Barbara Hamm)

Eat This Bread and Never Hunger (Daniel Charles Damon)
Eat This Bread, Drink This Cup (Taizé Community)
For Everyone Born, a Place at the Table (Shirley Erena
   Murray)
Haleluya! Pelo Tsa Rona/Hallelujah! We Sing Your Praises
   (South Africa)
I Come with Joy, a Child of God (Brian Wren)
Let Us Break Bread Together (African American spiritual)
Let Us Talents and Tongues Employ (Fred Kaan)
One Bread, One Body (John B. Foley)

Prayer of Thanksgiving for the Meal

A prayer thanking God for the blessings of bread and cup may be shared either before or after the elements are distributed.

Grant, O God, that your Holy Spirit may be with us, and that through the bread and cup set apart for remembrance and thanksgiving Christ may come to dwell among us, and through him we may know you, whom to know is life eternal. **Amen.**

Gracious God, in whom we live and move and have our being, we lift our hearts and offer thanks to you for the wonders of the world about us, for humankind and the richness of love, for each new day of forgiveness and grace. With thanksgiving we remember the One who was with you from the beginning, through whom all things were made, whose life is the light of the world and who became flesh and lived among us as Jesus the Christ. For his life and ministry, for his teaching and example, and for his love, we give you thanks, O God. **Amen.**

Lift up your hearts:
We lift them to God.
Let us give thanks to our God:
It is fitting and right for us to do.
What shall we offer back to the Holy One for all of God's
  benefits toward us?
**We shall offer to God our thanksgivings, for God is great,
  with power and glory and majesty forever!**
For your perfect wisdom and goodness and for the fullness
  of your love revealed to us through the body and blood
  of Jesus Christ our Savior:
With gratitude we worship and praise you, O God. Amen.

In remembrance of all that Christ has done for us, we offer
  praise and thanksgiving, proclaiming the good news of
  our faith:
Christ has died; Christ is risen; Christ will come again.
By your Spirit, Lord, make us one with Christ, one with
  each other, and one in ministry to all the world. **Amen.**

We Go Out Praising God

Bringing our Sabbath worship to a close is a high moment.
It deserves words that revitalize us and send us out to the
world with commitment and hope, equipped and sustained
for the week ahead. Following the blessing, worshipers can
share the ritual "passing of the peace." Words commonly
used (which can be varied, as desired) are:

May the peace of Christ be with you always.
And also with you. (*Please share signs of love and peace
  with your church family.*)

Historically, the Peace has been included in the liturgy prior to sharing the Lord's Supper or, in some churches, following the Confession and Words of Assurance. In our free church worship, it's up to the planners and ministry staff to determine the best time to include the Peace, preferably at a point in worship where it doesn't break the flow of the service: the hubbub of greetings, welcomes, and introductions is a joyful noise to be sure, but it may require an unpredictable period of settling down—or even a call to order! Many churches have found that placing the Peace at the end of the service works well, as the joyful greetings in the name of the Christ flow naturally into the time of fellowship that follows.

Blessing and Benediction; the Peace

May God bless you and keep you.
May God's face shine upon you and be gracious to you.
May God look upon you with love and give you peace.
  Amen.　　　　　　　　　　　　　　　—Numbers 6:24-26

Holy One, let your servants depart in peace; your word has been fulfilled.
We have seen the salvation which you have prepared for all people as a light revealing you to the nations.
Go in peace.
Amen.　　　　　　　　　　　　　—*Nunc Dimittis*, adapted

Jesus said, "Peace I leave with you; my peace I give to you, not as the world gives. Do not let your hearts be troubled, neither let them be afraid."
Peace be to the whole community, and love with faith, from God the Creator and from our Savior Jesus Christ.
　　　　　　　　　　　　　　　—John 14:27; Ephesians 6:23

May the God of hope fill you with all joy and peace in believing, so that you may abound in hope by the power of the Holy Spirit. **Amen.**   —Romans 15:13

The grace of Jesus Christ, the love of God, and the communion of the Holy Spirit be with you all. **Amen.**

—2 Corinthians 13:13

Now to our God, who by the power at work within us is able to accomplish abundantly far more than all we can ask or imagine, to God be glory in the church and in Christ Jesus to all generations, forever and ever. **Amen.**

—Ephesians 3:20-21

May the peace of God, which surpasses all understanding, guide your hearts and your minds in Christ Jesus. **Amen.**

—Philippians 4:7

Let us go forth secure in the knowledge of God's love for us, confident in the power of the resurrection, and encouraged by the communion of the saints.
Let us go forth to love and serve, to help and heal, to grow ever more fully into the likeness of Christ. Amen.

—Allison J. Tanner

Support us, God, all the day long, until the shadows lengthen, and the evening comes, the busy world is hushed, the fever of life is over, and our work is done; then, in your mercy, give us safe lodging, a holy rest and peace at the last, through Jesus Christ. Amen.

—*The Book of Common Prayer*, adapted

God be in your head, and in your understanding.
God be in your eyes, and in your looking.
God be in your mouth, and in your speaking.
God be in your heart, and in your thinking.
God be at your end, and at your departing.

—Sarum Liturgy, thirteenth century

Lord, you have spoken to us. Your word has instructed us.
Your music has inspired us. Your Holy Spirit has comforted
us. Help us to not forget you until next Sunday. Burn deep
desire in our hearts to volunteer our service to you, in our
churches, our homes, our communities, and in the world.
Amen.

—J. Alfred Smith Sr.

As you, O God, have blessed our coming, bless now our
going forth; and grant that when we leave your house we
may not leave your presence, but be ever near to us and
keep us near to you. **Amen.**

Deep peace of the running wave to you,
  deep peace of the flowing air to you,
deep peace of the quiet earth to you,
  deep peace of the shining stars to you,
deep peace of the gentle night to you,
  moon and stars pour their healing light on you,
deep peace of Christ the light of the world to you.
  The deep peace of Christ to you. Amen.   —Gaelic blessing

May the love of God, which is broader than the measure of
our minds; the grace of Jesus Christ, which is sufficient for
all our needs; and the communion of the Holy Spirit, which

shall lead us into all truth, go with us this day and all our days. **Amen.**
—Esther Hargis

Gracious God, as we go from worship into the world we pray that you will make us instruments of your peace; where there is hatred, let us sow love; where there is injury, pardon; where is doubt, faith; where there is despair, hope; where there is darkness, light; and where there is sadness, joy. **Amen.**
—Attributed to Francis of Assisi (1182–1226)

Go forth from this place in peace. Be watchful, stand firm in your faith, be courageous and strong. Let all that you do be done in love. And all God's people say:
Thanks be to God! Amen.

On what has now been sown your blessing, God, bestow;
The power is yours alone to make it spring and grow.
Do now in grace the harvest raise, and you alone shall have
the praise!
—John Newton (1725–1807)

Christ be with me, Christ within me,
Christ behind me, Christ before me,
Christ beside me, Christ to win me,
Christ to comfort and restore me.
Christ beneath me, Christ above me,
Christ in quiet, Christ in danger,
Christ in hearts of all that love me,
Christ in mouth of friend and stranger.
—Attributed to Patrick of Ireland (385–461)
May be sung to the tunes ALLELUIA (Jerry Sinclair) or
SCHMÜCKE DICH (Johann Crüger)

SUGGESTED HYMNS AND SONGS
For Benedictions and Blessings
(see hymnary.org or other sources as noted)

Go, My Children, with My Blessing (Jaroslav Vajda)
God Be with You Till We Meet Again (Jeremiah E. Rankin)
God of Our Life (Hugh Thomson Kerr)
Guide My Feet (African American spiritual)
Lord of All Hopefulness (Jan Struther)
May the God of Hope Go with Us/Canto de esperanza
    (Alvin Schutmaat)
Now Thank We All Our God (Martin Rinckart)
O Master, Let Me Walk with Thee (Washington Gladden)
On What Has Now Been Sown (John Newton)
Thuma, Mina/Send Me, Jesus (South Africa)

ADDITIONAL WORSHIP MATERIALS

The Lord's Prayer

Our Father, which art in heaven, hallowed be thy Name.
Thy Kingdom come.
    Thy will be done on earth, as it is in heaven.
Give us this day our daily bread.
And forgive us our trespasses,
    as we forgive those who trespass against us.
And lead us not into temptation, but deliver us from evil.
For thine is the kingdom, and the power, and the glory,
For ever and ever. Amen.

—Traditional, based on Matthew 6:9-13

Spanish

Padre nuestro, que estás en los cielos,
  santificado sea tu nombre.
Venga tu reino, hágase tu voluntad,
  asi en la tierra como en el cielo.
Danos hoy el pan de este día,
y perdona nuestras deudas
  como nosotros perdonamos nuestros deudores.
Y no nos dejes caer en al tentación
  sino que líbranos del malo.
Porque tuyo es el reino, el poder y la gloria,
  por los siglos de los siglos. **Amen.**

For the Lord's Prayer in additional languages, see
www.wordproject.org/bibles/resources/our_father/in_
  many_languages.htm.
For hymn or song versions of the traditional wording of
  the Lord's Prayer, see hymnary.org.

Father, hallowed be your name. Your kingdom come. Give
us each day our daily bread. And forgive us our sins, for we
forgive everyone indebted to us. And do not bring us to the
time of trial.   —Luke 11:2-4

Eternal Spirit,
  Earth-maker, Pain-bearer, Life-giver,
  source of all that is and that shall be,
  Father and Mother of us all,
  loving God, in whom is heaven:
The hallowing of your name echo through the universe!
  The way of your justice be followed by the peoples of
    the world!
  Your heavenly will be done by all created beings!

Your commonwealth of peace and freedom
   sustain our hope and come on earth.
With the bread we need for today, feed us.
   In the hurts we absorb from one another, forgive us.
   In times of temptation and test, strengthen us.
   From trials too great to endure, spare us.
   From the grip of all that is evil, free us.
For you reign in the glory of the power that is love,
   now and forever. Amen.
      —*A New Zealand Prayer Book – He Karakia Mihinare o Aotearoa*

O God, who gave us life and who loves us, let the glory of your love be felt by all. Bring grace and justice in your kingdom and to all people. Convince us that you alone are God and your will is the best we could want. Provide for us all that we need to enjoy this day. Forgive our desire to turn away from you. Forgive us for the pain we cause others and give us strength to forgive those who cause us pain. Help us to look to you, when the selfishness and pride of our spirits beg us to look away. You are the meaning of Love and Life and have made us new people today. Thank you. **Amen.**
      —Russell Rathbun

Eternal Spirit, Father and Mother of us all,
   holy is your name.
Let justice and mercy fill all creation and let us recognize
   that every thought and thing belongs to you.
Feed us with the bread we need for today. Forgive our sin as
   we forgive those who sin against us. Stand with us in trial
   and temptation. Free us from the grip of all that is evil.
For you alone are creating our universe, now and forever.
   Amen.

Doxologies

A doxology is a short hymn of praise to God. It can be included at various places in the service, although it is most typically sung as the offerings are brought forward. The texts shown below can be sung to the following tunes: OLD HUNDREDTH, TALLIS' CANON, DUKE STREET, TRURO, WINCHESTER NEW, O WALY WALY, and many others.

Trying a new tune for a familiar set of words (or new words for a familiar tune) can offer a refreshing change.

Praise God, from whom all blessings flow;
praise him, all creatures here below,
Praise him above, ye heavenly host;
praise Father, Son, and Holy Ghost.

—Thomas Ken (1637–1711)

Praise God, from whom all blessings flow,
Praise God, all creatures here below,
Praise God above, you heavenly host;
Creator, Christ, and Holy Ghost.

—(Inclusive version)

Spanish
A Dios el Padre celestial,
al Hijo nuestro Redentor,
y al eternal Consolador
unidos todos alabad.

To God Creator, God the Son,
and Holy Spirit, three in one,
unceasing praise and glory be,
now and through all eternity.

Praise God, Creator of the earth;
Praise Christ, the Word that came to birth;
Praise Holy Spirit, by whose grace
The Light of love shines on this place.   —N. H.

Praise God, from whom all blessings flow;
Praise Christ, all creatures here below;
Praise Holy Spirit evermore;
One triune God, whom we adore.

Psalms for Sabbath Worship

These psalm readings are designed for Sabbath worship during seasons or occasions in the Christian year other than Advent, Epiphany, Lent, or Easter. Most are based on the New Revised Standard Version of the Bible, but some are composites from several translations and paraphrases, and may not include the entire psalm; whenever possible, these sources are shown. Sung responses are suggested for some psalm readings; such responses can greatly enrich the congregational experience of the reading, but are optional. Two outstanding resources for including psalms in worship are Psalms for All Seasons: A Complete Psalter for Worship, *which includes every psalm, most in multiple versions, and Nan C. Merrill,* Psalms for Praying: An Invitation to Wholeness, *a classic devotional work of psalm paraphrases. (See the list of resources.)*

PSALM 20

God will answer you in the day of trouble!
   The name of the God of Jacob will protect you.
May God send you help from the sanctuary,

and give you support from Zion.
May God remember all your offerings,
    and regard with favor your burnt sacrifices.
May God grant you your heart's desire,
    and fulfill all your plans.
May we shout for joy over your victory,
    and in the name of our God set up our banners.
Now I know that the Holy One will help God's anointed;
God will give answer from heaven above
    with mighty victories.
Some take pride in chariots, and some in horses,
    but our pride is in the name of the Eternal One.
Earthly things will collapse and fall,
    but we shall rise and stand upright.
Give victory to us, O God; answer us when we call.

Suggested sung response, at beginning and end: "In the Lord I'll Be Ever Thankful" (see hymnary.org).

PSALM 29

Ascribe to God, O heavenly beings,
    ascribe to God glory and strength.
Ascribe glory to the name of God;
    worship the Eternal One in holy splendor.
The voice of God is over the waters;
    the God of glory thunders, over mighty waters.
The voice of the Holy One is powerful and full of majesty;
    a voice that breaks the cedars of Lebanon.
God makes Lebanon skip like a calf,
    and Sirion like a young wild ox.
The voice of God flashes forth flames of fire,
    shaking the wilderness.

The voice of God causes the oaks to whirl,
  and strips the forest bare;
and all in God's temple say, "Glory!"
The Holy One sits enthroned over the flood;
  as sovereign forever.
May God's people receive strength!
May God's people be blessed with peace!

Suggested sung response with psalm, at beginning and end:
"Come Light, Light of God" (see hymnary.org).

PSALM 84

God All-Powerful, your temple is so lovely!
Deep in my heart I long for your temple,
  and with all that I am I sing joyful songs to you.
God All-Powerful, my Sovereign and my Eternal One,
  sparrows find a home near your altars;
swallows build nests there to raise their young.
You bless everyone who lives in your house,
  and they sing your praises.
You bless all who depend on you for their strength
  and all who deeply desire to visit your temple.
When they reach Dry Valley, springs start flowing,
  and the autumn rain fills it with pools of water.
Your people grow stronger, and you, the God of gods,
  will be seen in Zion.
God All-Powerful, the God of Jacob,
  please answer my prayer!
You are the shield that protects your people,
  and I am your chosen one. Won't you smile on me?
One day in your temple is better
  than a thousand anywhere else.

I would rather serve in your house,
   than live in the homes of the wicked.
Our God, you are like the sun and also like a shield.
You treat us with kindness and with honor,
   never denying any good thing to those who live right.
God All-Powerful, Holy One, you bless everyone who
   trusts you.   —(CEV)

PSALM 111

Congregation begins by singing the refrain from "Great Is Thy Faithfulness"—All I have needed your hand has provided; great is thy faithfulness, God, unto me! —or the refrain from "How Great Thou Art"—Then sings my soul, my Savior God to thee, how great thou art, how great thou art!

Praise God! I will give thanks to God with my whole heart,
in the company of the upright, in the congregation.
Great are your works, O God,
   studied by all who delight in them.
Majesty and splendor mark your deeds,
   and your righteousness endures forever.
You help us remember your wonders;
   you are gracious and full of compassion.
You provide food for those who honor you, being ever
   mindful of the covenant you have made. (*sing response*)
You have shown the people your powerful works,
   in giving them the heritage of the nations.
The works of your hands are faithfulness and justice;
   all of your guidance is sound.
These stand fast forever and ever,
   because they are both trustworthy and fair.

You sent redemption to your people and made with us an eternal covenant. Holy and awesome is your name!

The most important part of wisdom is honoring God.

(*All:*) **All those who practice this prove themselves wise. Our praise to God endures forever!** (*sing response*)

PSALM 139:1-18

O God, you have searched me and known me:
you know when I sit down and rise up;
  you discern my thoughts from afar.
You mark my path, and the places where I rest:
  you are familiar with all my ways.
Even before there is a word on my tongue
  you know it, O God, completely.
You guard me from behind and before,
  and cover me with your hand.
It is beyond my knowledge;
  it is a mystery, I cannot fathom it.
Where can I escape from your spirit?
  Where can I flee from your presence?
If I ascend to heaven you are there:
  if I lie down in the grave you are even there.
If I take wing with the dawn
  and fly to the outermost parts of the sea,
even there your hand will lead me,
  and your right hand will guide me.
If I say, "Let the darkness cover me,
  and my day be turned to night,"
even darkness is not dark to you,
  the night is as clear as the day:
    for darkness and light to you are both alike.
It was you who created my inward parts,

and knit me together in my mother's womb.
I praise you, for you are awesome
   and I am wonderfully made.
Marvelous are your works, this I know very well,
   and you know me through and through.
My body was not hidden from you
   when I was being fashioned in secret,
   and woven together in the depths of the earth.
Your eyes saw my substance taking shape,
   while it was as yet imperfectly formed.
In your book, all the days of my life were written,
   even before they came to be.
How deep are your thoughts, O God:
   how great is the sum of them.
If I should try to count them, they are more in number than
   the sand.
I come to the end—I am still with you.

Suggested sung response: "To You, O Lord, I Lift My Soul," Val Parker, *Psalms from the Soul*, volume 1 (Oregon Catholic Press, 2008, ocp.org)

PSALM 145 (selected verses)

I lift you high in praise, my God,
   and I'll bless your name into eternity.
The Holy One is magnificent;
   we can never offer praise enough.
Generation after generation stands in awe of your works,
   O God. Your beauty and splendor have everyone talking,
   composing songs about your wonders.
Your marvelous doings are headline news;
   books are written to share the details of your greatness.

You are full of mercy, not quick to anger, but rich in love.
Goodness is showered on one and all;
   everything is covered in grace.
Your sovereignty is eternal;
   you never get voted out of office.
God lends a hand to those down on their luck,
   lifts up those who are ready to give up.
Everything God does is right;
   the trademark on all God's works is love.
God's always there, listening for all who pray,
   for all who pray trustingly.
(*All:*) Let everything living bless the Lord, bless God's holy
   name from now to eternity!   —*The Message*

Readings from Wisdom Literature

Wisdom shines bright and never grows dim;
those who love her and look for her can easily find her.
She is quick to make herself known
   to anyone who desires her.
Get up early in the morning to find her,
   and you will have no problem;
   you will find her sitting at your door.
To fasten your attention on Wisdom
   is to gain perfect understanding.
If you look for her, you will soon find peace of mind,
because she will be looking
   for those who are worthy of her,
and she will find you wherever you are.
She is kind and will be with you in your every thought.
      —Wisdom 6:12-20 (GNT)

All wisdom is from the Lord,
  and with God it remains forever.
The sand of the sea, the drops of rain,
  and the days of eternity: who can count them?
The height of heaven, the breadth of the earth,
  the abyss, and wisdom: who can search them out?
Wisdom was created before all other things,
  and prudent understanding from eternity.
The root of wisdom: to whom has it been revealed?
  Her subtleties: who knows them?
There is but one who is wise, greatly to be feared,
  seated upon the throne: the Lord.
It is God who created Wisdom;
  saw her and took her measure;
  poured her out upon all the living according to creation;
  Wisdom is lavished upon those who love God.

—Ecclesiasticus 1 (KJV, adapted)

If you choose, you can keep the commandments,
and to act faithfully is a matter of your own choice.
God has placed before you fire and water;
stretch out your hand for whichever you choose.
Before each person are life and death,
and whichever each one chooses will be given.
For great is the wisdom of God;
the One mighty in power, who sees everything;
Everything is seen by the eyes of God,
every human action observed and noted.
The Eternal One has not commanded anyone to be wicked,
nor has anyone been given permission to sin.

—Ecclesiasticus 15:15-20

Resources for Part 2

Berglund, Brad. *Reinventing Sunday*. Valley Forge, PA: Judson Press, 2001.

Bonn, Linda. *The Work of the Worship Committee*. Valley Forge, PA: Judson Press, 1998.

Calvin Institute of Christian Worship and Faith Alive Christian Resources. *Psalms for All Seasons: A Complete Psalter for Worship*. Grand Rapids, MI: Baker Books, 2012.

Calvin Institute of Christian Worship and Faith Alive Christian Resources. *The Worship Sourcebook*, 2nd ed. (includes CD). Grand Rapids, MI: Baker Books, 2013.

Cartwright, Colbert S., and O. I. Cricket Harrison, eds. *Chalice Worship*. Nashville: Chalice Press, 1997.

Duck, Ruth C. *Worship for the Whole People of God: Vital Worship for the 21st Century*. Louisville, KY: Westminster John Knox, 2013.

Faith Alive Christian Resources. *Reformed Worship Magazine* (quarterly journal), faithaliveresources.org.

Merrill, Nan C. *Psalms for Praying: An Invitation to Wholeness*. 10th anniversary ed. New York and London: Continuum, 2007.

Stevens, John G., and Michael Waschevski. *Rhythms of Worship*. Louisville, KY: Westminster John Knox, 2014.

Textweek.com. Online resource for weekly worship planning, featuring a vast array of scripture study, worship and liturgy links, and resources, www.textweek.com.

PART 3

Scriptures, Prayers, and Readings for the Christian Year

*It is the eternal cycle of the church year with its
re-presentation of God's story in interaction
with our human story that best orders our lives
within the Christian faith community.*

—John H. Westerhoff III, *A Pilgrim People*

THE CHRISTIAN YEAR, beginning with the first Sunday in Advent, celebrates the events of the gospel through the birth, life, death, and resurrection of Jesus Christ, as well as his ministry. The story of God's mighty works in Christ, the coming of the Holy Spirit, and the establishment of the church are told through the seasons of Advent, Christmas, Epiphany, Lent, Holy Week, Easter, Ascension, and Pentecost. In the remainder of the Christian Year, during the season following Pentecost, the church spends many weeks focusing on God's mission to the world.

A collection of scriptures, prayers, and readings for these seasons of the Christian Year are given here; they by no means exhaust the richness of seasonal resources for congregational worship. While these materials work well with the weekly readings from the Revised Common Lectionary (RCL), churches that do not follow a lectionary plan of specific readings should also find the materials in this chapter useful. When they are combined with the use of a lectionary, however, these prayers can enhance the presentation of God's acts in history and serve as a recurring reminder of the Creator's love for the world.

In most cases, the prayers and readings have not been labeled for a specific part of the service; worship planners can determine where each might best be used.

Advent

Advent begins the Christian Year and marks the season of preparation for the coming of the Christ, both in his incarnation as a human infant and in his coming again at the end of time. It is a season for reflection and anticipation, rich in both meaning and in symbolism; but this richness is often lost amid the commercial frenzy before Christmas. Reviving an awareness of the Sundays of Advent as a time of patient waiting can create a refuge of calm, blessing, and wonder for our congregations, and a reminder that waiting in hope and expectation is a holy activity. Observing Advent as a season of its own, set apart from the artificial "holiday season" swirling round about, can offer our church families a much-needed retreat for recentering their lives and hearts.

Scriptures

Lift up your heads, O gates!
  and be lifted up, O ancient doors!
  that the Glorious One may come in.
Who is this Glorious One?
God, strong and mighty, God, victorious.
Lift up your heads, O gates!
  and be lifted up, O ancient doors!
  that the Glorious One may come in.
Who is this Glorious One?
  The Sovereign of heaven, the God of glory.

—Psalm 24:7-10

In days to come the mountain of God's house shall be established as the highest of the mountains, and shall be raised above the hills; all the nations shall stream to it.
Many peoples shall come and say,
"Come, let us go up to the holy mountain, to the house of the God of Jacob;
that we may be taught the holy ways and that we may walk in holy paths."
For out of Zion shall go forth instruction, and the word of God from Jerusalem.
The Holy One shall judge between the nations, and shall arbitrate for many peoples;
they shall beat their swords into plowshares, and their spears into pruning hooks;
nation shall not lift up sword against nation, neither shall they learn war any more.
(*All:*) **O house of Jacob, come, let us walk in the light of God!**

—Isaiah 2:2-5

A shoot shall come out from the stump of Jesse, and a branch shall grow out of these roots. The spirit of God shall rest on this One, the spirit of wisdom and understanding, the spirit of counsel and might, the spirit of knowledge and the fear of God.

—Isaiah 11:1-2

"Comfort my people," says our God. "Comfort them!
  Encourage the people of Jerusalem.
Tell them they have suffered long enough
  and their sins are now forgiven."
A voice cries out,
  "Prepare in the wilderness a road for the Holy One!
Clear the way in the desert for our God!
Fill every valley; level every mountain.
The hills will become a plain,
  and the rough country will be made smooth.
Then God's glory will be revealed, and all people will see it.
God, our God has promised this to us."

—Isaiah 40:1-5 (GNT)

In the sixth month the angel Gabriel was sent by God to a town in Galilee called Nazareth, to a virgin engaged to a man whose name was Joseph, of the house of David. The virgin's name was Mary. And he came to her and said, **"Greetings, favored one! The Lord is with you."**

—Luke 1:26-28

Mary said: "My soul lifts up the Lord!
My spirit celebrates my Liberator!
For though I'm the Lord's humble servant,
  God has noticed me.

Now and forever,
   I will be considered blessed by all generations.
For the Mighty One has done great things for me;
   holy is God's name!
From generation to generation,
   God's lovingkindness endures
for those who revere the Holy One.
God's arm has accomplished mighty deeds.
The proud in mind and heart
   have been sent away in disarray.
The rulers from their high positions of power,
   God has brought down low.
And those who were humble and lowly,
   God has elevated with dignity.
The hungry God has filled with fine food.
The rich have been dismissed with nothing in their hands.
To Israel, God's servant, God has given help,
As promised to our ancestors, remembering Abraham and
   his descendants in mercy forever."

—Luke 1:46-55 (*The Voice*)

Jesus said: In those days, after the suffering of that time, the sun will become dark, and the moon won't give its light. The stars will fall from the sky, and the planets and other heavenly bodies will be shaken.
Then they will see the Human One coming in the clouds with great power and splendor. Then he will send the angels and gather together his chosen people from the four corners of the earth, from the end of the earth to the end of heaven. —Mark 13:24-27 (CEB)

Prayers and Readings

Blessed are you, eternal God:

In whom the heavens rejoice and the earth is glad, for you will judge the world with justice.

Blessed are you, Christ our Savior:

You come in humility to perfect God's realm, and to bring in those who were ransomed with songs of everlasting joy.

Blessed are you, holy and gracious Spirit:

You gladden our hearts and fill our mouths with praise.

Glory be to you, O God, forever and ever.

The Advent season is indeed a time of anticipation, for the new ideas that will move the world in a new direction are soon to be born. Let us celebrate the coming birth of Jesus by giving birth to a new idea; looking with wider vision, working toward change. In the season of giving, let us support and nurture those institutions that courageously recognize all life as divine, that work to acknowledge and change oppressive systems. As we await the birth of the divine, let us be open to the divine in those around us who may have been overlooked or discounted. We ask for your strength and your blessing, O God.

—Joy Troyer, *Looking for Truth*

Let us receive the light, and we will receive you, O God. Let us receive the light and become disciples of the Christ. Sing, O Word; reveal the Creator to us! Your words will save us and your songs will teach us. Since we are the people of God's love, let us sing and never cease, to the God of peace above. **Amen.**   —Clement of Alexandria (150–215), adapted

Just as the Christ-child makes God known at Christmas,
May we make God known in the week ahead.
May our hope provide confidence as we await God's reign.
May our peace provide comfort as we work for God's justice.
May our joy provide celebration as we embrace God's
    presence.
May our love provide wholeness as we accept God's healing.
As we prepare for the light of the world to illumine us anew,
May we share our light with the world.   —Allison J. Tanner

When the King shall come again, all his power revealing,
splendor shall announce his reign, life and joy and healing;
earth no longer in decay, hope no more frustrated,
this is God's redemption day, longingly awaited.

In the desert trees take root fresh from his creation;
plants and flowers and sweetest fruit join the celebration;
rivers spring up from the earth, barren lands adorning:
valleys, this is your new birth; mountains greet the morning!

—Christopher M. Idle, © 1982 Jubilate Hymns, Ltd.
(administered by Hope Publishing Company)
Sing to the tune TEMPUS ADEST FLORIDUM (Good King Wenceslas)

Suggested Hymns and Songs
(see hymnary.org or other sources as noted)

Come and Fill Our Hearts / Confitemini Domino (Taizé
    Community)
Come, Dear Christ, Your World Awaits (Mary Louise
    Bringle, *Joy and Wonder, Love and Longing*, GIA
    Publications, Inc.)
Comfort, Comfort You My People (John Olearius)
Let Justice Roll Down (Daniel Charles Damon, *Garden of
    Joy*, Hope Publishing Company and Hope Hymns Online)

Mary, Woman of the Promise (Mary Frances Fleischaker)
O Come, O Come Emmanuel (Latin, c. twelfth century)
O Day of Peace That Dimly Shines (Carl P. Daw Jr.)
Prepare the Way, O Zion (Frans Mikael Franzen)
Rejoice, Behold the One True Light (John A. Dalles)
Soon and Very Soon (Andraé Crouch)
We Wait the Peaceful Kingdom (Kathleen R. Moore)

Christmas Eve, Christmas Day, and Christmastide

The Christmas season is twelve days, beginning with the festival of the Nativity. This time of celebration centers upon the birth of Jesus, the good news that the heavenly host proclaimed for all people. Congregations should consider celebrating not just Christmas Day, but the entire season. This expands the time for sharing gospel stories and rich musical expressions of joy for Emmanuel, God with us.

Scriptures

O sing to the Lord a new song,
    for God has done marvelous things.
God's right hand and holy arm have gotten the victory.
God has remembered steadfast love and faithfulness
    to the house of Israel.
All the ends of the earth have seen the victory of our God.
Make a joyful noise to God, all the earth;
Break forth into joyous song and sing praises.

—Psalm 98:1, 3-4

The people who walked in darkness have seen a great light; those who lived in a land of deep darkness—on them light has shined.

For a child has been born for us, a son given to us; authority rests upon his shoulders; and he is named Wonderful Counselor, Mighty God, Everlasting Father, Prince of Peace. —Isaiah 9:2, 6

In those days a decree went out from Emperor Augustus that all the world should be registered. This was the first registration and was taken while Quirinius was governor of Syria. All went to their own towns to be registered. Joseph also went from the town of Nazareth in Galilee to Judea, to the city of David called Bethlehem, because he was descended from the house and family of David. He went to be registered with Mary, to whom he was engaged and who was expecting a child. While they were there, the time came for her to deliver her child. And she gave birth to her firstborn son and wrapped him in bands of cloth, and laid him in a manger, because there was no place for them in the inn. —Luke 2:1-7

In that region there were shepherds living in the fields, keeping watch over their flock by night. Then an angel of the Lord stood before them, and the glory of the Lord shone around them, and they were terrified. But the angel said to them, "Do not be afraid; for see—I am bringing you good news of great joy for all the people: to you is born this day in the city of David a Savior, who is the Messiah, the Lord. This will be a sign for you: you will find a child wrapped in bands of cloth and lying in a manger." —Luke 2:8-12

In the beginning was the Word, and the Word was with God, and the Word was God. Everything came into being through the Word, and without the Word nothing came into being. What came into being through the Word was life, and the life was the light for all people. The light shines in the darkness, and the darkness doesn't extinguish the light. The Word became flesh and made a home among us, full of grace and truth.

—From John 1 (CEB)

Prayers and Readings

Prepare for God's arrival! Make the road straight and
    smooth, a highway fit for our God.
Fill in the valleys, level off the hills,
    smooth out the ruts, clear away the rocks.
Then God's brilliance will shine, and everyone will see it.
Get out of bed, Jerusalem! Wake up!
    Raise your face to the sunlight.
(*All:*) **God's bright glory has arrived for all the earth.**
    O come, let us adore the Christ child!

—Based on Isaiah, chapters 40 and 60 (*The Message*, adapted)

Into a world of darkness you came;
    into a world that was too busy to notice you.
A world too distracted to give you attention,
    a world too caught up in their own struggles,
a world too proud of their own accomplishments.
And yet you came, and the few who noticed were amazed.
You came and those who felt your touch were healed.
You came and those who knew you learned a better way.
Those who followed you walked with God.
Thank you for coming, so long ago;
    thank you for coming again tonight.

Through the music, the stories, and the candlelight,
may we be touched by you, learn from you,
  know God through you.
Into a world of darkness we go;
  into a world too busy to pay you much attention.
And yet we go, to proclaim the story that is our salvation.
As we go into the world of darkness, may we carry your
  light and share it with others.   —Allison J. Tanner

Almighty and everlasting God, who sent Christ into the
  world not just for us but for all people, hear the prayers
  of your servants as we lift up our hearts in intercession:
Let us pray for the children who have no welcome room in
  the world. (*Silence*)
Let us pray for those who suffer from hunger and who are
  homeless. (*Silence*)
Let us pray for those in the world who endure injustice.
  (*Silence*)
You have heard the prayers of your people, O God. We
  who are your faithful ones do humbly ask your power
  and love, so we may guide others in unity, through Jesus
  Christ. **Amen.**

Christ is born, give glory! Christ comes from heaven, meet
  him! Christ is on earth, be exalted!
**All the earth, sing unto God, and sing praises in gladness,
  all peoples, for God has been glorified.**
Wisdom and Word and Power, Christ is the Song and the
  brightness of God; Christ was made human, and so has
  won us to God.
**All the earth, sing unto God, and sing praises in gladness,
  all peoples, for God has been glorified. Amen.**
                                        —Eastern Orthodox prayer

Lift up your hearts:
We lift them up to God.
Let us give thanks to our God:
It is right and good to do so.
We praise you, God, for all the joys of this season. We sing gladly our hymns and carols. We give our gifts to one another in delight. But above all we thank you for the matchless gift of our Savior, Jesus Christ.
Grant that our words and deeds will fully praise you, Holy One. Grant us loving hearts, that we may love him who has loved us and who gave himself for us, Christ our Lord. Amen.

Born in the night, Mary's Child,
    a long way from your home;
coming in need, Mary's Child,
    born in a borrowed room.

Clear shining light, Mary's Child,
    your face lights up our way;
light of the world, Mary's Child,
    dawn on our darkened day.

Hope of the world, Mary's Child,
    you're coming soon to reign;
Savior of all, Mary's Child,
    walk in our streets again.

—Geoffrey Ainger, © 1964 Stainer & Bell, Ltd.
(administered by Hope Publishing Company)
Sing to the tune MARY'S CHILD

Suggested Hymns and Songs
(see hymnary.org or other sources as noted)

Before the Marvel of This Night (Jaroslav Vajda)

Breath of God, Breath of Peace (Adam M. L. Tice)

From the Heights of Heaven (Herman G. Stuempfle Jr., *The Song of Faith Unsilenced*, GIA Publications, Inc.)

Go, Tell It on the Mountain (African American spiritual)

Good News for This New Age (Albert F. Bayly, *Holding in Trust*, Hope Publishing Company and Hope Hymns Online)

Jesus, Jesus, O What a Wonderful Child (African American spiritual)

Once in Royal David's City (Cecil Frances Alexander)

'Twas in the Moon of Wintertime (Jesse Edgar Middleton)

When God Is a Child/Hope Is a Star (Brian Wren)

Who Would Think That God Almighty (Joy F. Patterson)

Wonder of All Wonders (Timothy Dudley-Smith)

Epiphany Season

The season of Epiphany celebrates the manifestation of God's light and power in the Christ, beginning with the visit of the star-led Magi to the child Jesus. His recognition as the Light by Simeon and Anna, and the stories of his baptism and early miracles, highlight the church's mission to the world.

Scriptures

Blessed are those whose help comes from the God of Jacob, whose hope is centered in the Eternal their God—
who created the heavens, the earth, the seas,
and all that lives within them;

who stays true and remains faithful forever;
who works justice for those who are pressed down by the
    world,
    providing food for those who are hungry.
The Eternal frees those who are imprisoned;
    making the blind see,
lifting up those whose backs are bent in labor;
    cherishing those who do what is right.
The Eternal looks after those who journey
    in a land not their own;
taking care of the orphan and the widow,
    but frustrating the wicked along their way.
The Eternal will reign today, tomorrow, and forever.
People of Zion, your God will rule
    forever over all generations.
Praise the Eternal!   —Psalm 146:5-10 (*The Voice*)

Arise, shine; for your light has come,
    and the glory of God has risen upon you.
For darkness shall cover the earth,
    and thick darkness the peoples;
But God will arise upon you,
    and holy glory will appear over you.
Nations shall come to your light,
    and sovereigns to the brightness of your dawn.
                                      —Isaiah 60:1-3

The spirit of God is upon me,
    because God has anointed me
and has sent me to bring good news to the oppressed,
    to bind up the brokenhearted,
to proclaim liberty to the captives,
    and release to the prisoners;

to proclaim the year of God's favor,
and the day of vengeance of our God;
to comfort all who mourn;
to provide for those who mourn in Zion—
to give them a garland instead of ashes,
the oil of gladness instead of mourning,
the mantle of praise instead of a faint spirit.
They will be called oaks of righteousness,
the planting of God, displaying glory.
They shall build up the ancient ruins,
they shall raise up the former devastations;
they shall repair the ruined cities,
the devastations of many generations.   —Isaiah 61:1-4

The wise ones set out; and there, ahead of them went the
star that they had seen at its rising, until it stopped over the
place where the child was. On entering the house, they saw
the child with Mary his mother; and they knelt down and
worshiped him.   —Matthew 2:9, 11

Blessed be the God of Israel, who has looked favorably on
the people and redeemed them.
God has raised up a mighty savior for us in the house of
God's servant David.
And the child will be called the prophet of the Most High,
the One who will go before, to prepare God's ways,
To give knowledge of salvation to God's people by the for-
giveness of their sins.
By the tender mercy of our God, the dawn from on high
will break upon us, to give light to those who sit in darkness and in the shadow of death,

To guide our feet into the way of peace.

—Luke 1:68-69, 76-79

Holy One, now you are letting your servant depart in peace, according to your word; for my eyes have seen your salvation that you have prepared in the presence of all peoples, a light for revelation to the Gentiles, for glory to your people Israel."

—Luke 2:29-32

Jesus said: "I am the light of the world. Whoever follows me will never walk in darkness but will have the light of life."

—John 8:12

In the beginning the Word already existed; the Word was with God, and the Word was God. From the very beginning the Word was with God, who made all things; not one thing in all creation was made without the Word. The Word is the source of life, and this life brings light to the people. The light shines in the darkness, and the darkness cannot overcome it. Come into our hearts this day, Emmanuel! **Amen.**

—John 1:1-5

Prayers and Readings

Gracious God, come and scatter the shadows in our hearts by the light of your presence; that we may know you are the Light of the World and the one true God, blessed this day and forevermore. —*The Book of Common Prayer*

As the wise ones of old came bearing offerings, so we come to you, O God, with our gifts. Accept and transform them in the light of the gospel, that the world might believe and come to know him whom to know is life eternal, Christ Jesus, our Lord. **Amen.**

Holy are you, O God, our light and our salvation, and blessed is Jesus Christ, in whom you have revealed yourself. You sent a star to guide wise ones to where the Christ was born; and your signs and witnesses in every age have led your people from far places to his light. For Jesus Christ, we thank you. **Amen.**

From the rising of the sun to its setting,
   let the name of God be praised.
You are our lamp. You, O God, make our darkness bright.
Light and peace in Jesus Christ our Lord.
Thanks be to God. Amen.

O splendor of God's glory bright, from light eternal bringing light;
Thou light of life, light's living spring,
   true day, all days illumining.

O joyful be the passing day
   with thoughts as clear as morning's ray,
With faith like noontide shining bright,
   our souls unshadowed by the night.

All praise to God Creator be;
   all praise the Son, who sets us free;
whom with the Spirit we adore
   forever and forever more.

                —Ambrose of Milan (c. 340–397)
                Sing to the tune PUER NOBIS NASCITUR

Suggested Hymns and Songs
(see hymnary.org or other sources as noted)

Arise, Your Light Is Come (Ruth Duck)
Behold That Star (African American spiritual)

Christ Be Our Light (Bernadette Farrell)
Come Light, Light of God (The Sisters of the Community
   of Grandchamp, Switzerland)
From a Distant Home Land (George K. Evans, Puerto
   Rican carol)
I Want to Walk as a Child of the Light (Kathleen Thomerson)
Jesus, the Light of the World (George D. Elderkin)
O Holy Wisdom, Pour Forth Compassion (Delores Dufner,
   OSB, *And Every Breath a Song*, GIA Publications, Inc.)
Open Our Eyes, Lord, We Want to See Jesus (Robert Cull)
Thy Word Is a Lamp Unto My Feet (Amy Grant)
What Feast of Love (Delores Dufner, OSB)
When Jesus Came to Jordan (Fred Pratt Green)

Transfiguration Sunday

Transfiguration Day, observed on the final Sunday of the
Epiphany season, celebrates Christ's mountaintop experience as reported in the Gospels.

The Eternal One is Sovereign; let the peoples rejoice! God
   sits enthroned among the angels; let all the earth sing
   "Glory!"
The Holy One is majestic in Zion;
   God is exalted over all the peoples.
Let them praise your great and awesome name, O God.
   Mighty One, you have established justice, you have ac-
   complished righteousness.
The Holy One is majestic in Zion;
   God is exalted over all the peoples.
God spoke to the ancestors in the pillar of cloud; they tried
   to keep God's commands for the good of the people.

The Holy One is majestic in Zion;
  God is exalted over all the peoples.
You answered them, Gracious God, forgiving them when
  they did wrong and holding them in safety.
(*All:*) **We worship at the holy mountain**
  in the light of God's splendor. Alleluia!   —From Psalm 99

Jesus took with him Peter and John and James, and went
up to the mountain to pray. And while he was praying,
the appearance of his face changed, and his clothes became
dazzling white. Suddenly they saw two men, Moses and
Elijah, talking to him. They appeared in glory and were
speaking of his departure, which he was about to accomplish at Jerusalem. Now Peter and his companions were
weighed down with sleep; but since they had stayed awake,
they saw his glory and the two men who stood with him.
Just as they were leaving him, Peter said to Jesus, "Master,
it is good for us to be here; let us make three dwellings, one
for you, one for Moses, and one for Elijah"—not knowing what he said. While he was saying this, a cloud came
and overshadowed them; and they were terrified as they
entered the cloud. Then from the cloud came a voice that
said, "This is my Son, my Chosen; listen to him!"

—Luke 9:28-35

There is no mountain too high, no valley too low, for God
to find us. There is no limit on grace or forgiveness, and
God's steadfast love is immeasurable. Know that you are
beloved by God, forgiven, and restored. Now, go, share the
Good News, and live into God's ways of justice and peace,
knowing that the power of God's love is far beyond what
we could ever hope or imagine. **Amen.**

—Mindi Welton-Mitchell

How good, Lord, to be here! Your glory fills our sight;
your face and garments, like the sun, shine with unbor-
    rowed light.

How good, Lord, to be here, your beauty to behold,
where Moses and Elijah stand, your messengers of old.

This image we behold, we see your kingdom come;
we long to hold that vision bright, and make this mount
    our home!

How good, Lord, to be here! Yet we may not remain;
but since you bid us leave the mount, come with us to the
    plain. —Joseph Armitage Robinson, (1858–1933), adapted
                        Sing to the tune FESTAL SONG

Suggested Hymns and Songs
(see hymnary.org or other sources as noted)

Be Thou My Vision (Ancient Irish poem)
Christ Upon the Mountain Peak (Brian Wren)
I Want to Walk as a Child of the Light (Kathleen Thomerson)
O Wondrous Sight, O Vision Fair (Latin, fifteenth century)
Open the Eyes of My Heart, Lord (Paul Baloche)
Shine, Jesus, Shine (Graham Kendrick)
We Have Come at Christ's Own Bidding (Carl P. Daw Jr.)

Ash Wednesday and Lent

Lent is forty days for personal discipline and reflection beginning with Ash Wednesday, and through six weeks culminating in Palm Sunday. It is a season for spiritual growth
and repentance, a preparation for sharing in the passion
of Jesus Christ. A congregation that journeys together
through this somber yet rich season of worship will greet

the events of Holy Week and Easter with a deeper sense of meaning and engagement.

Scriptures

To you, O God, we lift up our souls. In you, O God, we trust; do not let us be put to shame; do not let our enemies triumph over us. Make us to know your ways, O God; teach us your paths and lead us in your truth. You are the God of our salvation; for you we wait all day long. Be mindful of your mercy, O God, and of your steadfast love, for they have been from of old. Do not remember the sins of our youth or our transgressions. According to your steadfast love remember us, for your goodness' sake, O God! —Psalm 25:1-2, 4-7

Be merciful to me, O God, because of your constant love. Because of your great mercy wipe away my sins! Wash away all my evil and make me clean from my sin! Create a pure heart in me, O God, and put a new and loyal spirit in me. Do not banish me from your presence; do not take your holy spirit away from me. Give me again the joy that comes from your salvation, and make me willing to obey you. Then I will teach sinners your commands, and they will turn back to you. You do not want sacrifices, or I would offer them; you are not pleased with burnt offerings. My sacrifice is a humble spirit, O God; you will not reject a humble and repentant heart. —From Psalm 51 (GNT)

I cry out to you from the depths, Lord—
    O God, listen to my voice!
Let your ears pay close attention to my request for mercy!
If you kept track of sins, my Lord,
    who would stand a chance?

But forgiveness is with you—that's why you are honored.
I hope, O Lord. My whole being hopes,
  and I await your promises.
My whole being waits for God—
  more than the night watch waits for morning!
O Israel, wait for the Holy One!
Because faithful love and great redemption are with God;
the Eternal One will redeem Israel from all its sin.

—Psalm 130 (CEB)

Jesus told his disciples: "If any want to become my follow-ers, let them deny themselves and take up their cross and follow me. For those who want to save their life will lose it, and those who lose their life for my sake will find it. For what will it profit them if they gain the whole world but forfeit their life? Or what will they give in return for their life?"

—Matthew 16:24-26

Hear the words of Jesus: "I am the good shepherd. The good shepherd lays down his life for the sheep."

—John 10:11

We know that all things work together for good for those who love God, who are called according to God's pur-pose. What then are we to say?
If God is for us, who is against us?
God, who did not withhold God's own Son but gave him up for all of us, will God not with him also give us ev-erything else?
Who will separate us from the love of Christ?
Will hardship, or distress, or persecution, or famine, or nakedness, or peril, or sword?

No, in all these things we are more than conquerors through the one who loved us.

For neither death, nor life, nor angels, nor rulers, nor things present, nor things to come,

Nor powers, nor height, nor depth, nor anything else in all creation, will be able to separate us from the love of God in Christ Jesus.   —From Romans 8:28-39

If we say we have no sin, we deceive ourselves, and the truth is not in us. If we confess our sins, God is faithful and just to forgive us our sins and cleanse us from all our sins. In this is love, not that we loved God but that God loved us and sent Jesus Christ to be the atoning sacrifice for our sins. Beloved, since God loved us so much, we also ought to love one another.   —1 John 4:8-11

Prayers and Readings

Jesus Christ, who for our sake fasted forty days and forty nights, we ask for grace to discipline ourselves during this season, so that our bodies, minds, and spirits may become fitting vessels of your grace. We raise our voices in praise to you for his days upon the earth, his victory over temptation, his acts of love and mercy, his simple teaching concerning your way, his faithfulness even to death, and his victory in the cross and resurrection. Thanks be to you, O God, for your immeasurable gift in Jesus Christ. **Amen.**

Lord Jesus, our Savior, let us now come to you:
Our hearts are cold;
  Lord, warm them with your selfless love.
Our hearts are sinful;
  cleanse them with your precious blood,

Our hearts are weak;
 strengthen them with your joyous spirit.
Our hearts are empty;
 fill them with your divine presence.
Lord Jesus, our hearts are yours;
 possess them always and only for yourself. Amen.

—Attributed to Augustine of Hippo (354–430)

Lord, we have fallen far short of your purpose for us here,
 and we have sinned in so many ways.
Forgive us for the times we have not heeded the guidance
 of your Holy Spirit.
We have not centered our lives in your Son, Jesus Christ.
Forgive us for the times when we have taken control of our
 own lives and stumbled.
We have not been mindful of our behavior and how it
 could cause others to turn away from you.
Forgive us for being mindful only of our own needs and
 neglecting the needs of others.
Lord, in your loving mercy, grant us new life as we dedicate
 our lives once more to you.
We ask this in your Son Jesus' name. Amen.   —Amy Pearson

God of all suffering, healing, grace, and mercy:
During this time of prayer our hearts and minds are directed
toward the cross. As we remember the passion and agony
of your Son's crucifixion, let us also remember to keep in
our thoughts and prayers those in our community who suffer daily from chronic, debilitating, and terminal diseases.
Give them the strength and the willingness to bear their
affliction but also the courage to continue to fight the good
fight. Gracious God, allow us to know the right words to

say that will give comfort and encouragement. We ask you, heavenly healer, to intercede on behalf of the afflicted and let them feel your presence daily. In the name of Jesus, the Great Physician, we pray. Amen. —Karen Lee Deweese

Jesus walked that lonesome valley,
   he had to walk it by himself;
O, nobody else could walk it for him,
   he had to walk it by himself.
**Help us walk our lonesome valleys, O God, knowing that
we are not forsaken, for you are always there beside us.**
—African American spiritual

Suggested Hymns and Songs
(see hymnary.org or other sources as noted)

Dust and Ashes Touch Our Face (Brian Wren)
Give Me a Clean Heart (Margaret Douroux)
In Christ Alone (Keith Getty and Stuart Townend)
Jesus, Tempted in the Desert (Herman G. Stuempfle)
Jesus Walked This Lonesome Valley (African American spiritual)
Lord, Who Throughout These Forty Days (Claudia Frances Hernaman)
Saranam, Saranam / Jesus, Savior, Lord, Now to You I Come (D. T. Niles)
What Wondrous Love Is This (American folk hymn)
When We Are Tested (Ruth Duck)
Wild and Lone the Prophet's Voice (Carl P. Daw Jr.)

Palm and Passion Sunday

There are two ways to observe the beginning of Holy Week. We can focus solely on Jesus' triumphal entry to Jerusalem as the prelude to coming events, or we can take the congregation further into the passion story. For those who may not have the opportunity to experience Maundy Thursday or Good Friday services, a reminder on Sunday of the passion story yet to come can point them toward Calvary and provide a sense of the drama that leads to Easter morning.

Scriptures

Lift up your heads, O gates!
   and be lifted up, O ancient doors!
   that the Glorious One may come in.
Who is this Glorious One?
God, strong and mighty, God, victorious.
Lift up your heads, O gates!
   and be lifted up, O ancient doors!
   that the Glorious One may come in.
Who is this Glorious One?
The Sovereign of heaven, the God of glory.   —Psalm 24:7-10

Open to me the gates of righteousness,
   that I may enter through them and give thanks to God.
This is the gate of the Lord;
   the righteous shall enter through it.
I thank you that you have answered me
   and have become my salvation.
The stone that the builders rejected
   has become the chief cornerstone.

This is God's doing; it is marvelous in our eyes.
This is the day that the Lord has made;
  let us rejoice and be glad in it!
Save us, we beseech you, O God! Give us success!
Blessed is the one who comes in the name of God.
  God, the Holy One, has given us light.
Bind the festal procession with branches,
  marching up to the altar.
You are God, and we give thanks to you;
  you are God, we extol you!
O give thanks to the Eternal One, for God is good.
God's steadfast love endures forever.   —Psalm 118:19-29

When they were approaching Jerusalem, at Bethphage and Bethany, near the Mount of Olives, Jesus sent two of his disciples and said to them, "Go into the village ahead of you, and immediately as you enter it, you will find tied there a colt that has never been ridden; untie it and bring it." Then they brought the colt to Jesus and threw their cloaks on it; and he sat on it. Many people spread their cloaks on the road, and others spread leafy branches that they had cut in the fields. Then those who went ahead and those who followed were shouting,

"Hosanna! Blessed is the one who comes in the name of the Lord!
Blessed is the coming kingdom of our ancestor David! Hosanna in the highest heaven!"   —Mark 11:1-2, 7-10

Prayers and Readings

Creator and Sustainer of all:
you see us at our best and rejoice with us,
  and call us to share our best with others;

you see us at our worst and grieve for our falling short,
and offer us your love and the gift of a new day.
You are with us in the vast world around us,
   and in the eyes of everyone we meet.
**You are with us throughout the week and throughout the
   year.**
Out of our week, we have set aside this hour to cherish and
   celebrate your presence.
Out of our year, we have set aside this week to remember
   that most turbulent week:
**in the time when you walked among us in Jerusalem,
when you called for the best in us,
   and suffered the worst from us.**
Be with us now in this hour, as in word and song
we celebrate the triumph and mourn the desolation of that
   week.
(*All:*) **We ask this in the name of the one
   who walked with us then
and walks with us still. Amen.**   —Mark Theodoropoulos

O merciful God, on this Palm Sunday we rejoice that you
love us still, with a love that does not grow weary but is
constant, year after year, age after age. Let our prayers of
intercession be as palm branches before you.
**We pray for all those who give their lives in service and
   sacrifice in their devotion to you.**
We pray for all who face great temptation,
**We pray for all who stagger under burdens too great for
   them to bear.**
We pray for all who live in surroundings that breed ignorance and evil.

We pray for people in need around the world and for refugees everywhere.
We pray for those in our own faith community.
(*Silence*)
Today may we offer ourselves to you through our actions as well as our prayers.
May all who come to you in prayer be filled with your grace. **Amen.**

God of history—we thank you for sending your Son, Jesus Christ, to dwell among us, living and dying to show us your great love for all humanity.
God of this very day—we thank you for all that we have and all that we are. Please accept the gifts we freely offer in praise of you.
God of the days to come—walk with us in our journey, keep us focused upon the cross, and help us to speak words of love, comfort, and welcome in the name of Jesus.
We offer this prayer in that great name, crying "Hosanna!" Blessed is the one who came among us and lives with us still. Amen.
                                                                —N.H.

Merciful God, your son Jesus steadfastly walked the road to Jerusalem, knowing that a cross stood at the journey's end. Grant us courage, that we, like Jesus, might walk toward the cross, strengthened by the one who is our Redeemer. **Amen.**

From the east the poor are marching,
    spreading branches as they come;
from the west the sound of soldiers marching,
    marching far from home.

Jesus on a colt comes riding
   down a dusty city street,
with a ragtag peasant chorus—
   hopeful, shouting as they meet.

Pilate comes imposing order
   on the festival each year—
warhorse, drumbeat, armored soldiers.
   Silent crowds look on with fear.

Two processions to the city—
   shepherd staff and Roman spear.
Blessed is the Son of David
   who will bring God's kingdom here.

—Daniel Charles Damon, Garden of Joy, © 2011
Hope Publishing Company and Hope Hymns Online

Suggested Hymns and Songs
(see hymnary.org or other sources as noted)

A Cheering, Chanting, Dizzy Crowd (Thomas H. Troeger)
All Glory, Laud, and Honor (Theodulf of Orleans)
Filled with Excitement/Mantos y palmas (Rubén Ruíz Ávila)
I Will Enter His Gates with Thanksgiving/He Has Made Me
   Glad (Leona Von Brethorst)
Ride On, King Jesus (African American spiritual)
Soon and Very Soon (Andraé Crouch)
The King of Glory Comes (Willard F. Jabusch)
We Sang Out Glad Hosannas (Mary Nelson Keithahn)
You, Lord, Are Both Lamb and Shepherd (Sylvia G. Dunstan)

Maundy Thursday

This day of Holy Week derives its name from the Latin *mandatum novum*, the "new commandment" that Jesus gave in John 13:34. Maundy Thursday worship services focus on Christ's last Passover meal with his disciples, and through the sharing of bread and cup "in remembrance" we recall the drama of the upper room. Some churches, as part of their Maundy Thursday worship, follow the example of Jesus with the washing of feet.

Scriptures

Hear my prayer, O God; let my cry come to you!
Do not hide your face from me in the day of my distress!
Incline your ear to me;
   answer me speedily in the day when I call!
All the day my enemies taunt me;
   those who deride me use my name for a curse.
For I eat ashes like bread, and mingle tears with my drink,
because of your indignation and anger;
   for you have taken me up and thrown me down.
My days are like an evening shadow;
   I wither away like grass.   —Psalm 102:1-2, 8-11

We love God, and therefore our voices and our supplications have been heard.
God inclines an ear to us, therefore, we will call on God as long as we live.
What shall we return to God for all these blessings?
We will lift up the cup of salvation and call on God's name.
We will pay our vows to God, in the presence of the faithful, in the courts of God's house.
We are your servants, O God.   —Psalm 116:1-2, 12-19

Whoever wishes to be great among you must be your servant, and whoever wishes to be first among you must be your slave; just as the Christ came not to be served but to serve, and to give his life as a ransom for many.

—Matthew 20:26-28

During the meal Jesus took some bread in his hands. He blessed the bread and broke it. Then he gave it to his disciples and said, "Take this and eat it. This is my body." Jesus picked up a cup of wine and gave thanks to God. He then gave it to his disciples and said, "Take this and drink it. This is my blood, and with it God makes his agreement with you. It will be poured out, so that many people will have their sins forgiven. From now on I am not going to drink any wine, until I drink new wine with you in my Father's kingdom." Then they sang a hymn and went out to the Mount of Olives.   —Matthew 26:26-30 (CEV)

Jesus got up from the table, took off his outer robe, and tied a towel around himself. Then he poured water into a basin and began to wash the disciples' feet and to wipe them with the towel that was tied around him. He came to Simon Peter, who said to him, "Lord, are you going to wash my feet?" Jesus answered, "You do not know now what I am doing, but later you will understand." Peter said to him, "You will never wash my feet." Jesus answered, "Unless I wash you, you have no share with me." Simon Peter said to him, "Lord, not my feet only but also my hands and my head!"   —John 13:4-9

For whenever we eat this bread and drink this cup,
    we proclaim Christ's death until he comes again.

Christ has died. Christ is risen. Christ will come again.

Prayers and Readings

Help us, O God, to take towel and basin and in humbleness of spirit to wash the feet of those in need; through Jesus Christ, who came and who served. **Amen.**

Almighty and merciful God, the fountain of all goodness,
   who knows the thoughts of our hearts:
We confess that we have sinned against you.
Wash us, we implore you, from our sins.
Give us grace and power to put behind us
   all that offends you.
Being delivered from the bondage of sin, may we bring
   forth fruits worthy of repentance, and at last enter into
   your promised joy;
Through the mercy of your blessed One, Jesus Christ.
Amen.   —Alcuin (c. 732–804; adapted)

The love of Christ has gathered us as one.
   Let us rejoice and be glad in him.
Let us honor and love the living God
   and in purity of heart let us love one another.
For where mercy and love are, there is God.
When we are gathered together
   let us not be divided in spirit.
Let strife and discord cease between us;
   let Christ be present in our midst.
Where mercy and love are, there is God.
With all the blessed ones may we see forever your face in
   glory, Christ, our Redeemer, in joy that is infinite and
   spotless for all the ages of eternity.
Where mercy and love are, there is God.   —Western Rite

Suggested Hymns and Songs
(see hymnary.org or other sources as noted)

An Upper Room Did Our Lord Prepare (Fred Pratt Green)
As We Gather at Your Table (Carl P. Daw Jr.)
Bind Us Together (Bob Gillman)
Eat This Bread, Drink This Cup (Taizé Community)
Jesu, Jesu, Fill Us with Your Love (Tom Colvin)
Let Us Break Bread Together on Our Knees (African American spiritual)
Stay with Me (Taizé Community)

Good Friday

The journey of Lent, which began with ashes, concludes on the wood of Calvary's cross. Worship on Good Friday is one of the holiest events of the Christian year. This solemn service should include scripture, prayer, and song that match the power of Christ's saving act of redemption.

Scriptures

My God, my God, why have you forsaken me?
Why are you so far from helping me,
  from the words of my groaning?
O my God, I cry by day, but you do not answer;
  and by night, but I find no rest.
Yet you are holy, enthroned on the praises of Israel.
In you our ancestors trusted;
  they trusted, and you delivered them.
To you they cried, and were saved; in you they trusted,
  and were not put to shame.   —Psalm 22:1-5

Is it nothing to you, all you who pass by?
Look and see if there is any sorrow like my sorrow.
He was despised and rejected by others;
a man of sorrows and acquainted with grief.
He was wounded for our transgressions,
crushed for our iniquities;
upon him was the punishment that made us whole,
and by his bruises we are healed.

—Lamentations 1:12; Isaiah 53:3, 5

If any want to become my followers, let them deny themselves and take up their cross and follow me. For those who want to save their life will lose it; and those who lose their life for my sake will find it. —Matthew 16:24-25

Christ Jesus emptied himself, taking the form of a servant, being born in human likeness. And being found in human form, he humbled himself and became obedient to the point of death—even death on a cross. —Philippians 2:7-8

Prayers and Readings

Thanks be to you, O God, for Jesus Christ, who for the road that was set before him endured the cross.
Thanks be to you, O God, for Jesus Christ, who in the cross triumphed over sin and death, principalities and powers, and over all who would seek to deny you.
Thanks be to you, O God, for Jesus Christ, who by the cross showed your great love for us in that he died for our sins.
Thanks be to you, O God, who in Jesus Christ calls us to take up the cross and follow him. Grant that we may eagerly answer the call and become his disciples. In his name we pray. Amen.

We saw him in the countryside, healing the sick, preaching the word, and we followed him.
Who was the guilty?
We threw our cloaks before him and promised him allegiance and danced in the streets.
Who was the guilty?
We gathered at the judgment seat, and in our doubt, we called instead for Barabbas to go free.
Who was the guilty?
(*All:*) **We stand at the foot of the cross and watch and in our hearts we know . . . we were the guilty.**

—Frank A. Hallock

We confess to you, our Lord and Savior, that we have betrayed and denied you, forgotten and doubted you. When our faith is tested, we wonder where you are. When we see injustice in the world, we often stand by, we turn our backs, we ignore the cries of others. Forgive us, O God, and help us to truly repent. Help us to remember your sacrifice, your love, and to know your forgiveness. In the name of the One who lived, who was crucified, and who lives again, Jesus the Christ, we pray. Amen.

—Mindi Welton-Mitchell

The Service of Tenebrae

The term *Tenebrae*, Latin for "darkness," comes from the practice of gradually extinguishing candles in the course of the service until all is in darkness; the worshipers then depart in silence. Choices of scripture readings may be used to frame a Maundy Thursday, Good Friday, or Easter Vigil service. Appropriate hymns or other music may be interspersed among the readings.

The Shadow of Betrayal—Matthew 26:20-25
The Shadow of Desertion—Matthew 26:31-35
The Agony of the Soul—Luke 22:39-44
The Unshared Vigil—Mark 14:32-41
"God, the hour is come"—John 17:1-6
"That they may all be one"—John 17:15-22
The Arrest at the Garden—John 18:1-5
The Shadow of the Cross—Mark 15:16-20
The Way of the Cross—Mark 15:21-32
"Truly, this was the Son of God!"—Mark 15:33-39

The Seven Last Words of Christ Service

In this Good Friday service, seven preachers, from within the congregation or across the church community, come together to proclaim the seven last words of Christ on the cross. The service is often held midday or can take place in the evening. The scripture passages are read one at a time, a vocal solo or a congregational hymn follows, and then each message is preached.

The First Word—"Forgive them, for they know not what they do." (Luke 23:34)

The Second Word—"You shall be with me in paradise." (Luke 23:39)

The Third Word—"Woman, behold your son! Behold your mother!" (John 19:26-27)

The Fourth Word—"My God, my God, why have you forsaken me?" (Mark 15:34)

The Fifth Word—"I thirst." (John 19:28)

The Sixth Word—"It is finished." (John 19:30)

The Seventh Word—"Into your hands I commend my spirit." (Luke 23:46)

Christ on the cross has brought me life,
  his love has made me free.
Now through the symbols of his strife
  his holy gifts I see.

In love he washed the pilgrim's feet,
  then asked I do the same,
And so whene'er his children meet,
  such humble love makes claim.

Spurred on by haste, poor Judas sold
  his Lord for tokens few.
How often I for idols cold in
  haste betray him, too.

When Peter did our Lord deny
  the rooster crowed its pain,
so all creation weeps when I
  refuse to own Christ's name.

Christ on the cross has brought me life,
  his love has made me free,
and now to guide me through the strife
  he comes and walks with me.

—Rodney R. Romney, © 1988 AmaDeus Group
Sing to the tune ST. PETER

Suggested Hymns and Songs
(see hymnary.org or other sources as noted)

Calvary (African American spiritual)
Go to Dark Gethsemane (James Montgomery)
He Never Said a Mumbalin' Word (African American
  spiritual)

I Know It Was the Blood (African American spiritual)
In Christ Alone (Keith Getty and Stuart Townend)
Jesus, Remember Me (Taizé Community)
Jesus, Keep Me Near the Cross (Fanny J. Crosby)
O Sacred Head, Now Wounded (variously attributed)
Were You There? (African American spiritual)
What Wondrous Love Is This (American folk hymn)
When I Survey the Wondrous Cross (Isaac Watts)

Easter and Easter Season

The festival of Easter celebrates Christ as the Savior of the world. It is the high point of the Christian year, a time of joyful celebration that focuses on our continuing life in union with Christ. The season of Easter, known as "the Great Fifty Days," gives congregations an extended time to rejoice in the resurrection. Consider continuing to sing the hymns and songs of Easter throughout this season—one day is hardly enough to celebrate the crowning event of our faith!

Scriptures

Praise God in this holy house of worship,
　　and under the open skies;
Praise God for acts of power and for magnificent greatness;
Praise with a blast on the trumpet,
　　praise by strumming soft strings;
Praise God with castanets and dance, with banjo and flute;
Praise with cymbals and a big bass drum,
　　with fiddles and mandolin.
Let every living, breathing creature praise God! Hallelujah!
　　　　　　　　　　　　　　—Psalm 150 (*The Message*, adapted)

After the sabbath, as the first day of the week was dawning, Mary Magdalene and the other Mary went to see the tomb. And suddenly there was a great earthquake; for an angel of the Lord, descending from heaven, came and rolled back the stone and sat on it. His appearance was like lightning, and his clothing white as snow. For fear of him the guards shook and became like dead men. But the angel said to the women, "Do not be afraid; I know that you are looking for Jesus who was crucified. He is not here; for he has been raised, as he said."

—Matthew 28:1-6

When he was at the table with them, he took bread, blessed and broke it, and gave it to them. Then their eyes were opened, and they recognized him; and he vanished from their sight. They said to each other, "Were not our hearts burning within us while he was talking to us on the road, while he was opening the scriptures to us?" That same hour they got up and returned to Jerusalem; and they found the eleven and their companions gathered together. They were saying, "The Lord has risen indeed, and he has appeared to Simon!" Then they told what had happened on the road, and how he had been made known to them in the breaking of the bread.

—Luke 24:30-35

Jesus came and stood among them and said to them, "Peace be with you." After he said this, he showed them his hands and his side. Then the disciples rejoiced when they saw the Lord.

—John 20:19-20

Christ has been raised from the dead,
  the first fruits of those who have died.
Thanks be to God, who gives us the victory
  through our Lord Jesus Christ.

Death no longer has dominion over him.
  The death he died, he died to sin, once for all;
But the life he lives, he lives to God.
So you also must consider yourselves dead to sin,
For we are alive to God in Jesus Christ.
                    —1 Corinthians 15:20, 57; Romans 6:9-11

If you have been raised with Christ, seek the things that are above, where Christ is, seated at the right hand of God. Set your minds on things that are above, not on things that are on earth, for you have died, and your life is hidden with Christ in God. When Christ who is your life is revealed, then you also will be revealed with him in glory.
                                      —Colossians 3:1-4

Let us run with perseverance the race that is set before us, looking to Jesus the pioneer and perfecter of our faith, who for the sake of the joy that was set before him endured the cross, disregarding its shame, and has taken his seat at the right hand of the throne of the God.   —Hebrews 12:1-2

"I am the first and the last," says the Lord. "I am the living one. I was dead, and see, I am alive forever and ever."
                                      —Revelation 1:17-18

Prayers and Readings

Eternal God, may we hear with new ears this morning: "Behold, I tell you a mystery! We shall not all die, but we shall all be changed, for the trumpet shall sound and the dead shall be raised. For, like Christ, our earthly bodies shall put on immortality and the saying shall be fulfilled:
'**Where, O death, is your victory?**
  Where, O grave, is your sting?'"

Thanks be to you, O God, who dwells with us here this morning, who gives us the victory through Jesus Christ. And as we say "Amen," Lord, we proclaim for all time: "I know that my redeemer lives!" Christ is risen!
Christ is risen, indeed! Hallelujah!

—N. H.

Praise be to you, our Creator, who brought forth your son from the dead and has raised him to eternal glory. Praise be to you, O Jesus Christ, who is the resurrection and the life. Praise be to you, O Holy Spirit, who makes God alive in our hearts. All praise and thanksgiving be to you, O most blessed three-in-one, now and forever, world without end. **Amen.**

Christ is risen:
The spirit of evil has fallen.
Christ is risen:
The angels of God are rejoicing.
Christ is risen:
The tomb is empty and still.
Christ has indeed arisen from the dead.
Glory and power are Christ's for ever and ever. Amen.

—From an Easter hymn attributed to Hippolytus (170–235)

Rejoice, heavenly choirs of angels.
  Rejoice, all creation around God's throne.
Jesus Christ, our Redeemer, is risen!
Sound the trumpet of salvation.
  Rejoice, O earth, in shining splendor,
radiant in the brightness of your Savior.
Christ has conquered death! Glory fills all creation!
Darkness has vanished forever. Alleluia!

Our God, through the mighty resurrection of your son, Jesus Christ, you have liberated us from the power of death and brought us into the realm of your love. Grant that as Christ was raised from the dead by your glory, so we may walk in newness of life and look for those things that are in heaven. In the name of Christ who is alive and reigns forever. **Amen.**   —Gelasian Sacramentary, adapted

Because you live, O Christ,
    the garden of the world has come to flower,
the darkness of the tomb
    is flooded with your resurrection power.

REFRAIN: The stone has rolled away
    and death cannot imprison!
O sing this Easter Day, for Jesus Christ has risen,
    has risen, has risen, has risen!

Because you live, O Christ,
    the spirit bird of hope is freed for flying,
our cages of despair
    no longer keep us closed and life-denying. (Refrain)

Because you live, O Christ,
    the rainbow of your peace will span creation,
the colors of your love
    will draw all humankind to adoration. (Refrain)

—Shirley Erena Murray, *In Every Corner Sing*, © 1987
Hope Publishing Company and Hope Hymns Online
Sing to the tune VRUECHTEN

Suggested Hymns and Songs
(see hymnary.org or other sources as noted)

Because He Lives (Gloria and Bill Gaither)

Come to Us, Beloved Stranger (Edith Sinclair Downing)

Cristo vive/Christ Is Living (Nicholas Martinez)

Day of Delight and Beauty Unbounded (Delores Dufner, OSB)

Halle, Halle, Halleluja (Traditional Caribbean)

He Lives (Alfred H. Ackley)

Jesus Christ Is Risen Today (Latin hymn)

Lift High the Cross (George William Kitchin)

Lord, I Lift Your Name on High (Rick Founds)

Now the Green Blade Rises (John M. C. Crum)

These Things Did Thomas Count as Real (Thomas H. Troeger)

Thine Is the Glory (Edmund Louis Budry)

This Is a Day of New Beginnings (Brian Wren)

Victory in Jesus (Eugene M. Bartlett)

Woman, Weeping in the Garden (Daniel C. Damon)

Ascension

This day, the fortieth day after Easter, marks the exaltation of the Christ as he takes his place at the right hand of God. Christ's ascension gives to us a share of his divinity and the promise of his continuing presence in our lives.

Scriptures

God has gone up with a shout, with the sound of a trumpet. Sing praises to the Holy One, sing praises! God is sovereign over all the earth; sing praises with a psalm. God rules over the nations and sits on the heavenly throne. —Psalm 47:5-8

I lift you high in praise, my God, O Sovereign! and I'll bless
   your name into eternity.
You are magnificent with boundless greatness
   and can never be praised enough.
Generation after generation stands in awe of your work;
   each one tells stories of your mighty acts.
Your beauty and splendor have everyone talking and com-
   posing songs on your wonders.
Your marvelous doings are headline news; I could write a
   book full of the details of your greatness.
The fame of your goodness spreads across the country;
   your righteousness is on everyone's lips.
You are all mercy and grace—not quick to anger, rich in
   love.
You are good to one and all; everything you do is suffused
   with grace. —Psalm 145:1-9 (*The Message*, adapted)

Now the eleven disciples went to Galilee, to the mountain
where Jesus told them to go. When they saw him, they
worshiped him, but some doubted. Jesus came near and
spoke to them, "I've received all authority in heaven and
on earth. Therefore, go and make disciples of all nations,
baptizing them in the name of the Father and of the Son
and of the Holy Spirit, teaching them to obey everything
that I've commanded you. Look, I myself will be with you
every day until the end of this present age."

—Matthew 28:16-20 (CEB)

Jesus led them out as far as Bethany, where he lifted his
hands and blessed them. As he blessed them, he left them
and was taken up to heaven. They worshiped him and

returned to Jerusalem overwhelmed with joy. And they were continuously in the temple praising God.

—Luke 24:50-53

And being found in human form, Christ humbled himself and became obedient to the point of death—even death on a cross. Therefore God also highly exalted him and gave him the name that is above every name.
That at the name of Jesus every knee should bend and every tongue should confess that Jesus Christ is Lord.

—Philippians 2:7-11

Prayers and Readings

Our Lord Jesus Christ ascended into heaven; let our hearts ascend with him. Listen to the words of the apostle: "If you have risen with Christ, set your hearts on the things that are above where Christ is, seated at the right hand of God; seek the things that are above, not the things that are on earth." For just as he remained with us even after his ascension, so we too are already in heaven with him, even though what is promised us has not yet been fulfilled in our bodies. We cannot be in heaven, as he is on earth, by divinity, but in him, we can be there by love.

—Augustine of Hippo (354–430)

Since in Jesus Christ we have a great high priest who has ascended to the heavens, we confidently draw near to your throne of grace, O God. Grant us mercy and help us to find grace in time of need. May we come to know the presence of him who said: "Lo, I am with you always, even to the close of the age." **Amen.**

He who descended is also ascended far above the heavens,
  that he might fill all things.
When Christ, our Life, appears,
  we shall appear with him in glory. Alleluia! Amen!

Suggested Hymns and Songs
(see hymnary.org or other sources as noted)

A Hymn of Glory Let Us Sing (The Venerable Bede)
All Hail the Power of Jesus' Name (Edward Perronet)
At the Name of Jesus (Caroline Maria Noel)
Christ, High Ascended, Now in Glory Seated (Timothy
  Dudley-Smith)
Christ, Whose Glory Fills the Skies (Charles Wesley)
Crown Him with Many Crowns (Matthew Bridges)
Hail the Day That Sees Him Rise (Charles Wesley)

Pentecost

The day of Pentecost is witness and celebration to the pour-
ing out of God's Spirit upon the disciples and is observed
in many congregations as the birthday of the church. The
miracle of the understanding of tongues reaffirms that the
good news has come for all peoples. It is a festival day for
worship, with vivid symbols of wind and flame.

Scriptures

There is so much here, O Eternal One,
  so much you have made.
By the wise way in which you create,
  riches and creatures fill the earth.
And all of these look to you to give them food
  when the time is right.

When you feed, they gather what you supply.
When you open your hand, they are filled with good food.
When you withdraw your presence, they are dismayed.
When you revoke their breath, the life goes out of them,
and they become, again, the dust of the earth
    from which you formed them.
When you send out your breath, life is created,
and the face of the earth is made beautiful and is renewed.
May the glorious presence of the Eternal
    linger among us forever.
And may God rejoice in the greatness of these works.
I will sing to the Eternal all of my life;
I will call my God good as long as I live.

        —From Psalm 104:24-35 (*The Voice*)

This is the day that God has made.
Let us rejoice and be glad in it.
This is the day of which Jesus declared: "You will receive
    power when the Holy Spirit has come upon you.
And you will be my witnesses in Jerusalem, in all Judea and
    Samaria, and to the ends of the earth."

        —Psalm 118:24; Acts 1:8

And at the coming of the day of Pentecost they were all together in one place. And suddenly from heaven there came
a sound like violent, driving wind, and it filled the whole
house where they were sitting. And among them appeared
divided tongues, as if of fire, and settled on each one of
them. And all were filled with a holy breath and began
talking in different tongues in the degree that this breath
gave them to speak out.

        —Acts 2:1-4, translated by Mark Theodoropoulos

In the last days I will pour out my spirit on all flesh; your sons and your daughters shall prophesy, your old men shall dream dreams, and your young men shall see visions.

—Joel 2:28

God's love has been poured into our hearts through the Holy Spirit that has been given to us.   —Romans 5:5

Prayers and Readings

Spirit of truth, Spirit of love, Spirit of Christ, Spirit of God, the Holy Spirit, we honor you for your many gifts to us. Fire our hearts and touch our lips, that we may sing forth praise worthy of your great power. **Amen.**

Fire of the Spirit, life of the lives of creatures,
    spiral of sanctity, bond of all natures,
glow of charity, lights of clarity, taste of sweetness
    to sinners, be with us and hear us. . . .
Composer of all things, light of all the risen,
    key of salvation, release from the dark prison,
hope of all unions, scope of chastities,
    joy in the glory, strong honor, be with us and hear us.

—Hildegard of Bingen (1098–1179; translated by Charles Williams)

Gracious God, we make these offerings as a pledge of our love and loyalty: to you, to each other, and to all our sisters and brothers in humanity. We commit ourselves to live in love for all, using heart, soul, mind, and strength, in the name of Christ our Redeemer. Grant that your spirit of grace and generosity will move in each of our hearts and catch fire throughout our community. In Jesus' name we pray. **Amen.**   —N. H.

Glory to you, O God, glory to you!
  Heavenly Ruler, Comforter, Spirit of truth,
Come and dwell within us.
You who are everywhere and who fills all things,
  treasury of all good and giver of life,
Come, Holy Spirit, and dwell among us.
Cleanse us from all sin and through your goodness,
  redeem our souls.
Come, Holy Spirit, and dwell among us. Amen.
—Orthodox prayer, adapted

And so the yearning strong, with which the soul will long,
shall far outpass the power of human telling;
for none can guess its grace, till Love create a place
wherein the Holy Spirit makes a dwelling.
—Bianco da Siena, (1350–1399)

Open your hearts. Open your minds.
Rejoice and be glad in what the Spirit is doing
  in the world around you.
Wisdom shouts in the streets. She stands in the public square.
The Spirit is poured out upon all flesh.
The world is in need of listeners, my friends,
people to offer one another
  the attention they so desperately need.
People need love, not programs.
  People need someone to hear them,
not to tell them what to believe,
  not to tell them what to think,
not to tell them anything except,
  "I hear you, and I understand."
Listening is an act of love.
—Tripp Hudgins

Teach us to love, with strength of heart and mind,
    each and all, humankind;
break down old walls of prejudice and hate,
    leave us not to our fate.
As you have loved and given your life
    to end hostility and strife,
O share your grace from heaven above,
    teach us, Lord, how to love.

—"Renew Your Church," Kenneth L. Cober,
© 1960 Judson Press
Sing to the tune ALL IS WELL

Suggested Hymns and Songs
(see hymnary.org or other sources as noted)

As a Fire Is Meant for Burning (Ruth Duck)
Come Down, O Love Divine (Bianco da Siena)
From All That Dwell Below the Skies (Isaac Watts)
I Am That Great and Fiery Force (*Singing in the Living Tradition*, Unitarian Universalist Association)
Renew Your Church (Kenneth L. Cober)
Send, O God, Your Holy Spirit (Sylvia G. Dunstan)
Shine, Jesus, Shine (Graham Kendrick)
Sing Out, Earth and Skies (Marty Haugen)
Spirit of the Living God (Daniel Iverson)
There's a Spirit in the Air (Brian Wren)
Veni, Sancti, Spiritus (Taizé Community)
Wa Wa Wa Emimimo / Come, O Holy Spirit, Come (Josiah Olunowo Ositelu)

Season of Pentecost
(*also known as Trinity or Kingdomtide*)

Encompassing half the Sundays in the year and stretching through most of summer and autumn, we sometimes call this "the long green season" for its designated liturgical color. The focus of the season is the church's mission, and how God works through each of us to bring Christ's message of grace and salvation to the world. Gospel readings include healing and teaching stories, miracles, and parables.

Scriptures

The heavens are telling the glory of God;
    and the firmament proclaims God's handiwork.
Day to day pours forth speech,
    and night to night declares knowledge.
There is no speech, nor are there words;
    their voice is not heard;
yet their voice goes out through all the earth,
    and their words to the end of the world.
The law of God is perfect, reviving the soul;
the rulings of God are sure, making wise the simple;
the teachings of God are right, rejoicing the heart;
the commandment of God is clear, enlightening the eyes;
(*All:*) **Let the words of our mouths**
    and the meditations of our hearts
be acceptable to you, Holy One,
    our rock and our redeemer.   —Psalm 19:1-4, 7-9, 14 (GNT)

I bless God every chance I get; my lungs expand with praise.
I live and breathe God; if things aren't going well, hear this

and be happy: join me in spreading the news; together let's get the word out. God met me more than halfway, freeing me from my anxious fears. Look at the Holy One; offer your warmest smile. Never hide your feelings from God. When I was desperate, I called out, and God got me out of a tight spot. The hosts of angels set up a circle of protection around us while we pray. Open your mouth and taste, open your eyes and see—how good the Eternal One is. Blessed are you who run to God. —Psalm 34:1-8 (*The Message*)

God is our mighty fortress, always ready to help in times of trouble. And so, we won't be afraid! Let the earth tremble and the mountains tumble into the deepest sea. Let the ocean roar and foam, and its raging waves shake the mountains. A river and its streams bring joy to the city, which is the sacred home of God Most High. God is in that city, helping it at dawn, and it won't be shaken. Nations rage! Kingdoms fall! But at the voice of God the earth itself melts. The Holy One All-Powerful is with us. The God of Jacob is our fortress. —Psalm 46:1-7 (CEV)

How lovely is your dwelling place, O God of hosts!
My soul longs, indeed it faints for the courts of God.
I would rather be a doorkeeper in the house of my God
than live in tents of wickedness.
For the Holy One is a sun and shield;
God bestows favor and honor.
No good thing does God withhold
from those who walk uprightly.
Happy is everyone who trusts in you, O Eternal One.
—Psalm 84:1-2, 10-12

Now when Jesus came into the district of Caesarea Philippi, he asked his disciples, "Who do people say that the Son of Man is?" And they said, "Some say John the Baptist, but others Elijah, and still others Jeremiah or one of the prophets." He said to them, "But who do you say that I am?" Simon Peter answered, "You are the Messiah, the Son of the living God." And Jesus answered him, "Blessed are you, Simon son of Jonah! For flesh and blood has not revealed this to you, but my Father in heaven."

—Matthew 16:13-17

One of the scribes came near and heard them disputing with one another, and seeing that Jesus answered them well, he asked him, "Which commandment is the first of all?" Jesus answered, "The first is, 'Hear, O Israel: the Lord our God, the Lord is one; you shall love the Lord your God with all your heart, and with all your soul, and with all your mind, and with all your strength.' The second is this, 'You shall love your neighbor as yourself.' There is no other commandment greater than these." —Mark 12:28-31

On the way to Jerusalem Jesus was going through the region between Samaria and Galilee. As he entered a village, ten lepers approached him. Keeping their distance, they called out, saying, "Jesus, Master, have mercy on us!" When he saw them, he said to them, "Go and show yourselves to the priests." And as they went, they were made clean. Then one of them, when he saw that he was healed, turned back, praising God with a loud voice. He prostrated himself at Jesus' feet and thanked him. And he was a Samaritan. Then Jesus asked, "Were not ten made clean? But the other nine, where are they? Was none of them found to return and give praise to God except this foreigner?" Then he said to him, "Get up and go on your way; your faith has made you well."

—Luke 17:11-19

When the crowds found Jesus on the other side of the sea, they said to him, "Rabbi, when did you come here?" Jesus answered them, "Very truly, I tell you, you are looking for me, not because you saw signs, but because you ate your fill of the loaves. Do not work for the food that perishes, but for the food that endures for eternal life, which the Son of Man will give you. For it is on him that God the Father has set his seal." Then they said to him, "What must we do to perform the works of God?" Jesus answered them, "This is the work of God, that you believe in him whom he has sent. I am the bread of life. Whoever comes to me will never be hungry, and whoever believes in me will never be thirsty."

—John 6:25-29, 35

Let love be genuine; hate what is evil,
   hold fast to what is good;
love one another with mutual affection;
   outdo one another in showing honor.
Do not lag in zeal, be ardent in spirit, and serve God.
Rejoice in hope, be patient in suffering, persevere in prayer.
Contribute to the needs of the saints;
   extend hospitality to strangers.
Bless those who persecute you; bless and do not curse them.
Rejoice with those who rejoice, weep with those who weep.
Live in harmony with one another;
   do not claim to be wiser than you are.
Do not repay anyone evil for evil.
If it is possible, so far as it depends on you,
   live peaceably with all.

—From Romans 12:9-18

For we do not proclaim ourselves; we proclaim Jesus Christ as Lord and ourselves as servants for Jesus' sake. For it is the God who said, "Let light shine out of darkness," who has shone in our hearts to give the light of the knowledge of the glory of God in the face of Jesus Christ. But we have this treasure in clay jars, so that it may be made clear that this extraordinary power belongs to God and does not come from us. We are afflicted in every way, but not crushed; perplexed, but not driven to despair; persecuted, but not forsaken; struck down, but not destroyed; always carrying in the body the death of Jesus, so that the life of Jesus may also be made visible in our bodies.

—2 Corinthians 4:5-10

The fruit of the Spirit is love, joy, peace, patience, kindness, generosity, faithfulness, gentleness, and self-control. There is no law against such things. If we live by the Spirit, let us also be guided by the Spirit.
Let the word of Christ dwell in us richly; let us teach and admonish one another in all wisdom; and with gratitude in our hearts sing psalms, hymns, and spiritual songs to God.

—Galatians 5:22-23, 25; Colossians 3:16

Now faith is the assurance of things hoped for, the conviction of things not seen. Indeed, by faith our ancestors received approval. By faith we understand that the worlds were prepared by the word of God, so that what is seen was made from things that are not visible. —Hebrews 11:1-3

Prayers and Readings

Creator, Christ, and Holy Spirit, one God, we adore you for the many ways in which you have made yourself known to humanity. Increase our thanksgivings, that they may be worthy of your greatness, and help us to sing your praises, that all the world may truly know how glorious you are. **Amen.**

Holy One, we your servants gather in your presence to be strengthened and healed, inspired and empowered so that our work may make your compassion known. Speak to us, so that we may be a community that celebrates and proclaims your saving work. May we be ever faithful to the call you have placed on our hearts. We ask this in the name of Jesus Christ, our Redeemer. **Amen.**

O God, by the gift of your Spirit establish and ground us in your truth. Reveal to us what we do not know; make perfect in us what is lacking; strengthen us in what we do know; and keep us ever in your service, through Jesus Christ. **Amen.**   —Clement of Rome, adapted

Why are we gathered at this place at this hour?
We are gathered as the people of God, so we may come to know and praise God as seen in Jesus Christ and as made known by the Holy Spirit.
Then let us call upon the presence of God, the One before whom we stand.
In the name of the Creator and of the Christ and of the Holy Spirit. Amen.

Blessed be you, O eternal God:
In whom the heavens rejoice and the earth is glad, for you will judge the world with justice.
Blessed be you, O Christ our Savior:

Who will one day come again in power and great glory
to perfect God's realm, and to liberate the captives with
songs of everlasting joy.

Blessed be you, O holy and gracious Spirit:

Who stirs our hearts and fills our mouths with praise.

(*All:*) **Glory be to you, O God, who is Creator, Christ, and
Spirit, forever and ever.**

May God be with you.

And with your spirit.

Beloved in Christ, in communion with the saints of all ages
let us boldly offer our prayers of intercession to almighty
God: O God, we pray for the church, which is set amid
the confusion of contemporary life and is facing enor-
mous tasks.

Be with your church, O God.

Help us boldly to proclaim that the realm of God is here
on earth.

Be with your church, O God.

Fill us with the prophet's scorn of oppression; give us a
Christlike tenderness for the burdened and exploited.
Increase our faith to defend the cause of all people.

Be with your church, O God.

Let us center ourselves not on the church itself, but be courageous in looking beyond our walls to a community and
a world in need, as did our leader, Christ, who gave up
his very life.

**Be with your church, O God. We pray this in the name of
the one we follow, Jesus the Christ. Amen.**

Almighty and gracious God, we pray that you would sow
the seed of your Word in our hearts,

Send down upon us your heavenly grace;
that we may bring forth the fruits of the Spirit,
**And on the great day of harvest may we be gathered with
your saints; through Jesus Christ we pray. Amen.**
—Canterbury Convocation of 1862, adapted

We thank you, our God, for the life of knowledge that you
have made known to us through Jesus Christ, your servant.
To God be glory forever!
As the broken bread, once scattered upon the mountains,
has been gathered together and made one, so may your
church be gathered together from the ends of the earth into
one kingdom;
**To God be the glory and the power through Jesus Christ
forever!**   —The Didache, second century, adapted

God of love and God of our salvation,
    to a broken hungry world you've come,
with your gifts of wholeness and abundance
    offered freely to us in your Son.
Yet our world is still with hate divided,
    ghettoed lives betray our desperate fear.
Walk again our streets of lonely living,
    show the kingdom in its beauty here.

Broader lands in space declare your glory,
    as beyond our earth we pierce the sky;
soaring flights beyond our highest dreaming,
    boundless ventures where new kingdoms lie.
Yet no flight can e'er outrun your presence,
    there's no realm your truth has not been spread,
there's no kingdom but your own eternal,
    bringing life where once all life seemed dead.

Let our journey be to new commitment,
  to a deeper life within your grace,
let us reach in love to one another,
  e'er we try to reach new worlds in space.
Glory be to God who rules the heavens,
  glory be to Christ the holy one.
Yours the kingdom, power, and the glory
  in this world and in all worlds to come.

—"Journey to Commitment," Rodney R. Romney,
© 1990 AmaDeus Group
Sing to the tune BLOTT EN DAG

Suggested Hymns and Songs

Consult your hymnal, songbooks, and hymnary.org for congregational music to include during the long Pentecost season, according to each Sunday's scriptures.

All Saints Sunday

Usually observed on the first Sunday of November (All Saints Day falling on November 1) this is an occasion when members of the church family who have passed away may be remembered and celebrated, along with all the saints of Christendom who have gone before. Such a celebration of the cloud of witnesses offers an opportunity for creative rituals of remembrance.

Scriptures

Praise God! Sing to God a new song,
let the assembly of the faithful sing praises.
Let Israel be glad in its Maker;
let the children of Zion rejoice in their Ruler.

Let them praise God's name with dancing,
making melody with tambourine and lyre.
For the Holy One takes pleasure in the people's praises;
God adorns the humble with victory.
Let the faithful ones exult in glory forever;
let them sing for joy from heaven!

—Adapted from Psalm 149:1-5

Then Jesus looked up at his disciples and said: "Blessed are you who are poor, for yours is the kingdom of God. Blessed are you who are hungry now, for you will be filled. Blessed are you who weep now, for you will laugh. Blessed are you when people hate you, and when they exclude you, revile you, and defame you on account of the Son of Man. Rejoice in that day and leap for joy, for surely your reward is great in heaven; for that is what their ancestors did to the prophets."

—Luke 6:20-23

I looked, and there was a great multitude that no one could count, from every nation, from all tribes and peoples and languages, standing before the throne and before the Lamb, robed in white, with palm branches in their hands. They cried out in a loud voice, saying, "Salvation belongs to our God who is seated on the throne, and to the Lamb!" And all the angels stood around the throne and around the elders and the four living creatures, and they fell on their faces before the throne and worshiped God, singing, "Amen! Blessing and glory and wisdom and thanksgiving and honor and power and might be to our God forever and ever! Amen."

—Revelation 7:9-11

Litany of Remembrance and Thanksgiving for the Saints

First Reader: Creator God, we thank you for the people who showed us the way to best give our lives in service to you. First, for your Son, Jesus Christ, and also for the men and women who have been touched and empowered by your love for all people—we call them Saints.

Second Reader: For those who first followed the gospel message, women and men who trusted in you and held onto the Good News even in the face of persecution.

People: **We remember them and give thanks.**

Third Reader: For the men and women of the Middle Ages, for mystics who sought deeper connection and the poets who sought to express their visions.

Fourth Reader: For the reformers, whose protests against the church allowed people to follow their consciences and to forge their direct connections with God.

People: **We remember them and give thanks.**

First Reader: For the missionaries sent out by congregations to spread your gospel across not just this continent but the entire world.

Second Reader: For leaders in justice; for contemporary theologians who continue to grapple with questions of being and liberation.

People: **We honor them and give thanks.**

Third Reader: For all the pastors, leaders, deacons, teachers, musicians, and caregivers who came before us and inspired us.

Fourth Reader: For these saints we wish to honor today by name: _____.

People: **We honor them and give thanks.**

(*All:*) **And especially, God, we give thanks for the saints we
stand among now, blessed companions and friends. We
honor each other and give you all the praise. Amen.**

—Paul Schneider

Suggested Hymns and Songs
(see hymnary.org or other sources as noted)

Blest Are They (David Haas)
For All the Saints (William Walsham How)
God of the Ages (Ruth Duck)
Living Stones (Mary Louise Bringle)
Rejoice in God's Saints (Fred Pratt Green)
Song of Faith That Sings Forever (Shirley Erena Murray,
    Faith Makes the Song, Hope Publishing Company and
    Hope Hymns Online)

Reign of Christ Sunday

Also known as Christ the King, Reign of Christ Sunday is
the last Sunday of the Christian year, before Advent and
the new liturgical year begin. Not only does it bring the
long season of Pentecost to a close, it centers on Christ as
Alpha and Omega—the Eternal Christ reigns over all and
in him all things will be fulfilled at the end of time.

Scriptures

I rejoiced with those who said to me, "Let's go to God's
    house!"
Now our feet are standing in your gates, Jerusalem!
Jerusalem is built like a city joined together in unity.
That is where the tribes go up—the Holy One's tribes!
It is the law for Israel to give thanks there to God's name,

because the thrones of justice are there—the thrones of the
   house of David!
Pray that Jerusalem has peace:
   "Let those who love you have rest.
Let there be peace on your walls;
   let there be rest on your fortifications."
For the sake of my family and friends,
   I say, "Peace be with you, Jerusalem."
For the sake of God's house we will work for peace, for the
   good of all.   —Psalm 122 (CEB)

May the God of our Lord Jesus Christ give you a spirit
of wisdom and revelation that makes God known to you.
May the eyes of your heart have enough light to see what
is the hope of God's call, what is the richness of God's
glorious inheritance among believers, and what is the over-
whelming greatness of God's power that is working among
us believers. This power was at work in Christ when God
raised him from the dead and sat him at God's right side
in the heavens. God put everything under Christ's feet and
made him head of everything. His body, the church, is the
fullness of Christ.   —Adapted from Ephesians 1:17-23 (CEB)

Suggested Hymns and Songs
(see hymnary.org or other sources as noted)

Eternal Christ, You Rule (Daniel Charles Damon)
How Great Is Our God (Chris Tomlin, Jesse Reeves, and
   Ed Cash)
How Great Thou Art (Carl Gustav Boberg)
Immortal, Invisible, God Only Wise (Walter C. Smith)
Jesus Shall Reign Where'er the Sun (Isaac Watts)
My Lord, What a Morning (African American spiritual)

Lead On O King (Christ) Eternal (Ernest W. Shurtleff)
O God, Our Help in Ages Past (Isaac Watts)
Open the Eyes of My Heart (Paul Baloche)
Praise Him! Praise Him! (Fanny J. Crosby)

Resources for Part 3

Berglund, Brad. *Reinventing Worship*. Valley Forge, PA: Judson Press, 2006.

Christian Resource Institute: www.crivoice.org/chyear_resources.html

Consultation on Common Texts. *The Revised Common Lectionary*. Minneapolis: Augsburg Fortress, 2012.

Gilmore, Rachel. *Church Celebrations for Advent and Christmas*. Valley Forge, PA: Judson Press, 2011.

Hollies, Linda H. *Trumpet in Zion, Worship Resources* (Years A, B, C). Cleveland: The Pilgrim Press, 2001, 2002, 2003.

Olsen, Charles M. *The Wisdom of the Seasons: How the Church Year Helps Us Understand Our Congregational Stories*. Lanham, MD: Rowman and Littlefield, 2009.

Pfatteicher, Philip H. *Journey into the Heart of God: Living the Liturgical Year*. New York: Oxford University Press, 2013.

Roberts, Mark D., and Patheos.com. *Introduction to the Christian Year*, www.patheos.com/blogs/markdroberts/series/introduction-to-the-christian-year/.

Wallace, Robin Knowles. *The Christian Year*. Nashville: Abingdon, 2011.

Webber, Robert E. *Ancient-Future Time: Forming Spirituality through the Christian Year*. Grand Rapids, MI: Baker Books, 2004.

PART 4

Scriptures, Prayers, and Readings for the Calendar Year

Let us consider all time, all days and seasons, as sacred.

WITHIN EACH congregation's annual cycle of worship there are significant days and occasions that are not part of the Christian liturgical year. Nevertheless, our worship life as families of God needs to reflect such times and seasons by giving praise and thanks. Some of these occasions are reflected here. This section also includes worship materials devoted to themes such as missions, education, stewardship, and other areas of focus that may be included in Sabbath worship or special days in church life.

Then, too, there are those unpredictable events that occur in our communities and beyond, such as a crisis or disaster. These are crucial moments in congregational life when we turn to God in prayer and lament.

This chapter offers worship materials—scripture passages, prayers, readings, and litanies—for a range of occasions. Hymn and song suggestions are included, as well as recommended additional resources. The events are in general chronological order as they appear in the calendar year, followed by those times and themes that take place more occasionally.

DAYS AND SEASONS

New Year's Eve and New Year's Day, Watchnight Service

Scriptures

Eternal One, you have been our dwelling place in all generations. Before the mountains were brought forth, or before you ever formed the earth, from everlasting to everlasting you are God.

For a thousand years in your sight are like yesterday when it is past, or like a watch in the night.

You sweep them away; they are like a dream, like grass that is renewed and flourishes in the morning; and by the evening it fades and withers.

Teach us to number our days that we may gain a wise heart.

Satisfy us in the morning with your steadfast love, O God, so that we may rejoice and be glad all our days.

Let your favor be upon us, and prosper for us the work of our hands—O prosper the work of our hands!

—From Psalm 90

I lift my eyes to the hills—from where will my help come?
Our help comes from God, who made heaven and earth.

God will not let your foot be moved; the one who keeps
  you will not slumber.
The one who keeps Israel will neither slumber nor sleep.
God is our keeper, God is our shade at our right hand.
The sun shall not strike us by day, nor the moon by night.
God will keep us from all evil; God will keep our lives.
**God will keep our going out and our coming in from this
  time forward and forevermore.**   —Psalm 121

For everything there is a season, and a time for every purpose under heaven:
a time to be born, and a time to die;
a time to plant, and a time to pluck up what is planted;
a time to kill, and a time to heal;
a time to break down, and a time to build up;
a time to weep, and a time to laugh;
a time to mourn, and a time to dance;
**a time to throw away stones, and a time to gather stones
  together;**
a time to embrace, and a time to refrain from embracing;
a time to seek, and a time to lose;
a time to keep, and a time to throw away;
a time to tear, and a time to sew;
a time to keep silence, and a time to speak;
a time to love, and a time to hate;
a time for war, and a time for peace.
(All:) **For everything there is a season, and a time for every
  purpose under heaven.**   —Ecclesiastes 3:1-8

If anyone is in Christ, there is a new creation: everything
old has passed away; see, everything has become new! All
this is from God, who is reconciled to us through Christ,

and has given us the ministry of reconciliation. So we are ambassadors for Christ, since God is appealing through us; we entreat you on behalf of Christ, be reconciled to God.

—2 Corinthians 5:17-18, 20

Prayers and Readings

As the old year passes, O God, we acknowledge your presence as ruler not only of the past, but of the present and future; we rejoice that you make all things new. Use us as your instruments, we pray, in the work and ministry needed in this world. Empower us through your grace, that through knowledge, creativity, and prayer we may find ways in the present day to search out your paths for the future. Make us strong witnesses to our faith, so that while others may despair we can bring them a word of hope. As we have received your love, may we in turn share the light of your love with our sisters and brothers. May your kindom on earth come and your will be done; through Jesus Christ, we pray. **Amen.**

Eternal God, as another year has drawn to its close, we give you thanks for all the ways you have led us in days past. For your goodness that has created us, for your abundance that has sustained us, for your wise counsel that has corrected us, and for your patience that has supported us:
We give you our thanks and praise, O God,
For the worship and fellowship of your church, which uplifts our hearts; for the light and inspiration of your Word, and for the comfort and guidance of your Holy Spirit:
We give you our thanks and praise, O God,

For all the lessons we have learned, for all the good you
have enabled us to do, for all victories won and for all
the many blessings of life:

We give you our thanks and praise, O God,

For Jesus Christ, who has called us to follow his way; his
life our model, his death and resurrection our salvation,
and his constant presence a sign of your holy love:

**We thank you, O God, to whom be all praise and gratitude
without end, now and forevermore. Amen.**

Ageless God, who laid the foundations of the earth, and
whose mercy is from everlasting to everlasting, as this
new year begins we raise our voices in thanksgiving to
you.

**For the old, which we cherish and hold dear; for the
new, with its untold promise and possibilities; for your
strength that sustains us when we are uncertain, for your
patience that bears with us when we fail,**

for your guidance that leads us when we are confused, and
for your comfort that helps us when we are in distress,
we offer our boundless thanks.

**Most of all, Gracious One, for your forgiveness and grace
in Jesus Christ, for the abiding presence of your Holy
Spirit, for our fellowship with you and with one another,
we lift up your holy name; we give you thanks.**

Therefore, as you again make all things new, we worship
and adore you:

**(*All:*) To God be glory, honor, and praise, now and forever.
Amen.**

Summer and winter and springtime and harvest,
sun, moon, and stars in their courses above

join with all nature in manifold witness
to thy great faithfulness, mercy, and love.

—Thomas O. Chisholm (1866–1960)

Suggested Hymns and Songs
(see hymnary.org or other sources as noted)

Gather Us In (Marty Haugen)
Great Is Thy Faithfulness (Thomas O. Chisholm)
Guide My Feet (African American spiritual)
Hold to God's Unchanging Hand (Jennie Wilson)
I Know Who Holds Tomorrow (Ira F. Stanphill)
I Want Jesus to Walk with Me (African American spiritual)
Now Thank We All Our God (Martin Rinckart)
Order My Steps (Glenn Burleigh)
Our God, Our Help in Ages Past (Isaac Watts)
This Is a Day of New Beginnings (Brian Wren)

Martin Luther King Jr. Day, African American History Month

Scriptures and Readings

Praise the Lord! O give thanks to the Lord, for God is good; God's steadfast love endures forever.

Who can utter the mighty doings of God, or declare all the praises due?

Happy are those who observe justice, who do righteousness at all times.

Remember me, Holy One, when you show favor to your people; help me when you deliver them.

May I see the prosperity of your chosen ones, may I rejoice in the gladness of your nation, that I may glory in your heritage.

Blessed be the Lord, the God of Israel, from everlasting to everlasting.

And let all the people say, "Amen."

Praise the Lord! Amen!   —Psalm 106:1-5, 48

Do not fear, for I have redeemed you; I have called you by name, you are mine. When you pass through the waters, I will be with you, they shall not overwhelm you. When you walk through fire you shall not be burned, the flame shall not consume you.

There is a balm in Gilead, to make the wounded whole.

Do not fear, for I am with you; I will bring your offspring from the east, and from the west I will gather you; everyone who is called by my name.

There is a balm in Gilead, to make the wounded whole.

Let all the nations gather together, and let the peoples assemble. I am about to do a new thing. I will make a way in the wilderness and rivers in the desert.

There is a balm in Gilead, to make the wounded whole.

For I give water in the wilderness to give drink to my chosen people, the people whom I formed for myself so that they might declare my praise.

(*All:*) Everlasting God, revive our souls, that we might drink from your spring and overcome discouragement; that we may praise your mighty acts. We are called by you to do a new work in your name. Amen.

—Isaiah 43 and an African American spiritual

With what shall I come before the Lord,
   and bow myself before God on high?
God has told you, O mortal, what is good;
   and what does the Lord require of you:
to do justice, and to love kindness,
   and to walk humbly with our God.   —Micah 6:6, 8

Every valley shall be filled, and every mountain and hill shall be made low, and the crooked shall be made straight, and the rough ways made smooth; and all flesh shall see the salvation of God.   —Luke 3:5-6

Now you are coming to the Lord as to a living stone. Even though this stone was rejected by humans, from God's perspective it is chosen, valuable. You yourselves are being built like living stones into a spiritual temple. You are being made into a holy priesthood to offer up spiritual sacrifices that are acceptable to God through Jesus Christ. Thus it is written in scripture, "Look! I am laying a cornerstone in Zion, chosen, valuable. The person who believes in him will never be shamed." But you are a chosen race, a royal priesthood, a holy nation, a people who are God's own possession.   —1 Peter 2:4-6, 9 (CEB)

We must work unceasingly to uplift this nation that we love to a higher destiny, to a higher plateau of compassion, to a more noble expression of humanness.

   —Martin Luther King Jr.

From every mountainside, let freedom ring. When we let freedom ring, when we let it ring from every village and every hamlet, from every state and every city, we will be able to speed up that day when all of God's children, black and white, Jews and Gentiles, Protestants and Catholics, will be able to join hands and sing in the words of the old Negro spiritual, "Free at last! Free at last! Thank God Almighty, we are free at last!"

—Martin Luther King Jr.
Lincoln Memorial Speech, 1963

Courage is an inner resolution to go forward despite obstacles.

Cowardice is submissive surrender to circumstances.

Courage breeds creativity; cowardice represses fear and is mastered by it.

Cowardice asks the question, is it safe?

Expediency ask the question, is it politic?

Vanity asks the question, is it popular?

But, conscience asks the question, is it right? And there comes a time when we must take a position that is neither safe, nor politic, nor popular,

but one must take it because it is right.

—Martin Luther King Jr.
From *Remaining Awake Through a Great Revolution*, 1968

Prayer When the Lord's Supper Is Included in Worship

Heavenly Parent, hear us as we offer our prayers. Look beyond our faults and failures with forgiving love. Guide us in learning and depending upon your presence and protection. Make real our love for your church. Bring harmony into our fragmented lives. Cure our sick bodies; heal our diseased minds. Bring sanity into our insanity, make strong our weak hearts. Give strength to our tired lives. Substitute inspiration for our discouragement and joy for our sorrows. Give us heavenly food for our spiritual hunger. Ease our drought and famine with showers of prayerful communion. Magnify your presence in this service. Erase doubt with faith. May the Lord's Supper make us more like Jesus. This is our prayer, offered in his name. **Amen.**

—J. Alfred Smith Sr.

In Celebration of Black History

God is Alpha and Omega, the beginning and the end.
We come to worship our Creator and our Sustainer.
God has provided for our daily needs.
We come to offer thanksgiving to our Provider.
God has been mighty good to us.
We have tasted, and we have seen that the Lord is good.
God is the Wonderful Counselor.
We have come to worship the Mighty God.
God has loved us, is loving us, and will love us even when we are unlovable.
(*All:*) **We love God because God first loved us. We will love the Lord, our God with all our heart, and with all our soul, and with all our strength, and with all our mind, and our neighbor as ourselves.** —Joseph Daniel Johnson Sr.

Suggested Hymns and Songs
(see hymnary.org or other sources as noted)

Ain't Gonna Let Nobody Turn Me Around (Traditional American song)
Come, Let Us Dream (John Middleton, *Worship & Song*, The General Board of Discipleship of The United Methodist Church)
Come Sunday (Duke Ellington)

Hold On (African American spiritual)
Holy God, You Raise Up Prophets (Harold T. Lewis)
I Shall Not Be Moved (African American spiritual)
If I Can Help Somebody (Alma Androzzo, www.lyrics.com)
Keep the Dream Alive (Robert Manuel Sr.)
Lift Every Voice and Sing (James Weldon Johnson)
Only What You Do for Christ Will Last (Raymond
    Rasberry)
Order My Steps (Glenn Burleigh)
Precious Lord, Take My Hand (Thomas A. Dorsey)
Some There Are Who by Their Living (David L. Edwards)
We Are Marching (Walking) in the Light of
    God/Siyahamba (Zulu traditional song, South Africa)
We've Come This Far by Faith (Albert A. Goodson)

Annual Meeting Sunday

As part of church governance and life together, many
churches hold an annual meeting. This is a time to reflect
on the year completed, which may include reports from
officers and committees, financial reports, and a remembrance of those congregation members who have passed
away since the last annual meeting. It can also be a time
to recognize people who have offered special gifts of time
and talent for church projects and congregational life. The
annual meeting need not be just another occasion for business; it can be a meaningful church event shared every year.
Included below is a combined Call to Worship and Call
to Order; opening worship with such a call underscores
that the business meeting following the service is itself a
worshipful act of the people of God as they seek to carry
out their mission.

Scriptures

Jesus said: "For where two or three are gathered in my name, I am there among them." —Matthew 18:20

When they had prayed, the place in which they were gathered together was shaken; and they were all filled with the Holy Spirit and spoke the word of God with boldness.

—Acts 4:31

I therefore beg you to lead a life worthy of the calling
  to which you have been called, with all humility and
  gentleness,
**with patience, bearing with one another in love, making
  every effort to maintain the unity of the Spirit in the
  bond of peace.**
There is one Body and one Spirit, just as you were called to
  the one hope of your calling,
**one Lord, one faith, one baptism, one God and Creator of
  all, who is above all and through all and in all.**

—Ephesians 4:1-6

Beloved, whatever is true, whatever is honorable, whatever is just, whatever is pure, whatever is pleasing, whatever is commendable, if there is any excellence and if there is anything worthy of praise, think about these things. Keep on doing the things that you have learned and received and heard and seen in me, and the God of peace will be with you. —Philippians 4:8-9

Prayers and Readings

Call to Worship and Call to Order

We come at God's invitation, our faces reflecting the joy and challenge of being called together as a sacred family.

We gather as the Body of Christ, as a congregation in love with God's wisdom and God's word.

We are sisters and brothers of the new covenant, the covenant of hope and promise.

We are here daring to trust that we can be transformed by the light of God's justice and love.

Then let us bring ourselves to holy order, surrounded by the Spirit, and taste the joys of being the people of God.

(All:) **May we boldly proclaim abundant and inclusive love to all the world, as we sing praises, do God's work, and celebrate our life together!**

Prayer of Remembrance for Those Who Have Passed

Loving God, who is with us from our first moment to our last breath, we thank you today for the lives of those saints who have passed from our earthly midst to eternal life with you. We hear and honor the names of our members and loved ones: *(read the list of names)*.

With gratitude and love, we remember them:

Those who served us well; who brought joy to our lives, helped us walk with Christ more fully and deeply, and did your sacred work among us.

May the memory and example of these your children be part of our fellowship for years to come. Let us recall them often by sharing their stories and recounting how they blessed our lives and our church.

We commend these souls to you, Eternal One, confident that your love comforts us in their loss, sustains us through their memory, and strengthens us to do our part in serving this church family by following Jesus. It is in Christ's name we pray. Amen.

Blessing to Close the Meeting

We are the people of God, sisters and brothers in Christ, bonded by grace through the Spirit.

We are encouraged and strengthened by the gifts of worship and community.

Let us go forward in faith, grateful for the past and carrying a vision of joyful hope for the future.

Let us embrace and transform our world with love. In the name of the Love that unites us. Amen!

We meet at your command, dear Lord,
relying on your faithful word:
Now send your Spirit from above,
now fill our hearts with heavenly love.

—Samuel Stennett (1727–1795)

Suggested Hymns and Songs
(see hymnary.org or other sources as noted)

Be Thou My Vision (Ancient Irish poem)
Christians, We Have Met to Worship (George Askins)
Gather Us In (Marty Haugen)
God Be with You Till We Meet Again (Jeremiah E. Rankin)
How Firm a Foundation (Rippon's *Selection of Hymns*)
O Master, Let Me Walk with Thee (Washington B. Gladden)

Renew Your Church, Its Ministries Restore (Kenneth C. Cober)
Take My Life and Let It Be (Francis Ridley Havergal)
Welcoming God (Carolyn Winfrey Gillette)

International Women's Day and Women's History Month

March has been designated Women's History Month, with International Women's Day occurring on March 8.

Scriptures

Praise God! Let my whole being praise the Holy One!
I will praise God with all my life;
   I will sing praises to my God as long as I live.
Don't trust leaders; don't trust any human beings—
   there's no saving help with them!
Their breath leaves them, then they go back to the ground.
On that very same day, their plans die too.
The person whose hope rests on God is truly happy!
God, the maker of heaven and earth,
   the sea, and all that is in them,
God; who is faithful forever, who gives justice to people who are oppressed, who gives bread to people who are starving!
Eternal One, who frees prisoners, who makes the blind see,
   who straightens up those who are bent low.
Eternal One, who loves the righteous, who protects immigrants, who helps orphans and widows, but who makes the way of the wicked twist and turn!
The Holy One will rule forever,
   from one generation to the next!
Praise God!   —Adapted from Psalm 146 (CEB)

THE NEW MANUAL OF WORSHIP

And Mary said: "My soul lifts up the Lord!
    My spirit celebrates my Liberator!
For though I'm God's humble servant,
    the Holy One has noticed me.
Now and forever,
    I will be considered blessed by all generations.
For the Mighty One has done great things for me;
    holy is God's name!
From generation to generation,
    God's lovingkindness endures
    for those who revere the Eternal One.
God's arm has accomplished mighty deeds.
The proud in mind and heart
    have been sent away in disarray.
The rulers from their high positions of power,
    God has brought down low.
And those who were humble and lowly
    have been elevated with dignity.
The hungry ones God has filled with fine food.
The rich have been dismissed with nothing in their hands.
To Israel, God's servant, God has given help,
As promised to our ancestors, remembering Abraham and
    Sarah and their descendants in mercy forever."

—Adapted from Luke 1:46-55 (*The Voice*)

Prayers and Readings

We believe in light beyond our seeing,
flowing from the flame of life in God
who creates us in her image, in his image.

We believe in healing beyond our knowing,
from the Christ who refuses to let the stones of our strug-
    gles be thrown,

but lays them at the foot of the cross;
who is the cornerstone of our hope and our empowerment.

We believe in the grace of God's Spirit,
as we journey on laughing and weeping in the centre of
  our pain,
celebrating in the power of our solidarity,
with all who stand for love and hope,
and the victory of right.   —Pamela Tankersley

A Confession for Women

Loving and holy Lord, we enter your presence full of reverence and full of need. As we remember your goodness and recall your teaching, our shortcomings are brought to mind. Guide us, Lord Jesus, as we recognize and confess our sin. We have accepted the inadequacy attributed to us by others, denying the wholeness in which you have created us.
Forgive and strengthen us, O Lord.
We have hesitated in fear to embrace your gifts and calling.
Forgive us and fill us with courageous faith, O Lord.
We have neglected to speak out on behalf of one another, choosing instead the safety of silence and continued oppression.
Forgive us, and cause freedom to break through among us, O Lord. Fill us with your Holy Spirit, that we might be your daughters indeed. Amen.   —Patricia Ciupek-Reed

An Affirmation

I am a beloved child of the universe, cherished daughter of
  the living God,

birthed and breathed, celebrated and sustained, by the
  Source of Life.
I am rooted and grounded, embraced, filled and surround-
  ed, in Infinite Love.
Ground of my being, in whom I live and move, thanks be
  to you, O God.   —Susan S. Vanderburgh

Of women, and of women's hopes we sing:
  of sharing in creation's nurturing,
of bearing and of birthing new belief,
  of passion for the promises of life.
We praise the God whose image is our own,
  the mystery within our flesh and bone,
the womanspirit moving through all time
  in prophecy, Magnificat and dream.

                              —Shirley Erena Murray, © 1992
                  Hope Publishing Company and Hope Hymns Online
                        Sing to the tune SURSUM CORDA (Smith)

Suggested Hymns and Songs
(see hymnary.org or other sources as noted)

A Mother Lined a Basket (Mary Nelson Keithahn)
A Prophet Woman Broke a Jar (Brian A. Wren)
A Widow of Zarepheth Town (Mary Nelson Keithahn)
For All the Faithful Women (Herman G. Stuempfle Jr.)
God of the Women Who Answered Your Call (Carolyn
  Winfrey Gillette)
God of Our Foremothers (Shirley Erena Murray, *Faith
  Makes the Song*, Hope Publishing Company and Hopes
  Hymns Online)
God, We Praise You for the Women (Daniel C. Damon)
Maker of the Sun and Moon (Peter Sharrocks)

Spirit, Spirit of Gentleness (James K. Manley)
To My Precious Lord (Chung Kwan Park)
We Praise You, God, for Women (Ruth Duck, *Circles of Caring*, The Pilgrim Press)
Woman in the Night (Brian A. Wren)
Womb of Life and Source of Being (Ruth Duck)

Earth Day / Celebrating the Environment

Since 1970, Earth Day has been held annually on April 22. From its origins in the United States, it's now observed in almost two hundred countries across the globe. God calls us, from the first words of Genesis, to care for our planet home and everything that dwells in it.

Scriptures

God said, "See, I have given you every plant yielding seed that is upon the face of all the earth, and every tree with seed in its fruit; you shall have them for food. And to every beast of the earth, and to every bird of the air, and to everything that creeps on the earth, everything that has the breath of life, I have given every green plant for food." And it was so. God saw everything that was made, and indeed, it was very good.   —Genesis 1:29-31

O God, our God,
    how majestic is your name in all the earth!
When we look at your heavens, the work of your fingers,
    the moon and the stars you have established, what are
    human beings that you are mindful of them?
Yet you have made us a little lower than the divine being,
    and crowned us with glory and honor.

**You have given us charge over the works of your hands;
you have put all things under our feet,**
All sheep and oxen, and also the beasts of the field, the
birds of the air, and the fish of the sea.
**O God, our God,
how majestic is your name in all the earth!** —From Psalm 8

God makes grass grow for the cattle and plants for us to
use, so that we can grow our crops and produce wine to
make us happy, olive oil to make us cheerful, and bread
to give us strength. The cedars of Lebanon get plenty of
rain—the trees that the Holy One planted. There the birds
build their nests; the storks nest in the fir trees. The wild
goats live in the high mountains, and the rock badgers hide
in the cliffs. You created the moon, O God, to mark the
months; the sun knows the time to set. You made the night,
and in the darkness all the wild animals come out. When
the sun rises, they go back and lie down in their dens. Then
people go out to do their work and keep working until
evening. Gracious One, you have made so many things!
How wisely you made them all! The earth is filled with
your creatures.   —Psalm 104:14-24 (GNT)

Look at the birds in the sky! They don't plant or harvest.
**They don't even store grain in barns. Yet God in heaven
takes care of them.**
Aren't you worth more than birds? Can worry make you
live longer? Why worry about clothes?
Look how the wild flowers grow. They don't work hard to
make their clothes.
**But truly, Solomon with all his wealth wasn't as well
clothed as one of them.**

God, who gives such beauty to everything that grows in the fields, even though it is here today and thrown into a fire tomorrow, will surely do even more for you!
Why, then, do we have such little faith?

—Matthew 6:26-30 (CEV)

Jesus told them a parable: "The kingdom of heaven is like this. A planter takes a mustard seed and sows it in a field. It is the smallest of all seeds, but when it grows up, it is the biggest of all plants. It becomes a tree, so that birds come and make their nests in its branches."

—Matthew 13:31-32 (GNT)

Prayers and Readings

When I admire the wonders of a sunset or the beauty of the moon, my soul expands in the worship of the creator.

—Mohandas Gandhi

God of all space, peoples, and cultures:
we give thanks this day for variety and difference.
God of the cosmos, mystery, and beauty:
we give thanks this day for our wonder and curiosities.
God of compassion, love, and sharing:
we give thanks this day for the bounty of your good earth.
God of hope, life, and revelation:
we pray this day to be enlightened with a deeper world consciousness.
God of grace, humility, and gentleness:
Teach us about our humanity as we celebrate your magnificent creation.

—Michael Burch

Like a seed planted
  in the darkened womb of Mother Earth, our Sister,
whose roots reach down to the depths of mystery
in search of water, living water, our Sister Water
to draw up sustaining life, to break ground, to find light.
As a young shoot rooted and rising,
reaching to touch the Son, Brother Sun,
  the Son of God, light and life.
Opening up in praise
branches in the wind
extended as a witness to the Christ.
Breathing in the Spirit
gathering in the grace
living in the love
which sustains
a tree. Amen.

—Lawrence Jay

The fire has its flame and praises God.
The wind blows the flame and praises God.
In the voice we hear the word which praises God.
And the word, when heard, praises God.
So all of creation is a song of praise to God.

—Hildegard of Bingen (1098–1179)

The garden needs our tending now—
  the water, soil, and air.
The very rocks and stones cry out
  for stewardship and care.
Creation groans, awaiting still
  the consummation of God's will:
Earth shall be green and new, Eden restored.
  Terra viridissima.

—Mary Louise Bringle, *Joy and Wonder, Love and Longing*,
© 2002 GIA Publications, Inc.

Suggested Hymns and Songs
(see hymnary.org or other sources as noted)

All Creatures of Our God and King/To You, O God, All
  Creatures Sing (Francis of Assisi)
Creating God, Your Fingers Trace (Jeffrey Rowthorn)
Creation Sings! Each Plant and Tree (Martin E. Leckebusch)
De colores/Sing of Colors (Mexican folk song)
For the Fruit of All Creation (Fred Pratt Green)
Learn from All the Songs of Earth (Thomas H. Troeger)
Morning Has Broken (Eleanor Farjeon)
Pray for the Wilderness, Vanishing Fast (Daniel Charles
  Damon)
Touch the Earth Lightly (Shirley Erena Murray)
We Are Children of Creation (Barbara Hamm)

Christian Home and Family Life,
Mother's Day and Father's Day

Scriptures

Hear, O Israel: The Lord is our God, the Lord alone.
**We shall love God with all our heart, and with all our soul,
  and with all our might.**
Keep these words that I am commanding you today in your
  heart. Recite them to your children and talk about them
  when you are at home and when you are away, when you
  lie down and when you rise.
Hear, O Israel: The Lord is our God, the Lord alone.

—Deuteronomy 6:4-7

Now therefore honor God, and serve God in sincerity
and in faithfulness. Choose this day whom you will serve,

whether the gods your ancestors served or the gods of the land in which you are living. But as for me and my household, we will serve God, the Holy One.

—From Joshua 24:14-15

Happy is everyone who honors God,
   who walks in God's ways.
They shall eat the fruit of the labor of their hands;
   they shall be happy, and it shall go well with them.
The parents will be like fruitful vines within their house;
   their children will be like olive shoots around their table.
Thus shall the ones who honor God be blessed.
May they see the prosperity of Jerusalem
   all the days of their lives.
May they see their children's children.
   Peace be upon Israel!

—Psalm 128

O God, you have searched me and known me.
You know when I sit down and when I rise up;
   you discern my thoughts from afar.
You search out my path and the places I rest;
   you are familiar with all my ways.
Even before a word is on my tongue, O God,
   you know it completely.
You guard me from behind and before,
   and lay your protecting hand upon me.
It is beyond my knowledge, it is a mystery;
   I cannot fathom it.
It was you who formed my inward parts; you knit me together in my mother's womb. I praise you, for I am fearfully and wonderfully made.

Wonderful are your works; this I know very well.
My frame was not hidden from you, when I was being
  made in secret, intricately woven in the mystery of clay.
Your eyes saw my substance taking shape;
  in your book my every day was recorded;
all my days became possible,
  even before any of them as yet existed.
How deep are your designs, O God!
  How vast is their number!
I try to count them, but they are more than the sand,
  I come to the end—I am still with you.

—Psalm 139:1-6, 13-18

People were bringing little children to him in order that he
might touch them; and the disciples spoke sternly to them.
But when Jesus saw this, he was indignant and said to
them, "Let the little children come to me; do not stop them;
for it is to such as these that the kingdom of God belongs.
Truly I tell you, whoever does not receive the kingdom of
God as a little child will never enter it." And he took them
up in his arms, laid his hands on them, and blessed them.

—Mark 10:13-16

Love is patient; love is kind; love is not envious or boastful
or arrogant or rude. It does not insist on its own way; it is
not irritable or resentful; it does not rejoice in wrongdoing, but rejoices in truth. Love bears all things, believes
all things, hopes all things, endures all things. Love never
ends.   —1 Corinthians 13:4-8

Prayers and Readings

Creator and Creating God, you formed the first human being out of the clay of the Garden, shaping our very form with tender care. Even now breathe your Spirit into us and throughout this space that we may be ever formed and re-formed into the people you would have us become. In Jesus's name we pray. **Amen.** —Jennifer W. Davidson

On this day, our God, we offer thanks for your gracious gift of home and family. We pray for those who live with poverty, who deal with addictions or loss of a stable home. We pray also for those who have everything of this world's wealth but lack a spiritual center in their hearts. We lift up these concerns to you, loving God, that all homes and families may be strengthened by your grace, your love, and your protection. This we ask through Jesus Christ. **Amen.**

God, teach us to work with love, knowing that work is love made visible.

Teach us to weave the cloth with threads drawn from our heart, even as if you, our beloved, were to wear that cloth.

To build a house with affection, even as if you were to dwell in that house.

To sow seeds with tenderness and reap the harvest with joy, even as if you were to eat the fruit.

To charge all things we fashion with a breath of our own spirit,

And to know that all who have gone before us are standing about us and watching.

—Kahlil Gibran (1883–1931; adapted)

Then here will I and mine today
a solemn covenant make and say:
Though all the world forsake God's word,
I and my house will serve the Lord.

Christoph von Pfiel (1712–1784; translated by Catherine Winkworth)

Suggested Hymns and Songs
(see hymnary.org or other sources as noted)

All Are Welcome (Marty Haugen)
God of Every Generation (Mary Louise Keithahn)
God of the Ages (Ruth Duck)
Grandmother God/Younger Than a Youth (Brian Wren)
How Can We Name a Love (Brian Wren)
I Was There to Hear Your Borning Cry (John Ylvisaker)
Koinonia (V. Michael McKay)
Lord of Our Growing Years (David Mowbray)
Love Is the Touch of Intangible Joy (Alison M. Robertson)
O, Blest the House, Whate'er Befall (Christoph von Pfiel)
Thank God for Saints of Seasoned Age (Ruth Duck, *The Poetry of Grace*, Hope Publishing Company and Hope Hymns Online)
Three Things I Promise (Daniel C. Damon)

Recognition of Graduates, Christian Education

Scriptures

We are like green olive trees in the house of God.
Lead us in your Word and guide us.
We trust in your faithful love, O God, forever and ever,
and thank you for all that you have done.
Lead us in your Word and guide us.

In the presence of your people we will proclaim your name,
  for it is good.
Lead us in your Word and guide us.   —Psalm 52:8-9

How can a young person live a clean life?
  By carefully reading the map of God's word.
I'm single-minded in pursuit of you;
  don't let me miss the road signs you've posted.
I've banked your promises in the vault of my heart
  so I won't sin myself bankrupt.
Be blessed, God; train me in your ways of wise living.
I'll transfer to my lips
  all the counsel that comes from your mouth;
I delight far more in what you tell me about living
  than in gathering a pile of riches.
I ponder every morsel of wisdom from you,
  I attentively watch how you've done it.
I relish everything you've told me of life,
  I won't forget a word of it.   —Psalm 119:9-16 (*The Message*)

Wisdom is radiant and unfading,
and she is easily discerned by those who love her,
and is found by those who seek her.
She hastens to make herself known to those who desire her.
One who rises early to seek her will have no difficulty,
for she will be found sitting at the gate.
To fix one's thought on her is perfect understanding,
and one who is vigilant on her account will soon be free
  from care,
because she goes about seeking those worthy of her,
and she graciously appears to them in their paths,
and meets them in every thought.

The beginning of wisdom is the most sincere desire for
  instruction,
and concern for instruction is love of her,
and love of her is the keeping of her laws,
and giving heed to her laws is assurance of immortality,
and immortality brings one near to God;
so the desire for wisdom leads to a kingdom.

—Wisdom 6:12-20

Trust in God with all your heart, and do not rely on your
own understandings. In all your ways acknowledge the
Holy One, and God will make straight your paths.

—Proverbs 3:5-6

Some people brought children to Jesus for him to place
his hands on them and to pray for them, but the disciples
scolded the people. Jesus said, "Let the children come to
me and do not stop them, because the Kingdom of heaven
belongs to such as these." —Matthew 19:13-15 (GNT)

Do not be conformed by this world; but be transformed by
the renewing of your minds. —Romans 12:2

You then, my child, be strong in the grace that is in Christ
Jesus; and what you have heard from me through many
witnesses entrust to faithful people who will be able to
teach others as well. —2 Timothy 2:1-2

Prayers and Readings

In times past, O God, you taught through your holy prophets your will and your way. We praise you that your voice
has not grown silent, but that you have given us teachers to

open before us your truth and to lead us into right paths. Continue to lead us, we pray, through Christ. **Amen.**

O God our eternal Father, we praise thee for gifts of mind with which thou hast endowed us. We are able to rise out of the half-realities of the sense world to a world of ideal beauty and eternal truth. Teach us, we pray thee, how to use this great gift of reason and imagination so that it shall not be a curse but a blessing. Grant us visions that shall lift us from worldliness and sin into the light of thine own holy presence. Through Jesus Christ we pray. **Amen.**

—Martin Luther King Jr.

Merciful and gracious God, hear the thanksgivings we bring before you, in the name of Jesus Christ. For your providence that sustains and supports us; for your love that corrects and heals us:
We thank you, God, our Creator.
For minds that make us restless until we rest in you; for faith that allows for both our questions and our doubts:
We thank you, God, our Creator.
For all who faithfully teach your word and patiently help us to know and understand your ways:
We thank you, God, our Creator.
For the labor of scholars that adds to our understanding; for the inspiration we receive from their deep engagement and their dedicated study:
We thank you, God, our Creator.
For the writers and publishers of books and other resources who help us come to a clearer understanding of your word:
We thank you, God, our Creator.

For all these blessings that you have given, that we might
use them wisely and well:
We thank you, God, our Creator. Amen.

Litany for the Journey

God, Spirit of compassion, you have brought us together
for a time as students: we give you thanks for the learn-
ing we have gained in these years; for our teachers and all
who have guided us, accept our gratitude.
**Soon we will prepare to go from this place out into the
world.**
For a while we have shared a common road. Now we de-
part to travel new paths and take varied journeys.
We have walked together, played together, grown together.
We shared our dreams, our fears, our joys, our visions; we
learned from one another.
**We grew, we changed. We became young women and men.
We are still becoming.**
We cannot fully know where our different roads will take us.
Yet, through Christ, we trust we will be guided wherever
we may go, and we know that you will journey with us.
God, walk beside us as we go, we pray.
May grace go with us.
May peace sustain us.
(*All:*) **May love empower us!**   —Peter Yuichi Clark

Come, teach us, Spirit of our God,
   the language of your way,
the lessons that we need to live,
   the faith for every day.

Excite our minds to follow you,
   to trace new truths in store,

new flight paths for our spirit space,
  new marvels to explore.

—Shirley Erena Murray, *In Every Corner Sing*,
© 1992 Hope Publishing Company and Hope Hymns Online
Sing to the tune AZMON

Suggested Hymns and Songs
(see hymnary.org or other sources as noted)

For the Splendor of Creation (Carl P. Daw Jr., *A Year of Grace*, Hope Publishing Company and Hope Hymns Online)

Hands of Blessing (Peggy Haymes)

Lord, We Bring to You Our Children (Frank von Christierson)

Praise the Course of Faith and Learning (Thomas H. Troeger)

Something Within (Lucie Campbell)

These Treasured Children Present Now (Jacque B. Jones)

We Praise You with Our Minds, O Lord (Hugh McElrath)

World Communion Sunday, Christian Unity (see also *Hope for the World*, p. 202)

Scriptures

Happy are those whom you choose,
  whom you bring to live in your sanctuary.
We will be satisfied with the good things of your house,
  the blessings of your sacred temple.
You answer us by giving us victory,
  and you do wonderful things to save us.
People all over the world and across the distant seas
  put their trust in you.

You set the mountains in place by your strength,
   showing your mighty power.
**You calm the roar of the seas and the noise of the waves;
   you calm the uproar of the peoples.**
The whole world stands in awe
   of the great things that you have done.
**Your deeds bring shouts of joy
   from one end of the earth to the other.** —Psalm 65:4-8 (GNT)

O give thanks to God, for the Eternal One is good; with
   steadfast love that endures forever.
**Let the redeemed of God declare this, those redeemed from
   trouble and gathered in from the lands, from the east and
   the west, from the north, and from the south.**
Some wandered in desert wastelands, finding no way to an
   inhabited town; hungry and thirsty, their soul faltered
   within them.
**Then they cried to God in their trouble, and were delivered
   from their distress;**
God led them by a straight way, until they reached an inhabited town, a place of rest and plenty.
**(*All:*) Let us thank the Holy One for this steadfast love and
   for all blessings to humankind.**   —Psalm 107:1-8

Be encouraged to live as people worthy of the call you received from God. Conduct yourselves with all humility,
   gentleness, and patience.
**May we accept each other with love, making an effort to
   preserve the unity of the Spirit with the peace that ties us
   together.**
You are one body and one spirit, just as God also called
   you in one hope.

There is one Lord, one faith, one baptism, and one God and Creator of all.

Some are apostles, some prophets, some evangelists, some are pastors and teachers.

We are to be equipped as God's people for the work of serving and building up the Body of Christ until we all reach the unity of faith and knowledge of God's Son.

God's goal is for us to become mature adults—to be fully grown, measured by the standard of the fullness of Christ.

By speaking the truth with love, let's grow in every way into Christ, who is the head.

The whole body grows from him, as it is joined and held together by all the supporting ligaments.

The body makes itself grow in that it builds itself up with love as each one does its part.

—From Ephesians 4 (CEB)

Prayers and Readings

God of all, who has called us to be your people, we rejoice that on this day the unity of your church is shown as the faithful throughout the whole earth gather at Christ's table and share in this holy meal. We pray that the faith and witness of all Christian people may increase, and that every wall that still separates us one from another may be broken down. May we celebrate our diverse paths and recognize that they all lead through Jesus Christ to you, Holy One. Amen.

We are all one family, made in the image of God.
We are all one family, each unique, each special.
We are all one family, given gifts and talents to share.
We are all one family, on a journey of faith.

We are all one family, united in love, united in peace.
May a thousand tongues across the world today lift up our voices in praise!

If there is radiance in the spirit, it will abound in the family.
**If there is radiance in the family,
it will abound in the community.**
If there is radiance in the community,
it will abound in the nation.
If there is radiance in the nation, the universe will flourish.

—Tao Te Ching, sixth century BCE

Behold, how good and pleasant it is when sisters and brothers dwell in unity! It is like vistas seen from atop a mountain one has climbed, or like the stillness of a sunset after a long day's work. It is like a shimmering rainbow, breaking through a refreshing rain.
(*All:*) **When people dwell together in unity, God's goodness and grace are clearly seen and celebrated. Be with us today as we worship and as we thank you, O Holy One! Through Jesus Christ, the world's Redeemer, we pray. Amen.**

—Based on Psalm 133

Great God, fill our hearts with gladness for the Scriptures, for the traditions and the teachings that have been passed down to us. Fill our minds with questions so that we can challenge the ways of the world and think differently so that we can follow you with full hearts. Fill our lives with the presence of one another, that we may know our neighbors and love them as ourselves. Help us to love deeply, and to live in peace with one another, caring for those in need as our brother and sister. In the name of Jesus the

Christ, our Brother, our Friend, and our Savior, we pray.
Amen.   —Mindi Welton-Mitchell

Litany for Unity

May the Holy Spirit guide our prayer toward Jesus the
  Christ and God the Creator:
Beyond the frontiers of language, race, and nation,
Unite us in our humanity.
Beyond our ignorance, our prejudices, and our hostilities,
Unite us in our hearts.
Beyond our intellectual and spiritual barriers,
Unite us in our minds.
O God, that goodness and trust may prevail,
Gather together all Christians.
O God, that there may be one flock and one Shepherd,
Gather together all Christians.
O God, that human pride may be confounded,
Gather together all Christians.
O God, that peace may at last reign on earth,
(*All:*) **Unite us, gather us, and bless us this day. Amen.**

Call to Communion

The cup of blessing that we bless, is it not a sharing in the
blood of Christ? The bread that we break, is it not a sharing in the body of Christ? Because there is one bread, we
who are many are one body, for we all partake of the one
bread.   —1 Corinthians 10:16-17

**Gather your church, O God, from the four winds into the
  kin-dom of your love.**

Have mercy, O God, on your church; deliver it from all
evil, and ground it in your love. Bring it out from many
nations into that unity you have prepared.

**Gather your church, O God, from the four winds into the
kin-dom of your love.**

Come, Jesus, come! Glory be to God forever and ever.

**Gather your church, O God, from the four winds into the
kin-dom of your love. Amen.**

He turned to say: "Come follow me."
   I joined his band to travel land and sea.
And so we go to whom he sends,
   no longer strangers, we're sisters, brothers, friends.
My world was small, my neighbors few,
   but now God's love gives me a larger view:
before the cross my world extends,
   no longer strangers, we're sisters, brothers, friends.

—Richard K. Avery and Donald S. March,
© 1978 Hope Publishing Company and Hope Hymns Online

Suggested Hymns and Songs
(see hymnary.org or other sources as noted)

God, You Link Our Hands Together (Herman G.
   Stuempfle Jr.)

In Christ There Is No East or West (John Oxenham)

Khudaya, rahem kar/Have Mercy on Us, Lord (*Sing with
the World*, GIA Publications, Inc.)

Let Us Break Bread Together (African American spiritual)

No Longer Strangers/He Turned to Say, Come Follow Me
   (Richard K. Avery and Donald S. Marsh)

Now I Have New Life in Christ (Houn Lee, translated by
   Ruth Duck)

O For a Thousand Tongues to Sing (John Wesley)

O for a World (Ruth Duck)
One Bread, One Body (John B. Foley, SJ)
O-so-so/Come Now, O Prince of Peace (Geonyong Lee)
Santo, Santo, Santo/Holy, Holy, Holy (Argentine folk song)
Song of Hope/Canto de Esperanza (Alvin Schumatt)
We Are Marching (Walking) in the Light of
   God / Siyahamba (Zulu traditional song, South Africa)

Blessing of the Animals (see also *Earth Day*, p. 166)

Many churches have adopted this tradition, observed on or around October 4, the feast day for Francis of Assisi. Commemorating this patron saint of animals and of all God's creation, guardians bring their pets into the church or to an area outside the sanctuary for a special blessing that celebrates the kinship of all living things.

Scriptures

Then God said, "It's not good that the human is alone. I will make him a helper that is perfect for him." So God formed from the fertile land all the wild animals and all the birds in the sky and brought them to the human to see what he would name them. The human gave each living being its name. The human named all the livestock, all the birds in the sky, and all the wild animals.

—Genesis 2:18-20 (CEB)

Praise God from the earth, you sea monsters and all you
   ocean depths!
Do the same, fire and hail, snow and smoke, stormy wind
   that does what God says!
**Do the same, you mountains, every single hill, fruit trees,
   and every single cedar!**

Do the same, you animals—wild or tame—you creatures
that creep along and you birds that fly!

**Do the same, you rulers and princes of the earth and every
single person!**

Do the same, you young men—young women too!—you
who are old together with you who are young!

**Let all of these praise the Holy One's name because only
God's name is high over all.**

Only God's majesty is over earth and heaven.

God raised the strength of the people, the praises of all
those faithful ones—the people whom God holds close.

Praise our God! —Psalm 148:7-14 (CEB)

Look at the birds of the air; they neither sow nor reap
nor gather into barns, and yet your heavenly Father feeds
them. —Matthew 6:26

Prayers and Readings

The greatness of a nation can be judged by the way its
animals are treated. —Mohandas Gandhi

For your creatures that breathe, move, and have life.

We give you thanks, O God.

That we may love and honor the work of God's hand.

We give you thanks, O God.

That each pet here may be treasured with care.

Hear us, O God.

For all animals who suffer pain, hunger, or neglect.

Hear us, O God.

For the hunted, and lost, for all in captivity or ill-treated,
and for those who must be put to death.

Hear us, O God.

For our pets who have died.

We thank you, and we give you praise; for your love is great.

For those who deal with animals we ask a heart of compassion, gentle hands, and kindly words. Make us true friends of animals and worthy followers of our merciful Savior, Jesus Christ. **Amen.**
—Mark Liebenow

God of Compassion, Source of All that is; Spirit of Life, Maker of countless expressions of life: cultivate among us a shared consciousness; guide us to faith and authentic spirituality. In the interest of wisdom, empathy, and respect enlighten us through the inspiring lives of animals and all creatures that share our world. Our desire is to understand the lives of others and find wisdom in their living. Through humility may we come to know kindness and in respectful living may we embrace and protect your glorious creation. **Amen.**
—Michael Burch

Christ has something in common with all creatures. With the stone he shares existence, with the plants he shares life, with the animals he shares sensation, and with the angels he shares intelligence. Thus all things are transformed in Christ since in the fullness of his nature he embraces some part of every creature.
—Bonaventure (c. 1217–1274)

Bless the beasts, all inhabitants of the earth!

Bless the large and mighty, the low and tiny, bless the birds that fly and the fish that swim,

bless all the animals that play under the trees, that race across the meadows with the joy of life.

All creatures are precious in God's sight!
Bless our pets who bring life into our homes!
who snuggle with us on cold, rainy days, who lay their
   heads on our laps when we watch TV,
who keep us company when we are sick, lonely, or de-
   pressed, who drag us outside for exercise
and give us a chance to stretch our legs.
**Bless them all and keep them safe; heal their wounds of
   body and mind.**
Watch over them as they watch over us and if they should
   die before our time,
may we never forget the sound of their voice, the smell of
   their fur, the vibrations of their purr,
the look of devotion in their eyes when we come home.
**Bless the animals of the world, all inhabitants of the
   earth!**
                                              —Mark Liebenow

Earth is full of wit and wisdom,
   sounding God's delighted laugh,
from the tiny roly-poly to the treetop tall giraffe.
All creation sings in wonder; even rocks and trees rejoice
as they join the ringing chorus: echoes of our Maker's voice.

Earth is full of wit and wisdom: penguin, platypus and snail,
cactus, sea slug, oak and algae,
   from the microbe to the whale.
In this great and strange creation,
   with a breath God gives us birth:
born of soil to live as stewards,
   called to love and serve the earth.

                          —Adam M. L. Tice, *Woven into Harmony*,
                               © 2009 GIA Publications, Inc.
                               Sing to the tune HOLY MANNA

Suggested Hymns and Songs
(see hymnary.org or other sources as noted)

All Things Bright and Beautiful (Cecil Frances Alexander)

Birds in the Mountains Sing of Your Praises (Patricia Lewis)

God of the Sparrow, God of the Whale (Jaroslav J. Vajda)

Mothering Earth, Our Mother Birthing (Norman Habel)

O God, Your Creatures Fill the Earth (Carolyn Winfrey Gillette, www.carolynshymns.com)

Reformation Day

This celebration, held on the Sunday on or before October 31, commemorates the events of the Protestant Reformation, and the witness of Martin Luther in particular. Among other reforms, Luther reestablished the priesthood of all believers, put the liturgy of the Latin Mass into the common tongue of the people, and translated the Bible from Latin into German, beginning an era of the scriptures' availability in the vernacular of readers worldwide.

Scriptures

Happy are those who do not follow the advice of the wicked, or take the path that sinners tread, or sit in the seat of scoffers; but their delight is in the law of the Lord, and on this law they meditate day and night. They are like trees planted by streams of water, which yield their fruit in its season, and their leaves do not wither. In all that they do, they prosper.   —Psalm 1:1-3

God is our refuge and strength,
   a very present in help in trouble.

**Therefore we will not fear, though the earth should change,
though the mountains shake in the heart of the sea.**
There is a river whose streams make glad the city of God,
the holy habitation of the Most High.
**God is in the midst of the city; it shall not be moved; God
will help it when the morning dawns.**
Come, behold the works of God; see what desolations have
been brought on the earth. God makes wars to cease to
the ends of the earth, breaking the bow and shattering
the spear.
The Lord of hosts is with us; the God of Jacob is our refuge.
"Be still, and know that I am God! I am exalted among the
nations, I am exalted in the earth."
**The Lord of hosts is with us;
the God of Jacob is our refuge.** —From Psalm 46

Therefore, since we are justified by faith, we have peace
with God through our Lord Jesus Christ, through whom
we have obtained access to this grace in which we stand;
and we boast in our hope of sharing the glory of God. And
not only that, but we also boast in our sufferings, knowing
that suffering produces endurance, and endurance produces character, and character produces hope, and hope does
not disappoint us, because God's love has been poured into
our hearts through the Holy Spirit that has been given to
us. God, who is rich in mercy, out of great love to us even
when we were dead through our trespasses, made us alive
together with Christ. —Romans 5:1-5; Ephesians 2:4-5

God has made us alive together with Christ.
By grace we have been saved.

We have been raised up with Christ and seated in heavenly places with him, so that in the ages to come we might know the immeasurable riches of God's grace.
By grace we have been saved.
For by grace we have been saved through faith, and this is not our own doing; it is the gift of God.
For we are what God has made us, created in Christ Jesus to do good as our way of life. —Ephesians 2:4-10

Prayers and Readings

Unless I am convinced by Scripture and plain reason—I do not accept the authority of the popes and councils, for they have contradicted each other—my conscience is captive to the word of God. I cannot and I will not recant anything, for to go against conscience is neither right nor safe. God help me. **Amen.** —Martin Luther

We thank you, our heavenly Creator, through Jesus Christ your dear child, that you have kept us from all harm and danger; and we pray that you would keep us this day from sin and every evil, that all we do and all we are may please you. Into your hands we commend ourselves, body and soul and all things. Let your holy angels be with us, that the forces of evil may have no power over us. **Amen.**

—Based on a prayer by Martin Luther

Our God, who has brought us into fellowship with one another through Jesus Christ: grant us grace and mercy to continue in this ministry together. Help us to do your will when other ways seem easier. Direct our thoughts to you through the reading and preaching of Holy Scripture, that we may always stand in the light of Christ. Bless us in our weakness, O God, that we may better love and serve one another. Make holy our willingness to be obedient to you. We ask this in the name of Christ. **Amen.**

A mighty fortress is our God, a stronghold never failing;
whose love supports us midst the storm
   of earthly wrongs prevailing.
Though nations rise and wane, and conflict seems to reign,
the Holy One is here, to soothe and still our fear;
   on this our hope is founded.

If we on our own strength relied,
   our struggles we'd be losing;
but there is one who takes our side,
   the One of God's own choosing.
You ask who that may be? Christ Jesus, it is he!
With love and not a sword, his very life outpoured:
   the Word, with God, victorious.

That Word above all worldly might, eternally abiding,
the Spirit and its gifts ignite in those whom God is guiding.
Let all possessions go, this mortal life also;
all flesh will fade away and peace shall rule the day:
   God's love endures forever!

—Martin Luther, paraphrased by N. H.

Suggested Hymns and Songs
(see hymnary.org or other sources as noted)

Christ Is Made the Sure Foundation (J. M. Neale)
Lord, Keep Us Steadfast in Your Word (Martin Luther)
My Hope Is Built on Nothing Less (Edward Mote)
Now Thank We All Our God (Martin Rinckart)
O Word of God Incarnate (William Walsham How)

Our God, We Are a Church Reformed (Carolyn Winfrey
   Gillette)
The Church's One Foundation (Samuel J. Stone)

Stewardship, Thanksgiving

Many churches have a time of stewardship emphasis during the fall season. Since the scriptures and prayers for
Thanksgiving are similar to those of stewardship, the two
themes are here combined.

Scriptures

You crown the year with your goodness; your paths over-
flow with rich food. Even the desert pastures drip with it,
and the hills are dressed in pure joy. The meadowlands are
covered with flocks, the valleys decked out in grain—they
shout for joy; they break out in song!

—Psalm 65:11-13 (CEB)

Be gracious to us, O God, and bless us, and may your face
   shine upon us, that your way may be known upon earth,
   your saving power among all nations.
Let the peoples praise you, O God;
   let all the peoples praise you.
Let the nations be glad and sing for joy, for you judge the
   peoples fairly and guide the nations upon earth.
Let the peoples praise you, O God;
   let all the peoples praise you.
The earth has yielded its increase;
   God, our God, has blessed us.
May you continue to bless us;
   let all the ends of the earth revere the Holy One.

—Psalm 67

The eyes of all look to you, and you give them their food in due season. You open your hand, satisfying the desire of every living thing. God is just in all ways, and kind in all deeds. God is near to all who call, to all who call sincerely.   —Psalm 145:15-18

Jesus sat down opposite the treasury, and watched the crowd putting money into the treasury. Many rich people put in large sums. A poor widow came and put in two small copper coins, which are worth a penny. Then he called his disciples and said to them, "Truly I tell you, this poor widow has put in more than all those who are contributing to the treasury. For all of them have contributed out of their abundance; but she out of her poverty has put in everything she had, all she had to live on."
                                              —Mark 12:41-44

Do not store up for yourselves treasures on earth, where moth and rust consume and where thieves break in and steal; but store up for yourselves treasures in heaven, where neither moth nor rust consumes and where thieves do not break in and steal. For where your treasure is, there your heart will be also.   —Matthew 6:19-21

The point is this: the one who sows sparingly will also reap sparingly, and the one who sows bountifully will also reap bountifully. Each of you must give as you have made up your mind, not reluctantly or under compulsion, for God loves a cheerful giver.
And God is able to provide us with every blessing in abundance, so that by always having enough of everything, we may share abundantly in every good work.

God, who supplies seed to the sower and bread for food,
will supply and multiply your seed for sowing and increase the harvest of your righteousness.
**We will be enriched in every way for our generosity, which
will produce gratitude to God through us.**
This ministry not only supplies the needs of the saints but
also overflows with many thanksgivings to the Holy One.
Thanks be to God for this inexpressible gift!

—From 2 Corinthians 9

Prayers and Readings

Creator of heaven and earth, you have studded the sky with
stars and made it bright with lights, enriched the earth with
fruits to satisfy our needs, given to humankind the clear
light and the shining stars to enjoy, and the earth's produce
to feed on. We pray you, send us rain, abundant, plentiful, fertilizing; and make the earth yield fruit and to spare;
for we know how you love us, we know your kindness.
Hear our petitions and prayers and bless the whole earth,
through Jesus Christ. May glory and power be yours, in the
Holy Spirit, now and age after age. **Amen.**

—Serapion of Thmuis, c. 339

Our God, we desire to serve you in every way:
Consecrate our lives so we may be a blessing today.
We desire to serve you with our money;
Consecrate our lives so we may be a blessing today.
We desire to serve you with our talents;
Consecrate our lives so we may be a blessing today.
We desire to serve you with our time;
Consecrate our lives so we may be a blessing today.

Gracious One, in our use of money, talents, and time, may we bring glory to your name.

May we find reconciliation with you and our world. May we find new life and new possibilities.

May we find hope for abundant life today and in the life to come. Amen. —Michael-Ray Mathews

Source of Love, Center of Life—do you hear our call?
We wish to return to you that which we have borrowed.
Blessed Assurance, Just and yet Merciful—
do you sense our passion?
We wish to thank you for what we have been given.
Tender Creator, Tender of the Garden—
do you accept our intention?
We wish to show you our commitment to serve.
Now let us walk together, joyfully and unreservedly, with no looking back, but looking forward to God, celebrating the ability to give what is due.

The harvest is ripe—the time to put up the harvest has come. Amen. —Matthew Henry

God and creator, our hearts are filled with joy and thankfulness to you on this day of festival. Unfailingly, year by year, you clothe the earth in radiant beauty and bid it bring forth its bounteous blessings.

O God, we worship you, our hearts sing your praises.

In humble acknowledgment of your boundless providence, our ancestors brought to your altars on this day the first fruits of their harvest. They chanted songs of gratitude to you for the many gifts of garden and field and for the ripening of the fruit of the spirit.

O God, we worship you, our hearts sing your praises.

Each year at this time your sons and daughters stand before you, celebrating this season and their covenant with
you. Let us heed your words of wisdom and do your
works of mercy.

O God, we worship you, our hearts sing your praises.

Sanctify us all for your service. Grant that the good seed we
sow may ripen into a harvest of righteousness and truth.

**O God, we worship you, our hearts sing your praises.
Amen.**

—from Evening Prayer for Shavuos,
Union Prayer Book for Jewish Worship, adapted

We thank you, Lord, for hand and heart
    to offer up your praise.
We thank you, Lord, for tongue to speak
    of all your loving ways.
For health and strength, for work and play,
    for loved ones far and near,
with grateful heart we thank you, Lord,
    for all that we hold dear.

—Mary Kay Beall, *God Gives Us a Song*,
© 1991 Hope Publishing Company and Hope Hymns Online

Suggested Hymns and Songs
(see hymnary.org or other sources as noted)

Called as Partners in Christ's Service (Jane Parker Huber)
Cantad al Señor/O Sing to the Lord (Brazilian folk hymn)
Come, Thou Fount of Every Blessing (Robert Robinson)
Come, You Thankful People, Come (Henry Alford)
Give Thanks with a Grateful Heart (Henry Smith)
God, Whose Giving Knows No Ending (Robert L. Edwards)
Here Within This Congregation (Jacque B. Jones, *Songs
    Unchanged, Yet Ever-Changing*, GIA Publications, Inc.)

In the Lord I'll Be Ever Thankful (Taizé Community)
Take My Life and Let It Be (Frances Ridley Havergal)
Together We Serve (Daniel C. Damon)
Total Praise (Richard Smallwood)
We Are an Offering (Dwight Liles)
We Give Thee But Thine Own (William Walsham How)
What Gift Can We Bring (Jane Marshall)

WORSHIP THEMES

Missions Home and Abroad

Scriptures

God looks down from heaven, seeing all humankind. God watches all the inhabitants of the earth, fashions their hearts, and observes their deeds.
Truly the eye of God is on those who give honor; on those who hope in God's steadfast love.
Our soul waits for God, who is our help and shield. We have a glad heart because we trust in this holy name.
Let your steadfast love, O God, be upon us, even as we hope in you. —Psalm 33:13-15, 18-22

O give thanks to God, for God is good;
With steadfast love that endures forever.
Let the redeemed of God say so, those rescued from trouble:
God's faithful love endures forever.
Let the people be gathered in from the lands, from the east and from the west, from the north and from the south. God satisfies the thirsty, and the hungry are filled with good things.

God's faithful love endures forever.

Some sat in the shadows and in gloom; they cried to God in their trouble, and God brought them out and broke their binding chains.

God's faithful love endures forever.

Let those who are wise listen to these mighty acts, and consider the unfailing love of God.

God's faithful and gracious love endures forever.

—Psalm 107:13, 9-14, 43

How beautiful upon the mountains are the feet of the messenger who announces peace, who brings good news, who announces salvation, who says to Zion, "Your God reigns."

—Isaiah 52:7

Jesus said: "All authority in heaven and on earth has been given to me. Go therefore and make disciples of all nations, baptizing them in the name of the Creator and of the Son and of the Holy Spirit, and teaching them to obey everything that I have commanded you. And remember, I am with you always, to the end of the age."

—Matthew 28:18-20

Jesus said: "I am the light of the world. Whoever follows me will never walk in gloom but will have the light of life."

—John 8:12

Prayers—Home Missions

God of all the earth, too often we have tried to be Christian with our words alone and have forgotten that the disciples of Jesus Christ are known also by their deeds. We have praised you within the sanctuary, while on the streets we have walked past human need. We have spoken of mission but forgotten that Christ went into all the cities, villages, and towns of his home country to preach the gospel, heal the sick, and comfort the sorrowing. Forgive us, God, when we have neglected so great a task. Grant that through Jesus Christ we may become disciples in deed as well as word, reaching out in love to our sisters and brothers nearby and across this land. **Amen.**

We ask, O God, your blessing upon all those who have dedicated their lives to Christ's mission in our land. As they work in cities, in rural areas, in local churches, in schools and colleges, community centers, and in whatever places you have called them, we pray that their insight and strength may continue to deepen. May their dedication and labor continue to bring the word of peace and hope to those with whom they minister. We ask in the name of the One who called all people to be his witnesses, wherever they serve, Jesus the Christ. **Amen.**

Prayers—Missions Abroad

Eternal God, you made the world and everything in it. You gave to all humankind life and breath and made from one woman and one man every nation on earth. We praise you and thank you for the calling you give to those who are special witnesses to the marvels of your grace. We thank you for prophets and apostles who have in times past spoken your truth, and for the ambassadors of Christ in every age who have gone forth into distant lands to bring light and healing to those who dwell in the shadow of death. Above all, we thank you for Jesus Christ, whom you sent as your witness in the world and who has given us the hope that the realms and lands of this world will become your realm here on earth, so that all may share abundantly in your love and in peace. **Amen.**

Remember in your mercy, God, all your children everywhere. Let the whole earth be filled with your praise and made glad by singing praises to your name.
May they proclaim the Good News and be a light to the nations.
Be with all missionaries and workers who are this day serving in distant lands. Help them come to know and cherish the ways and words of the people with whom they serve.
May they proclaim the Good News and be a light to the nations.
Help them to know when they should speak and when they should remain silent. Grant them the grace and humility to learn from those whom they are teaching.
May they proclaim the Good News and be a light to the nations.
Let them be ready and willing to entrust into the hands of those with whom they labor the care and leadership of your church, Holy One.
May they proclaim the Good News and be a light to the nations. Amen.

Hear this from a homeless stranger,
nameless face in shadowed crowd,
makeshift bed and scant possessions,
nothing here to make me proud.
It's so easy to ignore me,
hasten steps and hurry by:

better not to glimpse my struggle,
    better not to hear my sigh.

There are times you pass my pallet
    on your way to sing and pray.
In the church you join with others
    thanking God for each fine day.
I can hear your joyful music
    from my joyless hiding place.
I am thankful just for shelter,
    gentle word, or knowing face.

But you've places you must go to,
    you have people you must see;
busy lives and tending families,
    giving little thought to me.
Yet I wonder what would happen
    if our roles should rearrange:
you'd be sleeping on this threshold,
    I would be a voice for change.

—Jacque B. Jones, *Songs Unchanged, Yet Ever-Changing*,
© 2014 GIA Publications, Inc.
Sing to the tune BEACH SPRING

Suggested Hymns and Songs
(see hymnary.org or other sources as noted)

As a Fire Is Meant for Burning (Ruth Duck)
For All the World (Margaret Clarkson)
Go Forth for God (J. R. Peacey)
How Shall They Hear, Who Have Not Heard? (Timothy
    Dudley-Smith)
I Love to Tell the Story (Katherine Hankey)
Lord, You Give the Great Commission (Jeffrey Rowthorn)

Not Alone, But Two by Two (Carl P. Daw Jr.)
The Church of Christ in Every Age (Fred Pratt Green)
To Be Your Presence (Delores Dufner, OSB)
We All Are One in Mission (Rusty Edwards)

Hope for the World

Scriptures

By the rivers of Babylon, we sat and wept when we thought
of Zion, our home, so far away.
On the branches of the willow trees, we hung our harps
and hid our hearts from the enemy.
And those who surrounded us made demands that we clap
our hands and sing—
**Songs of joy from days gone by, songs from Zion, our
home.**
Such cruel ones taunted us—haunted our memories.
How could we sing a song about the Eternal in a land so
foreign, while still tormented, brokenhearted, homesick?
Please don't make us sing this song.
When the upright need help and cry to the Eternal, God
hears their cries and rescues them from all of their
troubles.
**When someone is hurting or brokenhearted, the Eternal
moves in close and revives them in their pain.**

—Psalm 137:1-4, 34:17-18 (*The Voice*)

The spirit of God is upon me, and has anointed me; God
has sent me to bring good news to the oppressed, to bind
up the brokenhearted,
**To proclaim liberty to the captives, and release to the
prisoners;**

To proclaim the year of God's favor, and the day of vengeance of our God; to comfort all who mourn.

For as the earth brings forth its shoots, and as a garden causes what is sown in it to spring up, so God will cause righteousness and praise to spring up before all the nations. —Isaiah 61:1-2, 11

God has told you, O mortal, what is good; and what does the Holy One require of you but to do justice, and to love kindness, and to walk humbly with your God?

Let justice roll down like waters, and righteousness like an ever-flowing stream. —Micah 6:8; Amos 5:24

When Jesus saw the crowds, he went up the mountain; and after he sat down, his disciples came to him. Then he began to speak, and taught them, saying:

Blessed are those who depend upon God alone, for they belong to the kingdom of heaven.

Blessed are those who mourn, for they will be comforted.

Blessed are the humble, for God's earth belongs to them.

**Blessed are those who hunger and thirst for justice,
for they will be filled.**

Blessed are the compassionate,
for they will be treated with compassion.

**Blessed are those whose hearts are wholesome,
for they will see God.**

Blessed are the peacemakers,
for they will be called children of God.

Blessed are those who are persecuted for doing the right thing, for they belong to the kingdom of heaven.

Blessed are you when people insult you, mistreat you, and tell all kinds of evil lies about you on my account.

(*All:*) Rejoice and be glad, for our reward is great in heaven! These same things have been done for ages to those we call "the prophets." —Matthew 5:1-12, adapted

Jesus said: "You are the light of the world. Let your light shine before others, so that they may see your good works and give glory to God in heaven." —Matthew 5:14, 16

Let mutual love continue. Do not neglect to show hospitality to strangers, for by doing that some have entertained angels without knowing it. Remember those who are in prison, as though you were in prison with them; those who are being tortured, as though you yourselves were being tortured. —Hebrews 13:1-3

Prayers and Readings

God within, live through us,
we are the embodiment and the voice of the Sacred.
God above, descend into our lives and into our hearts,
we are your prophets of peace and renewal.
God the Invisible One, be ever near,
we know your presence through kindness and generosity.
God the Compassionate and Merciful One,
you sustain us with gratitude and guide us by hope.
God of Mystery and Surprise,
(*All:*) **empower us with vision and joyful resolve to be your united people. Amen.** —Michael Burch

While you are proclaiming peace with your lips, be careful to have it even more fully in your heart.
  —Attributed to Francis of Assisi (1181–1226)

Like the salt and light of Jesus' teaching, let us remember, O God, that we who follow Christ enhance everything we touch. We are more important than we know; let us use our knowledge and our faith to influence the world toward love and acceptance. **Amen.**
                                                                            —Shavon Walker

O Great Spirit, whose voice we hear in the winds and the sea and the cloud, and whose power gives life to all the world: Hear us! We are among your many children. We see with humility and gratefulness your everlasting grace and love. We pray that with strength we may understand the mysteries you have hidden in every leaf and rock. Our wish is not to be superior to our brothers and sisters but to purify our hearts and minds, so that when life fades, as the sunset fades, we may come to you with clean hands and a grateful heart. **Amen.**

                                        —Traditional Lakota Sioux prayer,
                      translated by Chief John Yellow Lark (1887, adapted)

Today we join our hearts together to offer our thanksgivings and blessings for those who serve and have served our country; and for their family members and friends who support and love them. We ask God, known by many different names in our faith traditions, to bless those who are away from home and in harm's way, to keep them safe, and to grant them comfort and holy presence.

Bless those who are here today, with good company. Bless those who are hurt and need healing;

Bless those who will soon be returning to their homes and families. Let us never take for granted the sacrifices they have made in their own lives and the lives of their families, so that liberty and justice might be a reality in our nation and world. Let us honor the active military and veterans by treating one another with love, respect, and kindness, for they are among us and deserve our prayers. **Amen.**   —Nancy B. Smith

We pause to remember those who go to war in our name.
We give thanks for courage, for love of country, for those who work to bring peace to our world.
Remind us, O God, that the goal of any war needs to be justice and peace.
On this day, we pause in worship to give thanks to God for veterans,
And seek to bind up the wounds of those who served.
Enable us to know how to comfort, how to bind up their wounds,
And remind us, dear God, that the widow, the orphan, the widower, and the veteran—all know the cost of war.
Challenge us to love the warrior but hate the cost of war,
and we pray for a time when peace will reign and swords become plowshares once more, that war be known only in history books.
(*All:*) **And we give thanks, Gracious God, that you remain with us as we celebrate the service of all who dared to go forth in our name. Remind us that such service is not a movie, an adventure, nor something to be glorified. Remind us that war is a failure by us to overcome hatred with love, injustice with righteousness, violence with peace. We give thanks for those who protect us from such failures. May we truly be your people and be makers of peace. Amen.**   —Tom Williams

God, make us instruments of your peace.
Where there is hatred, let us sow love.
Where there is injury, pardon;
Where is doubt, faith;
Where there is despair, hope;
Where there is darkness, light;
Where there is sadness, joy.
O Divine One, grant that we may not so much seek to be
    consoled, as to console,
To be understood, as to understand,
To be loved, as to love,
For it is in giving that we receive;
It is in pardoning that we are pardoned;
It is in dying that we are born to eternal life. Amen.

—Attributed to Francis of Assisi (1181–1226)

A refugee is someone who owing to a well-founded fear of
being persecuted for reasons of race, religion, nationality,
membership of a particular social group or political opin-
ion, is outside the country of his nationality, and is unable
to, or owing to such fear, is unwilling to avail himself of the
protection of that country.

—United Nations Refugee Agency

Hymn for Refugees

We are looking for a homeland,
    for a place we can be free,
for a land of hope and blessing
    where the promise we can see.
We are looking for a homeland,
    for a place we can belong,
where we dare to speak our names and sing our song.

We have traveled in the desert,
  in the wilderness have died,
we have borne the pain of hatred
  with our anguish as our guide.
But we know that God is with us,
  that we journey not alone,
so we keep on moving, searching for a Home.

We have paused to build an altar
  and to pray we will be found,
but the sacred word reminds us
  where we stand is Holy Ground.
So our weary search is over,
  we have finally reached the goal,
God is dwelling in the Homeland of the soul.

—Rodney R. Romney, © 1992 AmaDeus Group

Suggested Hymns and Songs
(see hymnary.org or other sources as noted)

By the Babylonian Rivers (Ewald Bash)
Diverse in Culture, Nations, Race (Ruth Duck)
Hope of the World (Georgia Harkness)
How Firm a Foundation ("K" in Rippon's *Selection of Hymns*)
In Christ There Is No East or West (John Oxenham)
O for a World (Ruth Duck)
Sizohamba naye, wo wo wo/We Will Walk with God (Swaziland traditional hymn)
The Church of Christ Cannot Be Bound (Adam M. L. Tice)
Today We Sing with Thankfulness (Jacque B. Jones, *Songs Unchanged, Yet Ever-Changing*, GIA Publications, Inc.)
We Shall Walk through the Valley in Peace (A. J. Hatter)

Interfaith Worship

Increasingly, churches of the various Protestant traditions are engaging with sisters and brothers of other faiths for occasions of interfaith worship. Such a service may take place as a community Thanksgiving gathering, for instance, or a broad cross-section of people may need to come together because of a community or national time of crisis. As ministers and lay people, we can be ready to plan and lead such times of worship by having prayers and musical selections available that embrace all people of faith. A few possibilities are offered here.

Scriptures

May God bless you and keep you.
May God smile upon you and be gracious to you.
May God look upon you with favor and give you peace.

—Numbers 6:24-26

In days to come the mountain of God's house shall be established as the highest of the mountains, and shall be raised above the hills; all the nations shall stream to it.
Many peoples shall come and say,
"Come, let us go up to the holy mountain,
to the house of the God of Jacob;
that we may be taught the holy ways
and that we may walk in holy paths."
For out of Zion shall go forth instruction,
and the word of God from Jerusalem.
The Holy One shall judge between the nations,
and shall arbitrate for many peoples;

they shall beat their swords into plowshares,
  and their spears into pruning hooks;
nation shall not lift up sword against nation,
  neither shall they learn war any more.
(*All:*) **O house of Jacob, come,**
  let us walk in the light of God!   —Isaiah 2:2-5

With what should I approach the Holy One, and bow
  down before God on high?
God has told you, human one, what is good; and God requires from you:
to do justice, embrace faithful love,
  and walk humbly with your God.   —Micah 6:6, 8

Prayers and Readings

When I despair, I remember that all through history the
ways of truth and love have always won. There have been
tyrants, and murderers, and for a time they can seem invin-
cible, but in the end they always fall.   —Mohandas Gandhi

O Holy One of light, inscribe your wisdom upon our hearts
that we may receive your Spirit.
Through sacred words of old
  and brave pioneers of our day
strengthen our traditions with compassion
  and renew our optimism.
As we are called onward
  to a deeper understanding of our humanity,
by the ancient wisdom of world ancestors,
  and the brilliance of our children's imaginations,
May we embrace your hope!
May we know true joy!   —Michael Burch

In the name of God, the beneficent, the merciful:
Praise be to the Lord of the Universe
who has created us and made us into tribes and nations,
that we may know each other, not that we may despise
    each other.
If the enemy inclines towards peace,
do thou also incline towards peace, and trust in God,
For the Lord is the one that hears and knows all things.
And the servants of God, Most Gracious,
are those who walk on the Earth in humility,
and when we address them, we say PEACE.

—Muslim Prayer for Peace

Ineffable One of Many Names: we pause for a moment to embrace a sense of awe that now and again comes over us, an inexpressible impression that we belong to something much greater than just ourselves; that mystical moment when we seem to participate in a unifying and irresistible Mystery. May our yearning to share these mystical experiences lead us to greater understanding of the infinite dimensions of the Sacred. Let us recognize the foolishness of insisting that one view—our view—is the only way the Spirit can be described. May we see that our similarity of experience vastly outweighs the particularity of our descriptions. May we grow ever more aware of the depth and beauty of these experiences as we encounter the many ways our fellow human beings express them. We dedicate ourselves to deepening our exploration of these mysteries as we work together in peace, harmony, and joy. **Amen.**

—Sharon P. Burch

If there is to be peace in the world,
   there must be peace in the nations.
If there is to be peace in the nations,
   there must be peace in the cities.
If there is to be peace in the cities,
   there must be peace between neighbors.
If there is to be peace between neighbors,
   there must be peace in the home.
If there is to be peace in the home,
   there must be peace in the heart.

—Lao-Tzu, sixth century BCE

With the heavens we share gladness, with the earth we share joy, with the sea we roar with life and all that fills creation is alive. The fields exult without restraint and celebrate in symphony. The trees of the forest humbly boast their beauty and we who are of the earth sense the earth within us. For we will find peace in creation's Oneness and what we hold in common will bind us together.

We will live in joy and peace. The mountains and hills, the trees of the field—all will rejoice.

Where once were thorns, fir trees will grow; where briars grew, the myrtle trees will sprout up.

This miracle will make great the name of the Holy One, and be an everlasting sign of the Creator's power and love. —Michael Burch and Isaiah 55:12-13 (TLB)

Creator, we acknowledge our common heritage that makes us all related. You are our Holy Parent and we have come forth from you. We each have a song to sing, each song different, each song beautiful as it is sung to you. May our

songs that we sing acknowledge the sacredness of all life as
we join together in this Sacred Circle.

—Native American prayer

Creator of the intertwined,
  you made each soul unique:
each one with ears to hear faith's call,
  each one with voice to speak.
Each worships where the call is heard
  in forest, temple, dome,
on mountain top, in upper room—
  the soul must find a home.

The song of peace, best sung by all,
  strength born of unity.
In harmony we celebrate
  your gift: diversity.
Can we not sing each other's songs?
  Speak unfamiliar prayer?
Rejoicing in the bounty of
  the diff'rences we share?

Teach us to cherish what is strange
  and so the richer be,
to listen with our hearts and speak
  with loving honesty.
From diff'rent sources comfort comes,
  each seeks for the divine:
Your voice speaks many languages,
  just one of them is mine.

—Jacque B. Jones, *Songs Unchanged, Yet Ever-Changing*,
© 2004 GIA Publications, Inc.
Sing to the tune KINGSFOLD

Suggested Hymns and Songs
(see hymnary.org or other sources as noted)

All the Colors of the Rainbow (Carl P. Daw Jr., *Prayer Rising into Song*, Hope Publishing Company and Hope Hymns Online)

Deep in Our Hearts There Is a Common Vision (John Oldham)

Great God of All, We Sing Your Praise (Mary Nelson Keithahn)

In Star and Crescent, Wheel and Flame (Mary Louise Bringle)

Let All Things Now Living (Katherine Davis)

Make Me a Channel of Your Peace (Francis of Assisi, adapted by Sebastian Temple)

On Eagle's Wings (Michael Joncas)

Our God, Our Help in Ages Past (Isaac Watts)

Out of Joy and Out of Need (Daniel C. Damon, *My Child Is a Flower*, Hope Publishing Company and Hope Hymns Online)

People of Faith (Paul Stott)

Too Often, God, Your Name Is Used (Thomas H. Troeger)

When Hands Reach Out Beyond Divides (Keri K. Wehlander)

Social Justice

Scriptures

I will listen to you, God, because you promise peace to those who are faithful and no longer foolish. You are ready to rescue everyone who worships you, so that you will live with us in all of your glory. Love and loyalty will come together; goodness and peace will unite. Loyalty will sprout from the ground; justice will look down from the sky above. Our God, you will bless us; our land will produce wonderful crops. Justice will march in front, clearing a path for you, Holy One. —Psalm 85:8-13 (CEV, altered)

When you spread out your hands in prayer, I hide my eyes from you; even when you offer many prayers, I am not listening. Your hands are full of blood! Wash and make yourselves clean. Take your evil deeds out of my sight; stop doing wrong. Learn to do right; seek justice. Defend the oppressed. Take up the cause of the fatherless; plead the case of the widow. —Isaiah 1:15-17

I hate, I despise your religious festivals; your assemblies are a stench to me. . . . Away with the noise of your songs! I will not listen to the music of your harps. But let justice roll on like a river, righteousness like a never-failing stream! —Amos 5:21, 23-24 (NIV)

Jesus returned in the power of the Spirit to Galilee, and news about him spread throughout the whole countryside. He taught in their synagogues and was praised by everyone. Jesus went to Nazareth, where he had been raised. On the Sabbath he went to the synagogue as he normally did and stood up to read. The synagogue assistant gave him the scroll from the prophet Isaiah. He unrolled the scroll and found the place where it was written:
The Spirit of the Lord is upon me,
    because the Lord has anointed me.
God has sent me to preach good news to the poor,
    to proclaim release to the prisoners

and recovery of sight to the blind,
   to liberate the oppressed,
   and to proclaim the year of the Lord's favor.
Jesus rolled up the scroll, gave it back to the synagogue
assistant, and sat down. Every eye in the synagogue was
fixed on him. He began to explain to them, "Today, this
scripture has been fulfilled just as you heard it."

—Luke 4:14-21 (CEB)

When we speak about wisdom,
   we are speaking about Christ.
When we speak about virtue,
   we are speaking about Christ.
When we speak about justice,
   we are speaking about Christ.
When we speak about peace,
   we are speaking about Christ.
When we speak about truth and life and redemption,
   we are speaking about Christ.

—Ambrose of Milan (c. 340–397)

Ours is the journey and it is far from over. May we continue to follow where Jesus leads and courageously challenge our culture. May we dare to question those who deny
that God's inclusive love is for all people. May God give
us strength for a radical welcome, to love as Jesus loved.
Amen.   —Sharon Allen

Lord Jesus, you had compassion on the hungry, weak,
and lost. And you shared in our neediness, even becoming homeless yourself for a time. Look with compassion
on the homeless here in our city. Provide them with daily
bread, with healing, and with hope in you. We pray also

for all those who work to help the homeless. We pray for social structures and values that care for the vulnerable and to support families. And we pray for ourselves; for compassion, wisdom, humility, and skill in responding to the homeless, that they and we may see you in each other. For this we pray to God. **Amen.**   —Russell Yee

A small body of determined spirits fired by an unquenchable faith in their mission can alter the course of history.
—Mohandas Gandhi

I pray that the light of Christ finds the grain of reason, love, and hope in this great nation so that we may all go forth and thrive. May we produce a loaf of understanding that can be savored: God's abundance means there is room for all! **Amen.**   —Judge C. Purifoy

Till all the jails are empty and all the bellies filled;
till no one hurts or steals or lies,
   and no more blood is spilled;
till age and race and gender no longer separate;
till pulpit, press, and politics are free of greed and hate:
God has work for us to do.

In tenement and mansion, in factory, farm, and mill,
in boardroom and in billiard hall,
   in wards where time stands still,
in classroom, church, and office, in shops or on the street;
in every place where people thrive or starve or hide or meet:
God has work for us to do.

By sitting at a bedside to hold pale trembling hands,
by speaking for the powerless against unjust demands,

by praying through our doing and singing though we fear,
by trusting that the seed we sow
  will bring God's harvest near:
God has work for us to do.

—Carl P. Daw Jr., *New Psalms and Hymns and Spiritual Songs*,
© 1996 Hope Publishing Company and Hope Hymns Online
Sing to the tune WORK TO DO

Suggested Hymns and Songs
(see hymnary.org or other sources as noted)

As Colors in the Sky (Daniel C. Damon, *My Child Is a Flower*, Hope Publishing Company and Hope Hymns Online)

As a Fire Is Meant for Burning (Ruth Duck)

City of God/Awake from Your Slumber (Dan Schutte)

For Everyone Born, a Place at the Table (Shirley Erena Murray)

God Is Still Speaking (Barbara Hamm)

God of Grace and God of Glory (Harry Emerson Fosdick)

Hear This from a Homeless Stranger (Jacque B. Jones, *Songs Unchanged, Yet Ever-Changing*, GIA Publications, Inc.)

Inspired by Love and Anger (John L. Bell and Graham Maule)

Seek the Welfare of the City (Norman Goreham)

Show Us How to Stand for Justice (Martin Leckebusch)

The Church of Christ Cannot Be Bound (Adam M. L. Tice)

The Cry of the Poor (John B. Foley)

The Heart Will Choose the One It Loves (Barbara Hamm, www.uccfiles.com/pdf/The-Heart-Will-Choose.pdf)

What Does the Lord Require of You (Jim Strathdee)

Who Would Steal a Life (Shirley Erena Murray)

In Times of Crisis or Disaster in the Community, Nation, or World

In order to be fully present and pastoral in the lives of our people, ministers and worship planners/leaders need to be ready to make changes in our plans when there is a disaster or tragedy in our midst. Given the instantaneous nature of news from the media, such calamities are brought to our attention regularly. Including these concerns during prayer time in worship may be sufficient for some situations. But in other cases, we must drop "business as usual" and focus on providing comfort and hope, recognizing that God is there even in the midst of fire, flood, storm, earthquake, and human-caused catastrophe.

Scriptures, Prayers, and Readings

Awake! Why are you sleeping, O God? Rouse yourself! Do not reject us forever!

Why do you hide your face? Why do you forget our affliction and oppression?

For our soul is bowed down to the dust; our belly clings to the ground.

Rise up; come to our help! Redeem us for the sake of your steadfast love!

Let not the downtrodden turn back in shame; let the poor and needy praise your name.

Arise, O God, defend your cause; remember how the foolish scoff at you all the day!

Do not forget the clamor of your foes, the uproar of those who rise against you, which goes up continually!

But we your people, the sheep of your pasture, will give
thanks to you forever; from generation to generation we
will recount your praise.

Let us hear what God will speak, for peace will be spoken
to the people; but let them not turn back to folly.

Surely salvation is near to those who hold the Holy One in
awe, that glory may dwell in our land.

(*All:*) Restore us, O God; let your face shine, that we may
be saved. —From Psalms 44, 74, 79, 80, 85

God, how long will I call for help and you not listen?
I cry out to you, "Violence!" but you don't deliver us.
Why do you show me injustice and look at anguish
so that devastation and violence are before me?
There is strife, and conflict abounds. The law is ineffective.
Justice does not endure
    because the wicked surround the righteous.
Justice becomes warped. —Habakkuk 1:2-4 (CEB)

There is a wound in the heart of the world.
Scarred over, we tread upon that injury in all that we do.
Every blessing and every curse made upon the wounded
heart of the world.
I cannot say how the wound came to be, by what illness or
act of violence.
I cannot say how the healing happens, by what medicine or
act of caring and grace.
Yet, I know this wound. I know its edges. I know its depths.
I know that this same heart pours blessing upon blessing
upon the earth and all the earth's inhabitants.
It is the heart of the world. It is resilient. —Tripp Hudgins

Sometimes events in the world around us call us not only to mourning, but also to questioning, and in the midst of the questioning, to new attitude and action. Let us seek a way forward in this time and place as we lay before God our confession.

God of all peoples, we confess all the times when we divided the world into "us" and "them." We confess the times when we thought that we were somehow, automatically, better than others. We confess the times when we tried to find a reason to distance ourselves from "those people." We confess the times when we snuffed out our lights; kept our salt to ourselves; spoke without thinking of the hurt we might cause; let the hate-filled remark go unchallenged; missed an opportunity to support the struggling; and turned our back on your call to radical love. Forgive us; draw us into one human community; unite us as your beloved children. Amen.

The Good News is this and simply this: God is love. God calls us to love.

God loves the unloved. God loves even the unloving. Let us live in and into this love. —Beth W. Johnston

O Sabbath rest of Galilee! O calm of hills above,
where Jesus knelt to share with thee
the silence of eternity interpreted by love.
Drop thy still dews of quietness till all our strivings cease;
take from our souls the strain and stress,
and let our ordered lives confess the beauty of thy peace.
—John Greenleaf Whittier (1807–1892)

Serene Son of God, whose will subdued the troubled waters and laid to rest the fears of those disturbed, permit the majesty of your might to master the turbulence of our hearts. May your power of calm soothe us. For our doubts may we have faith and for disquietude perfect trust in you, whose control governs all things, world without end. **Amen.**   —J. Alfred Smith Sr.

Litany of Lament

Give ear to my prayer, O God; do not hide yourself from my supplication. Attend to me, and answer me; I am troubled in my complaint. I am distraught by the noise of the enemy, because of the clamor of the wicked. For they bring trouble upon me, and in anger they cherish enmity against me. (*Silence*)   —Psalm 55:1-8

Naming Oppressions and Injustices

In these moments ahead you are invited to call aloud specific oppressions and injustices as they exist in our world today. Where and how is God most needed in our world, in our cities, in our families, in our lives? (*Those gathered may express their concerns.*)

Sung Response: **I need thee, O I need thee; every hour I need thee; O bless me now, my Savior, I come to thee.**

Lament (unison)

My heart is in anguish within me, the terrors of death have fallen upon me. Fear and trembling come upon me, and horror overwhelms me. (*Silence*)

Naming Our Fears

When we are honest with ourselves, with one another, and with God, there is much in life that fills us with fear. In these moments ahead, you are invited to give voice to those fears in the confidence that the God who hears you and listens to you, is also the God who frees you from all fear. From what do you wish you could hide or flee? (*Those gathered may express their concerns.*)

Sung Response: I need thee, O I need thee; every hour I need thee; O bless me now, my Savior, I come to thee.

LAMENT (UNISON)

And I say, "O, that I had wings like a dove! I would fly away and be at rest; truly, I would flee far away; I would lodge in the wilderness; I would hurry to find shelter for myself from the raging wind and tempest."

—Jennifer W. Davidson

Hymns in Times of Crisis

The Hymn Society in the United States and Canada offers an excellent resource, "Hymns in Times of Crisis," noting: "When tragedy strikes, we often find ourselves at a loss for words to express our sorrow, rage, and helplessness. When a community needs to gather, congregational song can be a powerful force to help us express what we cannot articulate ourselves. It can be a healing, unifying force."

This material is available at no cost at www.thehymn society.org/hymnsintimesofcrisis.

Additional Suggested Hymns and Songs
(see hymnary.org or other sources as noted)

As We, Your People, Gather (Howard Maple)
Be Not Afraid (Robert J. Dufford, SJ)
Be Still My Soul (Kathrina von Schlegel)

By Gracious Powers (Fred Pratt Green)
God, Our Help and Constant Refuge (Fred Anderson)
God, Stir Compassion in Our Hearts (Barbara Hamm,
   Hope Publishing Company and Hope Hymns Online)
How Firm a Foundation (Rippon's *Selection of Hymns*)
How Long, O Lord, Will You Forget (Barbara Woollett)
We Walk by Faith and Not by Sight (Henry Alford)
When Aimless Violence Takes Those We Love (Joy F.
   Patterson)

Resources for Part 4

theafricanamericanlectionary.org has excellent resources for many
   occasions in church life and worship.
Gilmore, Rachel. *Church Programs and Celebrations for All Generations.*
   Valley Forge, PA: Judson Press, 2010.
Hardy, Nancy Elizabeth. *Worship in the City—Prayers and Songs for
   Urban Settings.* Toronto: United Church Publishing House, 2015.
Heckman, Bud, ed., with Rori Picker Neiss. *Interactive Faith—The
   Essential Interreligious Community Building Handbook.* Nashville:
   Skylight Paths, 2010.
Kirk-Duggan, Cheryl A. *More African American Special Days.* Nashville:
   Abingdon, 2005.
Linzey, Andrew. *Animal Rites: Liturgies of Animal Care.* Eugene, OR:
   Wipf and Stock, 2015.
Matlins, Stuart M., and Arthur J. Magida, eds. *How to Be a Perfect
   Stranger—The Essential Religious Etiquette Handbook.* Nashville:
   Skylight Paths, 2015.
National Disaster Interfaith Networks: ndin.org
oremus.org/labarum/mainremebrance.htm#Remembrance (Memorial or
   Veterans' Day).
presbyterianmission.org/resource/worship-times-disaster/
Roberts, Stephen B. *Disaster Spiritual Care: Practical Clergy Responses
   to Community, Regional, and National Tragedy.* Nashville: Skylight
   Paths, 2008.
seasonofcreation.com/worship-resources/liturgies/
socialjusticelectionary.com
uua.org/worship
Washington, James Melvin. *Conversations with God: Two Centuries of
   Prayers by African Americans.* New York: Harper Collins, 1994.

PART 5

Life Celebrations and Transitions

Baptism, Child Dedication, Marriage, Memorial

*Practicing rituals requires courage, vision, humor,
and creativity, as well as the belief
that ritual allows us to awaken
to something bigger than ourselves.
By marking the transitions of life
through meaningful ritual, worshipers tap into the
mystery of God's grace across time and space.*

—Brad Berglund, *Reinventing Worship*

WHILE THE SABBATH service provides a basic pattern for worship, significant life transitions for individual members of the church family call for community observances. Birth, adoption, baptism, and marriage bring the congregation together in festive celebration. A funeral or memorial is one of the most important worship services a minister and church can conduct, not only in mourning the loss and celebrating a life, but in providing support and comfort for grieving loved ones.

In addition to the meaning they carry for the individual members involved and for the church family as a whole, these occasions often bring into our midst people who are not regularly part of the congregation. Thus an essential backdrop to the actual words of the ceremonies is a warm welcome. A cordial greeting; providing a sense of ease and understanding, especially for the newcomer who may be hesitant, timid, uncertain, or simply not conversant with local custom; a gathered community acting as one in embracing the stranger with a loving invitation into true participation—such a ministry of hospitality is the essence of authentic evangelism.

As with any of the worship orders and materials offered in this manual, what follows can be used as shown or can be considered as suggestions serving as the springboard for crafting meaningful sacred occasions.

Baptism

Many congregations in the Protestant free church traditions hold a service of baptism within the regular Sunday/Sabbath time of worship. It is good and right that those coming into the faith family should do so in the presence of the whole congregation they are now joining, as well as having relatives and friends there to witness the rite.

Because baptism is an act of dedication, it makes liturgical sense that it come at the time of offering. But pastors and churches need to consider a number of factors, both sacred and practical, when planning a service that will include baptism, especially baptism by immersion. In some circumstances, a congregation may need to schedule a service of baptism at a separate time from regular weekly worship, such as when the congregation lacks its own baptismal facilities and holds the ceremony elsewhere.

Services shown in this section may be freely adapted. Some churches offer baptism of infants as well as believers' baptism. The first service shown below could include sprinkling, rather than immersion. The Dedication of a Child service can be adapted to include sprinkling of water for an infant.

Wherever the baptism occurs, this is a joyous moment for the one who is professing faith and publicly declaring a desire to follow Christ. It is also a renewing moment for those who relive their own commitment to Christ and the church.

The minister enters the water and may read one or more of the following scripture passages, or some other suitable readings:
As a deer longs for flowing streams, so my soul longs for you, O God. My soul thirsts for God, for the living God. When shall I come and behold the face of God? These things I remember, as I pour out my soul: how I went with the throng, and led them in procession to the house of God, with glad shouts and songs of thanksgiving, a multitude keeping festival. —Psalm 42:1-2, 4

I will sing of your steadfast love, O God, forever; with my mouth I will proclaim your faithfulness to all generations. I declare that your steadfast love is established forever; your faithfulness is as firm as the heavens. You said, "I have made a covenant with my chosen one, I have sworn to my servant David: 'I will establish your descendants forever, and build your throne for all generations.'" —Psalm 89:1-4

Then Jesus came from Galilee to John at the Jordan, to be baptized by him. John would have prevented him, saying, "I need to be baptized by you, and do you come to me?" But Jesus answered him, "Let it be so now; for it is proper for us in this way to fulfill all righteousness." Then John consented. And when Jesus had been baptized, just as he came up from the water, suddenly the heavens were opened to him and he saw the Spirit of God descending like a dove and alighting on him. A voice from heaven said, "This is my Son, the Beloved, with whom I am well pleased."

—Matthew 3:13-17

When the people heard Peter's message, they were cut to the heart and said to Peter and to the other apostles, "Brothers, what shall we do?" Peter said to them, "Repent, and be baptized every one of you in the name of Jesus Christ so that your sins may be forgiven; and you will receive the gift of the Holy Spirit." So those who welcomed the message were baptized, and that day about three thousand persons were added. They devoted themselves to the apostles' teaching and fellowship, to the breaking of bread and the prayers.

—Acts 2:37-38, 41-42

As they were going along the road, they came to some water; and the Ethiopian eunuch said, "Look, here is water! What is to prevent me from being baptized?" He commanded the chariot to stop, and both of them, Philip and the eunuch, went down into the water, and Philip baptized him. When they came up out of the water, the Spirit of the Lord snatched Philip away; the eunuch saw him no more, and went on his way rejoicing. But Philip found himself at Azotus, and as he was passing through the region, he

proclaimed the good news to all the towns until he came to
Caesarea. —Acts 8:36-40

On the sabbath day we went outside the gate by the river,
where we supposed there was a place of prayer; and we sat
down and spoke to the women who had gathered there. A
certain woman named Lydia, a worshiper of God, was listening to us; she was from the city of Thyatira and a dealer
in purple cloth. The Lord opened her heart to listen eagerly
to what was said by Paul. When she and her household
were baptized, she urged us, saying, "If you have judged
me to be faithful to the Lord, come and stay at my home."
And she prevailed upon us. —Acts 16:13-15

There is one body and one Spirit, just as you were called
to the one hope of your calling, one Lord, one faith, one
baptism, one God and Creator of all, who is above all and
through all and in all. —Ephesians 4:4-6

Just as the body is one and has many members, and all the
members of the body, though many, are one body, so it is
with Christ. For in the one Spirit we were all baptized into
one body—Jews or Greeks, slaves or free—and we were all
made to drink of one Spirit. —1 Corinthians 12:12-13

In Christ Jesus you are all children of God through faith.
As many of you as were baptized into Christ have clothed
yourselves with Christ. There is no longer Jew or Greek,
there is no longer slave or free, there is no longer male and
female; for all of you are one in Christ Jesus.
—Galatians 3:26-28

Those to be baptized enter the water and the minister says:
Hear these words of Jesus: "All authority in heaven and on earth has been given to me. Go therefore and make disciples of all nations, baptizing them in the name of the Father and of the Son and of the Holy Spirit, and teaching them to obey everything that I have commanded you. And remember, I am with you always, to the end of the age."

—Matthew 28:18-20

The minister, using his or her own words or the following, addresses the congregation and those who are to be baptized:
Baptism is one of the two sacraments (*or* ordinances) given by Christ to his followers. In baptism, through faith, we are made one with Christ. We are buried with Christ and with him raised from the dead to walk in new life. The washing of our bodies with water is the outward and visible sign of the cleansing of our inner being through the grace of our Savior Jesus Christ. We are baptized not only with water but also with the Holy Spirit, and by this same Spirit we are baptized into Christ's Body, the church, and made members of the whole people of God.
In obedience to Christ's command let us baptize these (this one) who have (has) professed faith in him.

The minister, stating the name of each person to be baptized, addresses each one with these words:
(*Name*), do you before God and this congregation affirm through this act of baptism your faith in Christ as your Savior, and do you promise to follow Christ in word and deed throughout your life?
The person to be baptized answers:
    I do.

Those who were baptized as children may desire to receive adult baptism as a sign of their continuing personal relationship with and faith in Jesus Christ. For them, baptism becomes an affirmation of the baptism which was given to them as children and the promises made on their behalf by parents and godparents. The following words may be used:

(Name), do you now confirm the vows taken by your parents on your behalf in infancy? Do you believe in God as your eternal Creator, in Jesus Christ as your Savior, and in the Holy Spirit as your Comforter?

The person to be baptized answers:

I do.

The minister says:

Let us pray: Loving God, may your Spirit fall upon (Name) and remain with *him/her* all the days of *his/her* life. And may the joy of this moment be *his/her*s forever. **Amen.**

The minister then baptizes each candidate according to the custom of the congregation (immersion or sprinkling), saying:

Upon the declaration of your faith and in obedience to Christ's command, on behalf of this congregation I baptize you, (*Full Name*), in the name of God: Creator, Christ, and Holy Spirit. **Amen.**

After all have been baptized, the minister says:

Those who have been baptized are now members of the household of God and we welcome them to this congregation. As we have witnessed them confess their faith and commit themselves to discipleship, let us now renew our own baptismal vows as we pray:

Gracious God, baptize us afresh with your Spirit. May we know once again the newness of life so abundantly shown to these who have been baptized here. Open our hearts to receive them into our midst, that they may know among us the same spirit of love that was in Christ, who loved us and gave himself for us. Amen.

The Lord's Supper may follow later in the service, with the newly baptized receiving Communion for the first time as members of the church.

(Note: Some churches welcome their newly baptized members on the next Communion Sunday following the baptism service, offering them the Right Hand of Fellowship.)

Prayers

Almighty and everlasting God, we give you abundant thanks for our Savior Jesus Christ, who died for our sins, was buried, and was raised. Graciously accept these your servants, that they, coming to you in baptism, may be united with Christ in his church, and receive the gift of the Holy Spirit according to your promise. Grant that by putting on Jesus Christ they may receive of his grace and always walk with him. Keep them strong in faith, steadfast in hope, and abounding in love. Defend them in all trials and temptations, so they may inherit eternal life; through Jesus Christ we pray. **Amen.**

Send your blessing, O God, upon these your servants, who today acknowledge before us their desire to be disciples of Jesus Christ. Strengthen them by your Spirit, so they may lead lives worthy of the confession they have made. Teach them to serve you with loyal and steadfast hearts; to give and not to count the cost; to labor and to ask for no reward, save that of knowing that they do your will; through Jesus Christ we pray. **Amen.**

Grant, O God, that these who have in baptism made public confession of Jesus Christ may in their lives continually show that they are his disciples. Through their witness, may others come to follow him whom to know is life eternal; in Christ's name we pray. **Amen.**

Holy One, may we, in witnessing the coming to you of these baptized, renew our covenant with you and continue to walk in newness of life; through the grace of our Savior Jesus Christ we pray. **Amen.**

Dedication of a Child

The dedication service should be a part of a regular worship service of the church as an act that signifies the offering of the child to God. An appropriate liturgical moment for this would be as the offerings are brought forward. An usher escorts family members (and godparents, if present) and the child to the front of the church. (Note: This service may be adapted for a single parent.)

After the dedication of the offerings the minister says:
We welcome (*Names of parents*), who have brought their child (*Name*) to be dedicated to God, the maker of all things and the giver of life. In doing so we follow the way of Jesus who said, "Let the little children come to me; for it is to such as these that the kingdom of God belongs."

The minister, addressing the parents and godparents, says:
In presenting (*Name*) to God, do you promise that through
the grace given you and in partnership with this congregation you will teach *him/her* the scriptures and the joys
and responsibilities of the Christian faith, seeking to lead
him/her into a living relationship with Jesus Christ?
The parents and godparents reply:
We will.

The minister addresses the congregation, saying:
Do you, the members of this congregation, accept the responsibility, together with this family, to teach this child,
so that *he/she* may be brought to full maturity in Jesus
Christ? If so, please signify your acceptance by standing.
Let us pray: Even as Mary and Joseph brought the child Jesus to your temple, O God, that he might be consecrated
to your service, so this family has brought this little one
to your house, that among your people they might present *him/her* to you. Give to these parents and this family
your special graces of insight and love, that under their
guidance (*Name*) may grow in wisdom and stature and
in favor with you and all people. Grant that we your
people may truly be a household of faith to (*Name*), providing *him/her* with food for the spirit to nourish *him/her*
through the years of growth into maturity. With gratitude to you for this child we dedicate *him/her*, the family,
and ourselves, so that *his/her* life may be a blessing to
you and a service to all people. **Amen.**
*The minister takes the child into his or her arms and gives
a blessing:*
(*Name*), may God bless you and keep you. May God's face
shine upon you and be gracious to you. May God look
upon you with favor and give you peace. **Amen.**

Here the minister may choose to take the child into the midst of the congregation to be introduced to his/her *new church family. After returning to the front of the sanctuary, the minister returns the child to the parents and may present them with a certificate of dedication. The worship service then continues.*

Additional Worship Materials for a Child Dedication

Loving God, we come this day to dedicate this little one (*Name*) to you. We bring to you the parents and family members (*brother, sister, specific names*) who recognize the importance of a spiritual education for this child you have entrusted to them. We come alongside the family as fellow believers, to support and uphold them in this decision. We know, O God, that a child is a precious gift and so we ask that you bless this family as they seek your will for the life of their (*son, daughter*). Grant them the patience and the strength they will need in the days ahead. Above all, grant them the wisdom that can only come from above. As they come to know the sacrifice that love will require, may they understand more fully the sacrifice you made of your own dear Son. We dedicate this child now in the name of Jesus Christ, our Savior. Amen.　　　　　　　—Marilyn Bennett

Litany for a Newborn Child

The gift of life is one the Lord alone gives.
We praise you, O God, for the gift of life.
The gift of life is one we must honor and nurture.
We praise you, O God, asking for the wisdom to fulfill our calling.
The gift of life flows from the love of God.

We praise you, O God, for your love.
The gift of life is a blessing from God.
We praise you for being the head of our lives.
Holy One, we dedicate the life of this newborn child to
you. We offer up our own lives that we might be empowered to fulfill your will for the direction of this child. We
thank you, God, for your presence in the life of this child,
the parents, the family, the church, and the community.
Lord, be with this child and with us. Amen.

—Albirda Rose-Eberhardt

Prayer for the Adoption of a Child

Today, O God, we are thankful for new life that has come
among us as this family has welcomed a new child into
their midst. We ask your blessing on (*name of child*) and
on this family as they all adjust to new relationships and
new experiences.

You created us to be in families that come in all forms and
expressions, families that are places of nurture, love, and
affirmation. Give this family wisdom, love, and faith to
provide a spiritual home for (*name of child*). Guide us,
as a church, that we may all grow together in unity and
love, through Christ. It is in his name we pray. Amen.

—Anne D. Kear, adapted

Child of promise, child of heaven, to our watchcare you
are given;
we return you with thanksgiving to our God for your safe
living.

We release you to God's keeping, in your waking and your
sleeping.

In your coming and your going may you journey in God's knowing.

May your life, a holy treasure, offer love in fullest measure. Neither life nor death shall sever you from God's own hand forever.

—Rodney R. Romney, © 1991 AmaDeus Group
Sing to the tune TRYGGARE KAN INGEN VARA

Additional Scripture Selections for Baptism and Dedication

Psalm 139
Mark 1:1-11
Luke 2:22-40
Acts 19:1-7; 22:16
Romans 6:3-4
Colossians 2:12; 3:1-17
Titus 3:4-7
Hebrews 10:19-25

SUGGESTED HYMNS AND SONGS
For Baptism and Dedication
(see hymnary.org or other sources as noted)

A Mother Lined a Basket (Mary Nelson Keithahn)
An Act of Faith Transcending Time (Jacque B. Jones, *Songs Unchanged, Yet Ever-Changing*, GIA Publications, Inc.)
Baptized in Water (Michael Saward)
Come, Thou Fount of Every Blessing (Robert Robinson)
I Have Decided to Follow Jesus (attributed to S. Sundar Singh)
I Was There to Hear Your Borning Cry (John Ylvisaker)
Sing Praise for Rain That Washes Earth (Herman G. Stuempfle Jr., *Redeeming the Time: A Cycle of Song for the Christian Year*, GIA Publications, Inc.)

Take Me to the Water (African American spiritual)
This Is a Day of New Beginnings (Brian Wren)
Wade in the Water (African American spiritual)
Wonder of Wonders, Here Revealed (Jane Parker Huber)

Wedding

Wedding services often need to be adapted to local needs and situations. The following is a suggested guide for a wedding that is a service of worship. The service may be used alone or, if desired by the couple, included in the regular Sunday worship service at the time of the offering. This service may be reinterpreted for the marriage of same-sex couples (see note below).

Order of Ceremony

Prelude music
Lighting of the candles
Entrance of the family members and participants (with appropriate music)
—Seating of the grandparents (groom's to the right of the center of the aisle facing the front of the sanctuary, bride's to the left)
—Seating of the parents (same sides as above)
Minister, groom, best man, and groom's attendants enter and take their places on the right, then turn and face the rear of the sanctuary
The bridal procession:
—Bride's attendants enter, come down the aisle, and take their places on the left, facing the rear of the sanctuary
—Maid/Matron of honor enters, comes down the aisle and takes her place on the left

—Ring bearer and flower girl enter, come down the aisle, and take their places, the ring bearer beside the best man and the flower girl beside the maid/matron of honor

—Bride enters, accompanied by her parent(s), another relative, or a friend, while the congregation stands and remains standing until the wedding party is seated

Words of welcome by the minister/presider

Invocation

Hymn

Scripture readings

Homily/brief message

Music selection (vocal, instrumental)

Bride, groom, and bridal party take their places in front and center facing the minister

—Declarations of acceptance, presentations, vows, exchange of rings, prayer, and pronouncement of marriage

Unity ceremony (optional; candles, sand, knot, jumping the broom, etc.)

Hymn

Pastoral prayer and blessing

Introduction of the newly married couple

Recessional music (bride and groom, followed by the bridal party and immediate family)

The Marriage Service

Each marriage ceremony is a unique occasion and one of the most important days in a couple's life. Ministers/presiders should work carefully and pastorally with each couple to create a ceremony that is an appropriate time of worship and blessing, as well as an expression of the two lives that are becoming one.

After the procession, the minister says:

Dear friends, (*Name*) and (*Name*) have come this day to offer themselves to God and to each other in the holy bond of marriage. Marriage has been established by God for human welfare and enjoyment, making sacred the bond between two individuals, and offering to each the opportunity to know more fully the love of God through the love which they share with one another. This union of two persons in body, mind, and spirit is a gift from God, and is for their mutual comfort and joy. It is to be entered into reverently and in good faith in accordance with the purposes for which it was instituted by God. It is to this sacred union that (*Name*) and (*Name*) now give themselves to one another, seeking the blessing of God upon their life together.

Let us pray: God of love, who has brought (*Name*) and (*Name*) to this place to offer themselves to one another in holy marriage, we pray that you will grant them every good and perfect blessing. May their love continue to grow in depth and meaning. Help them to share fully their mutual joys and sorrows and continually to carry one another's burdens. Grant that their temptations may be few, and may they always be ready and willing to forgive even as you forgive them. We ask these blessings in the name of Jesus Christ, who has taught us to say when we pray:

Our Father (Creator), who art in heaven . . .

A hymn may be sung, after which the wedding party and congregation are seated. Scripture lessons (see suggested scriptures below) are read and a brief pastoral message is given. After this the minister invites the bride, groom, and bridal party to come and stand at the front. The other attendants may take their assigned places.

The minister says to the groom:
(*Name*), will you have (*Name*) to be your wedded wife/ spouse, to live together in the holy bond of marriage, to love her, comfort her, honor and keep her; and forsaking all others be faithful to her as long as you both shall live? If so, answer, I will.

The groom answers:
I will.

The minister says to the bride:
(*Name*), will you have (*Name*) to be your wedded husband/ spouse, to live together in the holy bond of marriage, to love him, comfort him, honor and keep him; and forsaking all others be faithful to him as long as you both shall live? If so, answer, I will.

The bride answers:
I will.

[*Optional, may be asked of one or both families*]
The minister then says:
Who presents (*Name*) to be married to (*Name*)?

The one(s) making the presentation answer(s) as follows, or use(s) other appropriate words:
I (we) do.

The minister then says to the bride and groom:
Please join your right hands for the giving and receiving of the marriage vows.

(Note: *The couple may choose to exchange vows that they have written and previously shared with the minister.*)

The groom, following the minister, says to the bride:

I, (*Name*), take you, (*Name*), to be my wife. I promise before God and this community to be your loving and faithful spouse, to share with you in plenty and in want, in joy and in sorrow, in sickness and in health, and to join with you so that together we may serve God and others, as long as we both shall live.

While their hands are still joined the bride, following the minister, says to the groom:

I, (*Name*), take you, (*Name*), to be my husband. I promise before God and this community to be your loving and faithful spouse, to share with you in plenty and in want, in joy and in sorrow, in sickness and in health, and to join with you so that together we may serve God and others, as long as we both shall live.

They release their hands. The minister asks for the ring(s) with these words:

What token(s) have you brought to symbolize the faithful fulfillment of your marriage vows?

The best man takes the ring(s) from the ring bearer and gives it/them to the minister, who says:

This ring is (*or* These rings are) the outward and visible symbol of the inward and spiritual bond that unites (*Name*) and (*Name*) in abiding love.

The minister says to the groom:

(*Name*), will you place this ring upon (*Name*)'s finger and say after me:

Name, I give you this ring as a token of the promises made this day between us, and as a pledge of our enduring love. May the God of all love bless you now and forever.

If there is a second ring, the minister gives it to the bride and says:

(*Name*), will you place this ring upon (*Name*)'s finger and say after me:

Name, I give you this ring as a token of the promises made this day between us, and as a pledge of our enduring love. May the God of all love bless you now and forever.

The minister says:

Let us pray: Bless, O God, (*Name*) and (*Name*), that for them this ring (*or* these rings) may be a constant reminder of the promises made this day to one another and to you. **Amen.**

Then the minister says:

Since (*Name*) and (*Name*) have consented to join together in marriage and have witnessed the same before God and this gathering, and have pledged their mutual love to each other and have declared the same by the giving and receiving of a ring (*or* rings) and by joining hands, I declare that they are husband and wife (*or* life partners). The God of all love has joined you one to another. Go now in peace, and may the love which you now know forever make you one.

[*Optional*] *The bride and groom may now engage in a unity ceremony which may include candles, sand, a knot, jumping of the broom, or other expressions of partnership. This may be followed by family blessings. If desired, the bride and groom may kneel for the closing prayer and blessing.*

A hymn may be sung or a musical selection shared.

The minister says:

Let us pray: Gracious God, continue to show your love to (*Name*) and (*Name*), who in the presence of family and friends have given their mutual pledge to live together as marriage partners. Grant them the strength and patience, the affection and understanding, the courage and love to abide in peace according to your will for them. May God bless you and keep you. May God's face shine upon you and be gracious to you. May God look upon you with favor and give you peace. **Amen.**

The minister says:

It is my joy to now present (*Name*) and (*Name*), [husband and wife, life partners, etc.]

The service concludes with the recessional, after which the members of the congregation may greet the bride and groom.

A Note on Adapting the Marriage Ceremony for Same-Sex Couples

Creating a wedding service with an LGBTQ couple involves special attention to use of terms and pronouns. Be sure to ask, "How do each of you want to be referred to in the ceremony? As partners? As brides or grooms? Husbands or wives?"

Although the order of ceremony above refers to bride and groom, these terms can easily be changed. All the printed scriptures and prayers are gender-neutral.

Scriptures

O God, our God, how majestic is your name in all the earth!

When we look at your heavens, the work of your fingers, the moon and the stars you have established, what are human beings that you are mindful of them?

Yet you have made us a little lower than the divine being,
and crowned us with glory and honor.
You have given us charge over the works of your hands;
you have put all things under our feet,
All sheep and oxen, and also the beasts of the field,
the birds of the air, and the fish of the sea.
O God, our God, how majestic is your name in all the
earth! —From Psalm 8

Trust in God, and do good;
dwell in the land and befriend faithfulness.
Delight yourself in the Holy One,
who will give you the desires of your heart.
Commit your way to God with trust and confidence
and your righteousness will be as a light, and your justice
as the noonday. —Psalm 37:3-6 (ESV, adapted)

Arise, my love, my fair one, and come away; for now the
winter is past, the rain is over and gone. The flowers appear
on the earth; the time of singing has come, and the voice
of the turtledove is heard in our land. The fig tree puts
forth its figs, and the vines are in blossom; they give forth
fragrance. Arise, my love, my fair one, and come away . . .
for our vineyards are in blossom.

—Song of Solomon 2:10-13, 15b

Set me as a seal upon your heart, as a seal upon your arm;
for love is strong as death, passion fierce as the grave.
Its flashes are flashes of fire, a raging flame.
Many waters cannot quench love,
neither can floods drown it. —Song of Solomon 8:6-7

If I speak in tongues of human beings and of angels but I don't have love, I'm a clanging gong or a clashing cymbal. If I have the gift of prophecy and I know all the mysteries and everything else, and if I have such complete faith that I can move mountains but I don't have love, I'm nothing. If I give away everything that I have and hand over my own body to feel good about what I've done but I don't have love, I receive no benefit whatsoever.

Love is patient, love is kind, it isn't jealous, it doesn't brag, it isn't arrogant, it isn't rude, it doesn't seek its own advantage, it isn't irritable, it doesn't keep a record of complaints, it isn't happy with injustice, but it is happy with the truth. Love puts up with all things, trusts in all things, hopes for all things, endures all things.

Love never fails. As for prophecies, they will be brought to an end. As for tongues, they will stop. As for knowledge, it will be brought to an end. We know in part and we prophesy in part; but when the perfect comes, what is partial will be brought to an end. When I was a child, I used to speak like a child, reason like a child, think like a child. But now that I have become an adult, I've put an end to childish things. Now we see a reflection in a mirror; then we will see face-to-face. Now I know partially, but then I will know completely in the same way that I have been completely known. Now faith, hope, and love remain—these three things—and the greatest of these is love.

—1 Corinthians 13 (CEB)

Additional Scriptures

Genesis 1:26-31; 2:18-25
Matthew 5:13-16
John 2:1-11; 15:9-16
Romans 8:28-38; 12:1-2, 9-18

Galatians 5:22-23
Ephesians 4:1-3; 5:25-33
1 John 3:18-24; 4:7-21

Additional Prayers

Almighty God, we see a reflection of you in the beauty of the earth, we glimpse you through the joys of human love, we grasp for you through hands that reach out to others. Even now, Beloved, let us bask in the presence of your glory and wonder; let us stand before you in awe. Move among us, we pray, during this time of worship and celebration. Inspire within us your Spirit of goodness. Amen.

—Nancy B. Smith

Holy One, gracious and loving, who has brought together these two lives in order that they may share one future path, guide and keep them in the unity of your Spirit. Help them to find their shared vocation as a couple and to bless their community and the world with the joy and strength that comes from bonds that cannot be broken. May their lives always reflect the radiant love and hope that our celebration today has created. We pray all of this in thanksgiving for your perfect love and matchless blessings. Amen.

Now you will feel no rain,
   for each of you will be shelter for the other.
Now you will feel no cold,
   for each of you will be warmth to the other.
Now there will be no loneliness,
   for each of you will be companion to the other.
Now you are two persons,
   but there is only one life before you.

May beauty surround you both in the journey ahead and
 through all the years.
May happiness be your companion and your days together
 be good and long upon the earth.

—Traditional marriage blessing

Holy Spirit, bless your children,
 who now bind two lives as one.
May your hope and joy be with them
 now and in the days to come.
Make them holy, faithful servants;
 on these partners shine your face.
Fill them both, O Holy Spirit,
 with forgiveness, love, and grace.

Grant that we may be your blessing,
 joining them your name to praise.
May we be both friends and neighbors
 to support them all their days.
May we share their burdens gladly,
 every pain with joy replace.
Fill us all, O Holy Spirit,
 with forgiveness, love, and grace.

Live in us, O Holy Spirit,
 dwell with us where e'er we go.
In our serving one another,
 may your light within us glow.
May we share your love with others,
 resting in your warm embrace.
Fill the world, O Holy Spirit,
 with forgiveness, love, and grace.

—© 1997 Peter W. Rehwaldt
Sing to the tune BEACH SPRING

Unity Candle Lighting

(*Name*) and (*Name*), the lighting of the unity candle represents the joining of your two lives as one. As you light the center candle, may you be reminded of your commitment this day before God and these witnesses to live together and love together all the days of your life. Today, two have become one.

—Lawrence Jay

Blessing of a Civil Marriage

This service may be used alone or, if desired by the couple, included in the regular Sunday worship service at the time of the offering. The following is a suggested order.

Words of Welcome by the minister/presider
Prayer
Scripture reading
Brief homily/message (if part of a stand-alone ceremony)
Reaffirmation of promises
Blessing of the rings and those who wear them
Affirmation of the marriage
Prayer and blessing
Benediction (if part of a stand-alone ceremony)

The Service of Blessing

The minister states the purpose of the service, using the following or other words:
(*Name*) and (*Name*) have joined in marriage according to the laws of the state. They now come to declare their love for one another and to receive the blessing of God and the church upon their marriage.

The minister says:

Let us pray: Loving God, we bring before you (*Name*) and (*Name*) who come seeking your blessing and that of the church as they confirm their marriage vows. Be with them and make of this a holy moment filled with your gracious presence. Amen.

If the service is used alone, scripture readings and a brief message are included here.

The minister then addresses the groom, saying:

(*Name*), you have given yourself to (*Name*) to be united in marriage. Do you reaffirm the promises you have made to love her and keep to her in the holy bond of marriage, to stand by her side in sickness and in health, in plenty and in want, in joy and in sorrow, as long as you both shall live? If so, answer by saying, I do.

The groom shall answer:

I do.

The minister addresses the bride, saying:

(*Name*), you have given yourself to (*Name*) to be united in marriage. Do you reaffirm the promises you have made to love him and keep to him in the holy bond of marriage, to stand by his side in sickness and in health, in plenty and in want, in joy and in sorrow, as long as you both shall live? If so, answer by saying, I do.

The bride shall answer:

I do.

The minister shall place a hand upon the rings(s) and say:

Grant your blessing upon (*Name*) and (*Name*) as they wear this symbol (these symbols) of the covenant made between them, and may this ring (*or* these rings) be for them a constant reminder of the perfect love made known in Jesus Christ, in whose name we pray. **Amen.**

The minister then joins the right hands of the man and woman and says:

You have been joined by God, therefore let no one separate you. (*Name*) and (*Name*), your marriage is honored by God and the church. Give yourself unselfishly to one another; be united in love and live in peace. God be with you always.

Let us pray: Gracious God, continue to show your love to (*Name*) and (*Name*), who in the presence of family and friends (and in the midst of this congregation) have reaffirmed their marriage vows and pledged their mutual assent to live together as partners in marriage. Grant them the strength and patience, the affection and understanding, the courage and love to abide in unity according to your will for them.

May God bless you and keep you. May God's face shine upon you and be gracious to you. May God look upon you with favor and give you peace. Amen.

At the conclusion of the service opportunity may be given for the members of the congregation to give their personal blessings and congratulations to the couple.

Renewal of Marriage Vows / Celebration of a Wedding Anniversary

This is a suggested ceremony for couples wishing to renew the vows made on their wedding day. It is also appropriate for anniversaries or other special occasions in the couple's life, or may be used for a couple who remarries. It is a gender-neutral ceremony.

A welcome to guests may be given by the minister, followed by a scripture reading and/or other readings chosen by the couple (see list of readings on p. 244-247). A hymn or song may be sung. Then the minister asks the couple to come forward.

(*Name*) and (*Name*), (*number, if desired*) years ago you stood together before God and gave your vows to one another. You made promises to love and keep the bonds of marriage, to stand by each other's side in sickness and in health, in plenty and in want, in joy and in sorrow. Many life experiences have taken place since then, many times of challenge, sadness, and celebration. As you look back and reflect on your life together, do you wish to reaffirm the vows you once made?

The couple shall answer:

We do.

Please join your hands and face each other. (*The couple gives these vows each in turn, prompted by the officiant.*) (*Name*), do you reaffirm the promises you made to (*Name*) on the day you became partners for life (*or husband and wife*)? Do you pledge to continue loving and honoring your spouse, standing together with God and as one, today and for all the seasons still to come?

The couple each responds by answering:

I do.

Let us pray: Gracious and loving God, who has ordained that two may become one in holy marriage and join together their lives, we thank you for this couple who has reaffirmed their love and commitment to each other. We know you blessed the years (*Name*) and (*Name*) have already spent together; we ask now that they might enjoy many more days and seasons on this earth and serve as witnesses to your abiding love for all people. Be with us all as their family and friends, that we would continue to uplift and support their relationship, enjoy their company, and celebrate their accomplishments. Give them your guidance, O God, your strength, and your constant presence. We pray in the name of Christ. **Amen.**

SUGGESTED HYMNS AND SONGS
For Marriage or Renewal Ceremonies
(see hymnary.org or other sources as noted)

Come Down, O Love Divine (Bianco da Siena)
I Was There to Hear Your Borning Cry (John Ylvisaker)
Jesus, Partner, Lover, Friend (Daniel C. Damon)
Joyful, Joyful, We Adore You (Henry Van Dyke)
Love Divine, All Loves Excelling (Charles Wesley)
Love Is the Touch of Intangible Joy (Alison M. Robertson)
Now Thank We All Our God (Martin Rinckart)
O, Blest the House, Whate'er Befall (Christoph von Pfiel)
O God in Whom All Life Begins (Carl P. Daw Jr.)
O Perfect Love (Dorothy F. Gurney)
The Gift of Love/Though I May Speak with Bravest Fire
    (Hal H. Hopson)
True Union Is a Gift of God (Daniel Charles Damon, *My Child Is a Flower*, Hope Publishing Company and Hope Hymns Online)

Memorial

The funeral or memorial service, within the context of Christian faith, is most appropriately a time for community worship. We come together to remember and celebrate the life of one who has died and to offer comfort to the bereaved. If possible, the service should be held in the church where the family of the deceased attends or is associated. Even if held in a mortuary chapel or other location, the memorial should remain an act of worship and include congregational participation.

While a funeral (with the body present) is almost always held soon after a death, a memorial may be held weeks or even months later. As a matter of pastoral care, the minister needs to determine what's best for the surviving family members, regarding the time, place, and nature of the service. Careful consideration should be given to creating a time of worship that is personal and honors the memory of the loved one, as well as to giving comfort and reassurance to the family.

It has been said that our greatest responsibility in ministry comes when we prepare for and conduct services that remember and celebrate a life. As presider, when we are fully present and prepared as well as compassionate, we play a crucial role in helping the family to express their grief, and also to begin moving forward.

Music is shared as the people gather. The minister then offers words of welcome to those present and says one or more of the following:
Hear these words from scripture:
God is our refuge and strength, a very present help in trouble.
Blessed are those who mourn, for they will be comforted.
Therefore we will not fear, though the earth should change, though the mountains shake in the heart of the sea; though its waters roar and foam, though the mountains tremble with its tumult.

Blessed are those who mourn, for they will be comforted.
There is a river whose streams make glad the city of God, the holy habitation of the Most High. God is in the midst of the city; it shall not be moved; God will help it when the morning dawns.
Blessed are those who mourn, for they will be comforted.
The Lord of hosts is with us; the God of Jacob is our refuge. —Psalm 46:1-5, 7; Matthew 5:4

How lovely is your dwelling place, O Lord of hosts! My soul longs, indeed it faints for the courts of God; my heart and my body sing to the living God. Even the sparrow finds a nest where she may lay her young, at your altars, O Lord of hosts, my God. Blessed are those who live in your house, ever singing your praise, in whose heart are the highways to Zion. O Holy One, hear my prayer; give ear, O God of Jacob! Behold our shield, O God; look on the face of your anointed. For a day in your courts is better than a thousand elsewhere. I would rather be a doorkeeper in the house of my God than live in the tents of sinners. For God is a sun and shield, bestowing favor and honor. O Lord of the heavens, blessed is everyone who trusts in you.

—Adapted from Psalm 84

Lord, you have been our dwelling place in all generations. Before the mountains were brought forth, or ever you had formed the earth and the world, from everlasting to everlasting you are God. You turn us back to dust, and say, "Turn back, you mortals." For a thousand years in your sight are like yesterday when it is past, or like a watch in the night. You sweep them away; they are like a dream, like grass that is renewed in the morning; in the morning it flourishes and is renewed; in the evening it fades and withers. So teach us to count our days that we may gain a wise heart. —Psalm 90:1-6, 12

Do not fear, for I am with you; do not be afraid, for I am your God. I will strengthen you, I will help you, I will uphold you with my victorious hand. —Isaiah 41:10

Jesus said, "I am the resurrection and the life. Those who believe in me, even though they die, will live, and everyone who lives and believes in me will never die."

—John 11:25-26

A congregational hymn or song may be sung at this time, after which the minister says:
Let us pray: Eternal Spirit, before whom the generations rise and pass away, even in the presence of death our first words to you are in gratitude for your tender mercies. For the memory of this loved one now departed, we praise you. For their courage, their faith, and their love we give you thanks. As we remember (*Name*) and celebrate *his/her* life, give to us a sure knowledge that the victory over death has been won through the resurrection of Jesus Christ. It is in his name we pray. **Amen.**
   or
Eternal God, in whom we live and move and have our being, and who by your mighty power raised Jesus Christ from the dead, give us the light and life of your presence. Help us to put our trust in your wisdom and to open ourselves to the ministry of your love. Open our hearts, that we may truly hear your words of encouragement as they come to us from the scriptures, and that by their comfort

and consolation we may be lifted out of our sorrow to
know that in Christ there is life eternal. **Amen.**

*Psalm 23 may be read or sung. (Other appropriate Psalms
are 16; 39:4-7; 116:12-15, 17-19; 121; 130; 139:1-18.)*
God, you are my shepherd: I shall not want.
You make me lie down in green pastures
    and lead me beside the still waters.
You restore my soul and lead me in right paths.
Even though I walk through the darkest valley,
    I fear no evil, for you are with me;
      your rod and your staff, they comfort me.
You prepare a table before me
    in the presence of my enemies;
      you anoint my head with oil; my cup overflows.
Surely goodness and mercy shall follow me
    all the days of my life,
      and I shall dwell in your house, O God, forever.

—Psalm 23, adapted

The minister then says:
We are gathered to hear God's word of hope as we remem-
    ber with thanksgiving the life of (*Name*).
*It is customary at this point in the service to give a brief
    biographical statement of the deceased.*

*Then selections from the following or other suitable pas-
sages of scripture may be read.*
Jesus said, "Do not let your hearts be troubled. Believe in
God, believe also in me. In God's house there are many
dwelling places. If it were not so, would I have told you that
I go to prepare a place for you? And if I go and prepare a
place for you, I will come again and will take you to myself,

so that where I am there you may be also. Peace I leave with you, my peace I give to you. Do not let your hearts be troubled, and do not let them be afraid." —John 14:1-3, 27

We know that all things work together for good for those who love God. If God is for us, who is against us? Who will separate us from the love of Christ? Will hardship, or distress, or persecution, or famine, or nakedness, or peril, or sword? No, in all these things we are more than conquerors through him who loved us. For I am convinced that neither death, nor life, nor angels, nor rulers, nor things present, nor things to come, nor powers, nor height, nor depth, nor anything else in all creation, will be able to separate us from the love of God in Christ Jesus our Lord.

—From Romans 8:28-39

Christ has been raised from the dead, the first fruits of those who have died. For since death came through a human being, the resurrection from the dead has also come through a human being, for as all die in Adam, so all will be made alive in Christ. But someone will ask, "How are the dead raised? With what kind of a body do they come?" What you sow does not come to life unless it dies. And as for what you sow, you do not sow the body that is to be, but a bare seed, perhaps of wheat or of some other grain. But God gives it a body as God has chosen, and to each kind of seed its own body. So it is with the resurrection of the dead. What is sown is perishable, what is raised is imperishable. It is sown in dishonor, it is raised in glory. It is sown in weakness, it is raised in power. It is sown a physical body, it is raised a spiritual body. When this perishable body puts on imperishability, then the saying that is written will be fulfilled:

"Death has been swallowed up in victory."

"Where, O death, is your victory?

Where, O death, is your sting?"

Thanks be to God, who gives us the victory through our Lord Jesus Christ.   —From 1 Corinthians 15 (KJV, adapted)

Do not lose heart. Though our outer nature is wasting away, our inner nature is being renewed day by day. For this slight momentary affliction is preparing us for an eternal weight of glory beyond all measure, because we look not at what can be seen but at what cannot be seen; for what can be seen is temporary, but what cannot be seen is eternal. For we know that if the earthly tent we live in is destroyed, we have a building from God, a house not made with hands, eternal in the heavens.   —2 Corinthians 4:16–5:1

May grace and peace be yours in abundance. By God's great mercy we have been given a new birth into a living hope through the resurrection of Jesus Christ from the dead, and into an inheritance that is imperishable, undefiled, and unfading, kept in heaven for you, who are being protected by the power of God through faith for a salvation ready to be revealed in the last time. In this you rejoice even if now for a little while you have had to suffer various trials.

—1 Peter 1:2-6

I saw a new heaven and new earth, for the first heaven and the first earth had passed away, and the sea was no more. And I saw the holy city, the new Jerusalem, coming down out of heaven from God, prepared as a bride adorned for her husband. And I heard a voice from heaven saying,

"See, the home of God is among mortals. God will dwell with them; they will be God's peoples. God will wipe every tear from their eyes. Death will be no more; mourning and crying and pain will be no more, for the first things have passed away."   —Revelation 21:1-4

The Doxology or a hymn of affirmation may be sung, followed by a brief homily or message on one of the scripture texts dealing with the victory of Christ over death and the hope which Christ's victory brings to humankind.

An appropriate anthem or solo may be presented.

One or more of the following prayers, or an extemporaneous prayer, may then be offered.

In this time of sorrow it is natural for us to focus on our grief. But we know the God of the living. We experience that God is the inner strength that sees us through our dark times, in the care that others bestow when we are fragile, through the little moments that connect us beyond our expectations, and within the memories of lives well lived. And this God of living brings resurrection and hope to our lives. May all who are in sorrow be blessed. **Amen.**

—Joy Troyer, *Looking for Truth*

God of all grace and glory, who sent Jesus Christ to bring us eternal life, we give you thanks that by his death on the cross Christ destroyed the power of death. By his resurrection he gave assurance that because he lives we too shall live, and that neither death nor life, nor things present nor things to come, shall be able to separate us from your love, which we have seen in Christ Jesus. **Amen.**

Eternal God, let your mercy rest upon us as with grateful affection we remember (*Name*), who has departed this life. We thank you for *his/her* days upon the earth and the joy that *he/she* brought to many. May our remembrance of *him/her* live long among us and be to us a source of guidance and strength. Give to those who miss *him/her* most deeply wells of consolation from which to draw comfort, and enable us to be your ministers of mercy to them in their time of need. We pray in the name of the great Comforter, Jesus Christ. **Amen.**

The congregation joins the minister in the Lord's Prayer, after which the minister says:
Support us, God, all the day long, until the shadows lengthen, and the evening comes, the busy world is hushed, the fever of life is over, and our work is done; then, in your mercy, give us safe lodging, a holy rest and peace at the last, through Jesus Christ. **Amen.**

—Adapted from *The Book of Common Prayer*

or

May God bless you and keep you. May God's face shine upon you and be gracious to you. May God look upon you with favor and give you peace. **Amen.**

or

Go in peace, and may the blessing of God the Creator, Christ the Redeemer, and the Holy Spirit the Comforter be with you, and remain with you now and forever. **Amen.**

The benediction is followed by music, as first the family departs the worship space, and then the rest of the assembly.

Graveside or Committal Service

The service of committal is generally held at the grave site, the place of interment, or when ashes are scattered.

After the family and others have taken their places, the service begins as the minister says one or more of the following scripture sentences:

I know that my Redeemer lives, and will stand upon the earth at the last; then I shall see God.   —Job 19:25-26

Jesus said, "I am the resurrection and the life. Those who believe in me, even though they die, will live, and everyone who lives and believes in me will never die." —John 11:25-26

"Death has been swallowed up in victory. Where, O death, is your victory? Where, O death, is your sting?" Thanks be to God, who gives us the victory through our Lord Jesus Christ.   —1 Corinthians 15:54-55, 57

The home of God is among mortals. God will dwell with them; they will be God's peoples. God will wipe every tear from their eyes. Death will be no more; mourning and crying and pain will be no more, for the first things have passed away.   —Revelation 21:3-4

Then shall be said the words of committal:
Eternal God, whose loving care is over all, we commit the earthly remains of (*Name*) to the *earth/sea/elements*, in the sure knowledge that *his/her* spirit is with you, whom to know is life eternal. **Amen.**

At this time those present may place a flower on the casket, may place a handful of dirt on the gravesite, or the ashes may be scattered or interred in a niche.

Then the minister shall say:
Let us pray: Almighty God, who by the death and resurrection of Jesus Christ revealed your victory over death, grant that we may live in the power of that victory. We honor and bless the life of (*Name*), confident in the hope that we will one day be reunited for eternity. May our whole lives be a witness to Christ who is the resurrection and the life and who lives and reigns with you and the Holy Spirit, world without end. **Amen.**

Let us go forth in the Spirit of Christ, and may God bless you and keep you. May God's face shine upon you and be gracious to you. May God look upon you with favor and give you peace. **Amen.**

Memorial for a Child

After music has been shared as the people gather, the minister may offer words of welcome to those present. The minister then shall say:
Let us pray: Loving God, we come to you this day, our hearts sorrowful over the loss of your child and ours. We turn to you and give ourselves to your loving care. Speak to us words of consolation and comfort. Lift us out of the darkness of our distress into the light and peace of your presence. For as Jesus said, "Blessed are those who mourn, for they will be comforted." In the name of Christ, our loving Savior, we pray. **Amen.**

Psalm 23 may be said or sung, followed by the reading of one or more suitable scripture selections (see also 1 Corinthians 13; Revelation 21:1-6; 22:1-5):

The disciples asked: "In the kingdom of heaven, who is the greatest?" Jesus called over a little child. He put his hand on the top of the child's head. "This is the truth: unless you change and become like little children, you will never enter the kingdom of heaven. In that kingdom, the most humble who are most like this child are the greatest. And whoever welcomes a child in my name, welcomes me."

—Matthew 18:1-5 (*The Voice*)

People brought little children to Jesus in order that he might touch them. He said, "Let the little children come to me, for it is to such as these that the kingdom of God belongs." And he took them up in his arms, laid his hands on them, and blessed them. —Mark 10:13-14, 16

Jesus said, "Do not let your hearts be troubled. Trust in God, trust also in me. In God's house there are many dwelling places. If it were not so, would I have told you that I go to prepare a place for you? And if I go and prepare a place for you, I will come again and will take you to myself, so that where I am, there you may be also. Peace I leave with you; my peace I give to you. I do not give to you as the world gives. Do not let your hearts be troubled, and do not let them be afraid." —John 14:1-3, 27

A brief homily or message may then be given, followed by a hymn or special music.

The minister then prays extemporaneously, or with one of the following prayers:

Let us pray: God of love and mercy, we thank you for (*Name*), who has lived for a brief time among us. We have been blessed by *his/her* presence and *he/she* has brought a blessing to those who have been closest to *him/her*. We thank you for the love which *he/she* has given and received and for the memories that will continue to bless the family of which *he/she* has been a part. Grant that those who have cared for (*Name*) and who have poured out their love upon *him/her* may be comforted in their sorrow. **Amen.**

Gracious God, who in Jesus Christ promised comfort to those who mourn, be present with these who have suffered the loss of their child. Grant that in their sorrow they may be brought closer to you and to each other and that their hearts may be filled with your presence and peace. Loving Christ, you took little children into your arms and said, "to such belong the kingdom of God." We rest in the assurance that this little one is now with you, resting in your everlasting joy. **Amen.**

Then the Lord's Prayer may be said, followed by a hymn and the blessing.

The minister shall say:

Go in peace; and the blessing of God: Creator, Redeemer, and Comforter be upon you and remain with you always. **Amen.**

Graveside or Committal for a Child

At the place of interment the minister may read one or more of the following or other suitable scripture passages (see above):
Jesus said, "Let the little children come to me; for it is to such as these that the kingdom of God belongs."

—Mark 10:14

Jesus said, "Peace I leave with you; my peace I give to you. I do not give to you as the world gives. Do not let your hearts be troubled, and do not let them be afraid."   —John 14:27

Then shall the minister say the words of committal:
Eternal God, whose loving care is over all, we commit the earthly remains of (*Name*) to the *earth/sea/elements*, in the sure knowledge that *his/her* spirit is with you, whom to know is life eternal. **Amen.**

At this time those present may place a flower on the casket, may place a handful of dirt on the gravesite, or the ashes may be scattered or interred in a niche.

The minister then says:
Let us pray: God of love and grace, we entrust to your tender care this child. Be our guide and comfort, giving us a sure sense of your never-failing love. As we remember the life of this little one may we be consoled by the joy *he/she* brought to our lives and receive your unending grace and peace. In the name of Jesus, who took the little ones into his arms and blessed them, hold us now and in the days to come. **Amen.**

May God bless you and keep you. May God's face shine
upon you and be gracious to you. May God look upon you
with favor and give you peace. **Amen.**

Will you hold me in the light with prayer and song?
  Hold me in the light of God.
Will you weep and cry with me?
  Will you ache and sigh with me?
Hold me in the light of God.

We will hold you in the light and walk with you.
  Come into the light of God.
We will share your tears with you;
  we will face your fears with you.
Come into the light of God.
  —Adam M. L. Tice, *Stars Like Grace*, © 2013 GIA Publications, Inc.

SUGGESTED HYMNS AND SONGS
For Funerals or Memorials
(see hymnary.org or other sources as noted)

Be Still My Soul (Kathrina von Schlegel)
For All the Saints (William Walsham How)
Give Thanks for Life (Shirley Erena Murray)
God Weeps with Us Who Weep and Mourn (Thomas H.
  Troeger)
How Great Thou Art (Stuart K. Hine)
I Am Jesus' Little Lamb (Henriette Louise von Hayn)
I Was There to Hear Your Borning Cry (John Ylvisaker)
I'll Fly Away (Albert E. Brumley)
In the Bulb There Is a Flower (Natalie Sleeth)
It Is Well with My Soul (Horatio Gates Spafford)
Like a Flowing Stream (Daniel C. Damon)
My Shepherd Will Supply My Need (Isaac Watts)

Precious Lord, Take My Hand (Thomas A. Dorsey)
Shall We Gather at the River (Robert Lowry)
Shepherd Me, O God (Marty Haugen)
We Shall Walk through the Valley in Peace (A. J. Hatter)
What a Friend We Have in Jesus (Joseph M. Scriven)
Whatever Be the Love (Mary Louise Bringle)

Resources for Part 5

Ayers, Tess, and Paul Brown. *The Essential Guide to Lesbian and Gay Weddings*. New York: The Experiment, 2012.

Cartwright, Colbert S., and O. I. Cricket Harrison. *Chalice Worship*. Atlanta: Chalice Press, 1997.

Church Publishing, Inc. *Liturgical Resources 1: I Will Bless You and You Will Be a Blessing* (revised and expanded 2015). Online resource for marriage ceremonies: churchpublishing.org/products/liturgicalresources1.

Engle, Paul E. *Baker's Wedding Handbook: Resources for Pastors*. Grand Rapids, MI: Baker Books, 1994.

Francesca, Lisa. *The Wedding Officiant's Guide: How to Write and Conduct a Perfect Ceremony*. San Francisco: Chronicle Books, 2014.

Gleason, John J. *The Pastoral Caregiver's Casebook: Ministry in Crisis*. Valley Forge, PA: Judson Press, 2015.

Hiscox, Edward T. *The Star Book for Ministers*. 3rd rev. ed. Valley Forge, PA: Judson Press, 2014.

Kingma, Daphne Rose. *Weddings from the Heart: Contemporary and Traditional Ceremonies for an Unforgettable Wedding*. New York: MJF Books, 1995.

Lehman, Victor D. *The Pastor's Guide to Weddings and Funerals*. Valley Forge, PA: Judson Press, 2001.

Moncada, Luisa. *Poems and Readings for Funerals and Memorials*. London: New Holland Publishers, 2009.

Reid, Dayna. *Funerals and Memorials: Creating the Perfect Service to Remember a Loved One*. CreateSpace Independent Publishing Platform, 2015.

Roberts, Howard H. *Pastoral Care through Worship*. Macon, GA: Smyth and Helwys, 1995.

PART 6

Special Occasions in the Life of the Congregation

God of rainbow, fiery pillar, leading where the eagles soar.
We your people, ours the journey now and evermore.

—Julian B. Rush

I T IS A PRIVILEGE, a responsibility, and a profound joy to nurture and affirm those who receive a call from God to a life of ministry and service. Licensing, ordination, and installation of ministers are times when the congregation celebrates and supports those it will send out to serve, or when a church welcomes a new shepherd into its midst. Likewise, it is important to recognize the gifts of lay members by commissioning those who will serve as deacons, officers, or teachers.

In the life cycle of congregations we are also called to celebrate the dedication of buildings and anniversaries of our church as a Body of Christ. And sometimes we must say farewell. All these occasions are offered here as a guide for blessing the ties that bind our hearts.

Licensing of a Minister

This service is for recognizing those who are preparing for the pastoral ministries. Generally, it will take place in the student's home church as he or she begins professional training, but it may be adapted for use by a church to which the student has been called as a minister, or may also be adapted for the recognition of a lay minister.

The licensing should be set within a full worship service and the act of licensing can be included at the time of the offering. The licensee, escorted by the moderator or another officer of the congregation, comes forward to the front of the sanctuary.

The worship leader presents a prayer of dedication, saying:
We present to you, O God, these gifts in thankfulness for your abundant love. Today we bring before you this one who is offering *himself/herself* for special ministry in your church. We also offer ourselves, that our lives may be faithfully spent in the ministries to which you have called each of us. We give praise and thanks in Jesus' name. **Amen.**

The minister then says:
The church is composed of many members with a variety of gifts. Every member is called to exercise a unique gift in ministry. The church also recognizes those who are called by God into church vocations for which special training is needed. It is customary for a congregation to support such a vocational decision by presenting a License to Minister (*or* License to Preach). (*Name*) now offers *himself/herself*

for the Christian ministry and comes before this congregation to be affirmed in this decision.

The church officer says:
Upon recommendation of the (*official board of the church*) and by vote of the congregation, I present to (*Name*) a License to Minister. This license represents not only our support as you continue your preparation for ministry through theological study, but also our declaration of confidence in you and our assurance that in your vocational preparation you will have our ongoing blessing and prayers.

The church officer then presents the license, after which the minister asks the licensee:
(*Name*), by accepting this License to Minister do you promise to faithfully serve God and the church, both in your studies and in your ministry?
He/she replies:
I do, trusting in God's help.

The minister then says to the congregation:
Do you, the members of this congregation, acknowledge and receive (*Name*) as a fully licensed minister of the gospel and promise to give *him/her* your encouragement and cooperation in the fulfillment of *his/her* calling? If so, please show your support by standing and uniting in the prayer of consecration:
Spirit of the Living God, fall afresh on (*Name*). Consecrate *him/her* for the work of ministry. Grant wisdom to discern the mind of Christ, compassion for human need, and love toward all those to whom *he/she* is called to

minister. Strengthen and nourish (*Name's*) faith, both through the challenges and rewards of study, and through ever more fruitful work in your church. May God's Spirit rest upon *him/her* this day and in all the days to come. Amen.

After the prayer the newly licensed minister may be congratulated by the pastor and other church leaders, perhaps being invited to share in the serving of the Lord's Supper, if included in the worship service.

Ordination of a Minister

In the free churches the service of ordination is an act of the local congregation. Often, however, local churches of the same denomination are invited to share in the celebration as witnesses and guests, along with clergy colleagues from the community who may be asked to participate. The many gifts that God bestows will also bring opportunity for a local church to ordain members to ministries other than that of a pastor, such as a chaplain or spiritual caregiver in a healthcare setting or the military, a missionary (local or international), associate minister, seminary professor, pastoral counselor, spiritual director, and others.

The service is generally held at a time when representatives of other area churches and denominational leaders can attend and participate, as well as the ordaining congregation and ordinand's family and friends. It is set in a full service of worship that may include the Lord's Supper. At the appropriate point in worship, the ordinand offers himself or herself to be set apart for the gospel ministry. The service given below is intended as a guide. Changes or additions may be made by the presiding minister and the ordinand as they plan the worship celebration.

The Service of Ordination

Call to Worship

How beautiful upon the mountains are the feet of the messenger who announces peace, who brings good news, who announces salvation, who says to Zion: "Your God reigns" (Isaiah 52:7).

Gracious God, you have brought us together to proclaim your mighty works and your word as made evident by one who has answered the call to become a minister of the gospel.

We celebrate that your Spirit is moving among us today, resting upon each of us, according to your abundant gifts. Let us worship and praise you, Holy One, through Jesus Christ and the power of the Holy Spirit!

Congregational Hymn(s) of Praise

Welcome and Sharing of Purpose

The presiding minister says:

As followers of Christ we are all called to be ministers of the gospel; but beyond this, some are called by God to focus their professional life and vocation in service to God's people. We are gathered today to acknowledge the call of (*Name*) to the pastoral (*if other than pastoral, substitute the appropriate term, such as* educational, spiritual caregiving, counseling, *etc.*) ministry of the church of Jesus Christ. On behalf of the whole people of God we will affirm and bless *his/her* ministry through prayer and the laying on of hands. We invite all who are gathered here to join in this celebration.

The presiding minister may at this time welcome and acknowledge other leaders/participants in the service.

The presiding minister or another worship leader says:
Let us pray: Worthy are you, O God, to receive glory, honor, and power. We praise you for the church, the Body of Christ and a dwelling place of your Holy Spirit. We praise you that through that same Spirit you call women and men into your service and give them gifts fitting for ministries to and with your people. Especially we thank you today for (*Name*), whom we are lifting up and affirming as a minister of the gospel. Bless us with your holy presence, Eternal One, and grant that this may be for (*Name*) and for us a joyful time of worship. May your grace and love rest upon *him/her* this day and through all the days of ministry ahead. In Christ's name we pray. **Amen.**

A sung response or hymn may be included here by the congregation, ensemble, choir, or soloist. [See list of suggested hymns and songs at the end of this section.]

Ministry of the Word

The scripture lesson(s) are read; musical selections may be interspersed with the readings. Some suitable passages are:
Isaiah 6:1-8
Jeremiah 1:4-10
Matthew 4:18-22; 28:16-20
Romans 10:13-17; 12
1 Corinthians 12
1 Corinthians 13

2 Corinthians 5
Ephesians 4:1-16
2 Timothy 1:11-14

The scripture readings are followed by a sermon appropriate for ordination.

After the sermon, the people may stand and sing a hymn or song of commitment. A general prayer for the ministry of the whole church and/or special prayers for the occasion may be offered.

As an act of offering himself or herself to the service and ministry of the church, the ordinand is escorted to the front of the sanctuary by the moderator (or chief officer) of the church. Note: The presiding minister may first give an invitation for an offering to be gathered; as the gifts are brought forward, the ordinand would also come forward as a doxology or hymn is sung.

At this time, any who are invited to bring a charge to the ordinand may give brief words of affirmation and encouragement.

The Act of Ordination

The moderator presents the ordinand to the congregation, saying:

Upon recommendation of the Ordination Council/Commission of the (*name of region or association*), I have the joy of presenting (*Name*) to this congregation for ordination to the gospel ministry.

The ordinand stands and the presiding minister says to him or her:

Before God and this congregation you are called upon to answer in all truthfulness the questions I now ask you. Do you believe that you are truly called to be an ordained minister in the church of Jesus Christ and, with the help of God, to serve faithfully in the responsibilities of this ministry?

I do, trusting in God's help.

Do you promise to be faithful in prayer and in the reading of the scriptures, and through study to deepen your knowledge of God's word? Will you continue to learn and grow in the many skills required for ministry with the Body of Christ?

I will, trusting in God's help.

Will you seek to bring others into an acceptance of the cost and joy of discipleship, and through faithful teaching lead them into a full understanding of Christian commitment?

I will, trusting in God's help.

Will you have a loving concern for all people, giving yourself to minister to them without regard to any biases?

I will, trusting in God's help.

The presiding minister then says:

People of God, you have heard the commitment made by (*Name*). What is your desire?

We find *him/her* prepared and worthy! In the name of Christ and relying on God's grace, let us ordain *him/her*.

Will you give *him/her* your full support in this ministry?

We will, relying on God's grace.

Then let us acknowledge and affirm this ordination by the laying on of hands in prayer.

The presiding minister invites the ordinand to kneel, and requests that those who are to share in the laying on of hands come forward and place their hands upon his or her head. This may include all who are ordained ministers or the entire congregation. Family members of the ordinand may be invited to come first.

The minister then says:

From the earliest times, the church has recognized God's call to ministry through the laying on of hands in prayer, and by this symbolic act sets apart men and women for service to the Body of Christ.

Let us pray: Eternal God, you have called (*Name*) into your service and to the ministry of your church. Affirm that call through your Holy Spirit, as with prayer and the laying on of hands we ordain this one to the office and work of ministry. Grant *him/her* wisdom to understand and power to proclaim the Good News as a leader of your people in worship. Give (*Name*) the grace to be a pastor (*or* educator, spiritual caregiver, counselor, *etc.*) whose love is like your own, a teacher who imparts light and understanding, and a priest who reveals your presence to every brother or sister in need. Keep *him/her* true to your high calling so that in your good time *he/she* may hear your words, "Well done, good and faithful servant." To this ministry we consecrate (*Name*), and give you all the praise and glory, now and forever. **Amen.**

The newly ordained minister stands and the presiding minister says:

By the authority of this church and its sister churches, and in the name of Jesus Christ, we declare you to be ordained to the office and work of the Christian ministry.

Through this act you have been commissioned to preach and teach the word of God, to lead the worship of the church, and to administer the sacraments (*or* ordinances) of baptism and the Lord's Supper, to perform other services associated with the ministry, to be a faithful leader of your people, to inform the conscience of the congregation concerning the personal and social issues of the day, and to be a witness to those who have not yet come to know for themselves the love of God in Christ.

(*For one being ordained to a ministry other than pastoral, the wording above may be modified, as appropriate.*)

I charge you in the presence of God and this congregation to be faithful in the commitment you have now accepted and to give yourself fully to this ministry and to the people of God.

May God bless you and keep you.

May God's face shine upon you and be gracious to you.

May God look upon you with favor and give you peace. **Amen.**

Those who have come forward return to their seats. The moderator or another church official then presents the newly ordained minister with a certificate of ordination, saying:

May this certificate of ordination be a continual reminder to you that on this day and in this place you were set apart for the holy and joyful work of ministry to the Body of Christ.

A representative of the congregation may give a Bible or other gift, such as stole or robe, to the newly ordained minister.

Ministry of the Table

If the Lord's Supper is to be shared, the presiding minister leads the newly ordained minister to the table and, taking his or her right hand, says:

I welcome you into the ministry of the church of Jesus Christ. On behalf of this congregation I invite you to begin your ministry by leading us in sharing the Lord's Supper.

The service may proceed as found in Part 1, Worship on the Sabbath Day – I, Gathering at Christ's Table.

Following the sharing of bread and cup, the presiding minister or the newly ordained minister says:

May the peace of Christ be with you always.

And also with you.

The congregation and worship leaders greet one another with a handshake or an embrace and repeat the words of peace.

Closing Hymn or Song of Celebration

The newly ordained minister gives the Benediction/Blessing, after which the presiding minister leads a recessional to the church entryway, where the new minister may be greeted by the members and friends of the congregation.

SUGGESTED HYMNS AND SONGS
For Ordination or Installation Services
(see hymnary.org or other sources as noted)

Be Thou My Vision (Ancient Irish poem)
Called as Partners in Christ's Service (Jane Parker Huber)

Come Celebrate the Call of God (Brian Wren)

God, the Spirit, Guide and Guardian (Carl P. Daw Jr.)

Here I Am, Lord/I, the Lord of Sea and Sky (Daniel L. Schutte)

I Have Called You by Your Name (Daniel C. Damon)

I Have Chosen This New Journey (Jacque B. Jones, *Songs Unchanged Yet Ever-Changing*, GIA Publications, Inc.)

In Christ Called to Worship (Ruth Duck, *Circles of Caring*, The Pilgrim Press)

Lord, Whose Love through Humble Service (Albert F. Bayly)

Ours the Journey (Julian B. Rush)

Take My Life and Let It Be (Frances Ridley Havergal)

Will You Come and Follow Me (John L. Bell)

Installation of a Minister

While this service is intended primarily for the installation of a pastor, it can be easily adapted as an installation for another specialized ministry of the church, such as associate pastor, minister of Christian education or music, and others. Usually, an installation service is held at a time other than Sunday morning, in order that the congregation may invite representatives of the denomination, other local clergy, and colleagues of the pastor-elect to attend and give leadership in worship.

The service may be followed by a reception, at which time words of welcome can be given by church and civic representatives and a response may be made by the newly installed minister.

Following a Call to Worship and the singing of a hymn or song, the presiding minister gives words of welcome to those assembled.

The minister then says:
As an act of dedication, in the name of Jesus Christ, the head of the church, we install (*Name*) as pastor of this congregation. We shall first hear the steps that led to the call of (*Name*) to be pastor of this people. Then both pastor-elect and this people shall declare their mutual covenant with one another and with God that they will faithfully work together for the ministries and mission of this church and the whole people of God.

A representative of the congregation then makes a statement concerning the church's selection and call of the pastor-elect.

A representative group of congregational members escorts the pastor-elect to the front, where he or she is met by the presiding minister, who says:
We believe that the call to the pastorate comes both from God and God's people. (*Name*), you are presenting yourself in this place and at this time to be installed as pastor of (*name of church*). Will you affirm now your covenant with God and with this congregation?
The pastor-elect answers:
I will.
Do you affirm your faith in God, the Creator, and in Jesus Christ, the Redeemer, and in the Holy Spirit, the Abiding Presence? Do you believe that in Jesus Christ humankind is called to live fully into the Good News of the gospel, and that the church is called to proclaim it to the world?

I do.

Do you believe that you have been truly called of God to be the pastor of this church?

I do.

Do you promise before God and this congregation to be a faithful teacher and preacher of the word of God as found in the holy scriptures, to lead this congregation in worship that is worthy of the glory of God, to be a nurturing pastor to this people, and to equip them for their own ministries in the world?

I promise to do so, with God's help.

The presiding minister then says to the congregation:

Do you, the members of this congregation, receive (*Name*) as your pastor, and before God and in the presence of one another promise to give *him/her* your loyalty and support? If so, please stand for the prayer of installation.

Prayer is then offered extemporaneously or as follows:

We thank you, Gracious God, for (*Name*), who has answered the call of your people to be their pastor. Filled with your Spirit, may *he/she* be ready to do every good work and give a full measure of devotion while serving in this place. Through *his/her* preaching and teaching of your word, may those who hear be drawn to Christ, be strengthened in their faith, and be equipped for Christ's service in the world. May (*Name*) be so filled with your love that *he/she* will care tenderly for all your people— in their joy and sorrow, their sickness and health, their doubt and faith—standing beside them so that they may come to know the gift of your abundant love. Bestow upon this congregation openness to receive the ministry of (*Name*) for its strengthening, renewal, and mutual service. We pray all this through Jesus Christ. **Amen.**

The presiding minister then says:
In the name of Jesus Christ, I declare you, (*Name*), to be the duly installed pastor of (*full name of church*). May God bring you great joy, and a continuing sense of purpose in the challenges and blessings of this ministry. **Amen.**

The presiding minister, the church officers, and any others appointed to do so extend on behalf of the congregation the Right Hand of Fellowship and welcome the newly installed pastor.
Further greetings, statements, or a preached message may follow.

The presiding minister then escorts the newly installed pastor to the table to lead in the Lord's Supper (if included in the worship service) and bring the service to its conclusion. The newly installed pastor gives a Benediction/Blessing and the Peace.
[The list of suggested hymns and songs shown above for the Service of Ordination may also be used for an installation service.]

Commissioning of Deacons

Since the earliest days of the church, deacons have occupied a special place in the church's ministry. It is therefore fitting that they should be set apart and commissioned in a special service of the church. The commissioning of deacons should take place within regular Sunday worship, usually at the time of the offering.

As the gifts are brought forward the deacons-elect, as an act of self-offering, come and take their places in front of the congregation. After the dedication of the gifts the minister or moderator of the church addresses the congregation, saying:

These who stand before you have been called to be servants of Christ and as deacons to join with the minister in the pastoral work, spiritual development, and administration of the congregation.

The names of those to be commissioned are then read.

The following scripture or some other suitable passage (such as Mark 10:42-45 or 1 Corinthians 12:4-13) may be read:

For as in one body we have many members, and not all the members have the same function, so we, who are many, are one body in Christ, and individually we are members one of another. We have gifts that differ according to the grace given to us: prophecy, in proportion to faith; ministry, in ministering; the teacher, in teaching; the exhorter, in exhortation; the giver, in generosity; the leader, in diligence; the compassionate, in cheerfulness.   —Romans 12:4-8

The minister shall say to the deacons-elect:

You have been called by God through this congregation to the office of deacon. Do you promise, with God as your helper, to faithfully serve God and this congregation? If so, will each of you answer, I do.

I do.

The deacons-elect may then kneel, if appropriate. The minister and those who are already deacons lay their hands on them, and the minister prays extemporaneously or as follows:

To you, O God, we offer these chosen to serve as deacons. By your Holy Spirit give them that grace whereby they may fulfill with devotion the duties and opportunities of their calling. Grant them wisdom to administer with integrity the ministries of the congregation. May they be open to all human need, especially the needs of the hungry and the homeless, the sick and the sorrowing, the fearful and the lonely, and those who find life's burdens too heavy to bear. To this service and in the name of the One who came not to be served but to serve, Jesus Christ, we set them apart as your servants and as leaders of this congregation. **Amen.**

The newly commissioned deacons stand and are given the Right Hand of Fellowship by the minister and their fellow deacons, after which the minister says:

May God bless you and keep you. May God's face shine upon you. May God look upon you with favor and give you peace. **Amen.**

Dedication of Church Officers

The act of dedication usually takes place within Sunday worship and may be included at the time of the offering. Some congregations may prefer to dedicate their officers as part of the church's annual meeting (see Part 4 for worship materials).

As the offerings are presented, the new officers come forward and stand before the congregation.

The minister says:

We are called today to dedicate these who have been chosen for special service in this congregation. As they give themselves to the work of their ministries, so we give them our support and encouragement and pray that they will carry out their tasks with faithfulness and to the glory of God.

The minister presents each of those who are to be dedicated, and names the office in which each is to serve.

The minister may then read one of the following scripture passages:

As God's chosen ones, clothe yourself with compassion, kindness, humility, meekness, and patience. Above all, clothe yourselves with love, which binds everything together in perfect harmony. Let the peace of Christ rule in your hearts, and be thankful. Let the word of Christ dwell in you richly; teach and admonish one another in all wisdom; and with gratitude in your hearts sing psalms, hymns, and spiritual songs to God. And whatever you do, in word or deed, do everything in the name of Jesus Christ, giving thanks to God through him.   —Colossians 3:12, 14-17

Like good stewards of the manifold grace of God, serve one another with whatever gift each of you has received. Whoever speaks must do so as one speaking the very words of God; whoever serves must do so with the strength that God supplies, so that God may be glorified in all things through Jesus Christ. To the Holy One belong the glory and the power forever and ever.   —1 Peter 4:10-11

The minister addresses those being dedicated with these words:

You have been called to special service in this congregation. Are you willing to undertake this ministry for the glory of God? If so, will each of you answer, I am.

I am.

Do you promise to give yourselves faithfully to this ministry and to serve with integrity? If so, answer: With God's help, I do.

With God's help, I do.

The minister addresses the congregation, saying:

You have heard the promises of these who have been called to special service in this congregation. Let us stand and affirm our commitment to support them in their ministry:

We are thankful that you have responded to our call and the call of God to serve in the life and work of this congregation. We promise to honor and support you in your ministry so that this church may be ever faithful to its calling in Christ.

The congregation remains standing and the minister says:

Let us pray: Eternal God, we thank you that from among us you have chosen these persons to serve you in the ministry of this congregation. Send your Holy Spirit upon them, that they may be faithful in their service. By that same Spirit give us grace to support them in their tasks, that the ministry and mission of the church may go forward for your glory. Through Christ we pray. **Amen.**

The minister may then, on behalf of the congregation, extend a welcome to the newly dedicated officers. A hymn may be sung as they take their place among the worshipers.

Dedication of Church School Teachers and Officers

This service may be held during Sunday worship. As the offerings are presented, the newly appointed church school teachers and officers come to the front of the church and stand before the congregation.

The minister says:
Hear these words of scripture:
God gives wisdom, and from God's mouth come knowledge and understanding; God stores up sound wisdom for the upright and is a shield to those who walk blamelessly. Trust in God with your whole heart, and do not rely on your own insight. In all your ways acknowledge God, and your paths will be made straight.

—Proverbs 2:6-7; 3:5-6

The minister, after presenting each of the appointed teachers and officers, addresses them, saying:
You have answered the call of God and of this congregation to become teachers and officers in our church (*or* Sunday) school. Do you promise to give yourself fully to this calling? If so, answer, I do.
I do.
Let us pray: For the call that has come to these who will serve as teachers and officers in our church (*or* Sunday) school, we give you thanks, O God. May their minds be open to your teachings, and with understanding hearts may they be sensitive to the needs of those whom they are called to instruct and lead. Grant that they may listen

with care to the questions they are asked and always to answer with patience and love. May their words and their lives commend Christ to those whom they serve. Enable them to work as effective partners with their fellow teachers and officers, and do all things to your honor and glory. **Amen.**

A hymn may be sung as the newly dedicated officers and teachers take their places in the congregation.

Reception of Church Members

The reception of new members into the congregation takes place in the main weekly worship service of the church. This is often done on the first Sunday of the month or when the Lord's Supper is to be shared.

As the offerings are brought to the table the new members come forward. After the dedication of the offerings, the minister, addressing the congregation, says:
We welcome in the name of Jesus Christ these who have come to join in the life and ministry of this congregation. As you receive them, do you promise before God and in their presence to give them your love and encouragement as they grow in their Christian life and commitment?
The congregation answers:
We do.

The minister may read one or more of the following scripture passages and offer words concerning the meaning and responsibilities of church membership.
As in one body we have many members, and not all the members have the same function, so we, who are many, are

one body in Christ and individually we are members of one another. We have gifts that differ according to the grace given to us. —Romans 12:4-6

Lead a life worthy of the calling to which you have been called, with all humility and gentleness, with patience, bearing with one another in love, making every effort to maintain the unity of the Spirit in the bond of peace. There is one Body and one Spirit, just as you were called to the one hope of your calling, one Lord, one faith, one baptism, one God and Creator of all, who is above all and through all and in all. Speaking the truth in love, we must grow up in every way into him who is the head, into Christ, from whom the whole body, joined and knit together by every ligament with which it is equipped, as each part is working properly, promotes the body's growth in building itself up in love. —Ephesians 4:1-6, 15-16

The minister then addresses each new member by name:
(*Name*), do you promise to be a faithful follower of Jesus
    Christ and to serve him gladly in this congregation?
Each person addressed answers:
I do.

Then the minister prays extemporaneously, or as follows:
We thank you, O God, for these who have come to join our
    family of faith. May they find among us a deep love and
    concern for them and for their well-being. Enable each
    to find their place of service among us. Grant that they
    may grow up in every way into him who is the head of
    the church, Jesus Christ. **Amen.**

The minister takes in turn the hand of each new member and says:

In the name of Jesus Christ and on behalf of this congregation, I welcome you into the membership of this church and extend to you its hand of fellowship.

A certificate of church membership may be presented to each new member. A representative of the congregation says:

This certificate indicates that you are a member of this church in good standing with all the rights, privileges, and responsibilities that such membership grants.

After each new member has been welcomed and presented with a certificate, the minister says:

You are now citizens with the saints and also members of the household of God, built upon the foundation of the apostles and prophets, with Christ Jesus himself as the cornerstone. In him the whole structure is joined together and grows into a temple in the Lord, in whom you also are built together spiritually into a dwelling place for God.   —Ephesians 2:19-22

The service then continues.

Dedication of a Church Building

The service of dedication may be held at a time separate from Sunday morning, or it can be included in the regular time of worship. Shown below are two parts of the ceremony: the opening of the doors, and the act of dedication itself (which may be included early in worship or may be done at the time of the offering). This service may be adapted for a remodeled building or for another structure, such as a family life center.

Opening of the Doors

The congregation may form a procession marching from the former church building, if nearby, or assemble before the closed doors of the new building. The minister, standing before the doors, shall say:

Lift up your heads, O gates! and be lifted up, O ancient doors! that the Holy One of Glory may come in. Who is this One? It is the Eternal and Sovereign God.

—Psalm 24:9-10

The keys are presented to a representative of the congregation, who shall throw open the doors and say:

In honor of God, whom we love and serve, I open the doors of this church (*or name of building*) for the use of this congregation and as a place of (*worship, prayer, learning, etc.*) for all people.

Then the minister shall pray extemporaneously or as follows:

Eternal God, as we open the doors to this house of (*worship, education, etc.*), we open our hearts to you. Go with us as we cross this threshold, that this place may always be filled with your presence. May these doors be open to everyone who is part of our community. May they be wide enough to welcome all who need your comfort and care. And may these doors also be the way through which your people go out into the world to serve and minister in your name. Through Christ we pray. **Amen.**

Processional music may be played as the people enter the church building, or a simple hymn or song may be chanted by the congregation as they enter and are seated.

Act of Dedication

Call to Worship

How lovely is your dwelling place, O Lord of hosts!
My soul longs, yes, faints for your courts;
Blessed are those who dwell in your house, ever singing your praise!
For a day in your courts is better than a thousand elsewhere.
For God is a sun and shield, bestowing favor and honor.
No good thing does our God withhold from those who walk uprightly.
O Lord of hosts, blessed are those who trust in you!

—From Psalm 84

After a hymn of praise is sung, the minister says:
Let us pray: With great joy we come before you, O God. We praise you for your marvelous works, but especially we praise you for this new place of (*worship, education, etc.*), brought into being by the vision and work of your people. We dedicate this building to your glory and to the service of all people. **Amen.**

The scripture lessons are read. Suitable passages include:
  1 Kings 8:12-21
  Ezra 3:10-13
  Psalm 24; 84; 121
  Ephesians 2:19-22

1 Peter 2:4-7
Revelation 21:15-26

After the readings a sermon is preached, followed by the time of offering. As a fitting part of the offerings the congregation presents its new building as a gift of thanksgiving dedicated to God's glory and service.

The act of dedication may be symbolized by the laying of the blueprints or some other suitable symbol upon the altar/table, after which the minister says:

As a congregation we are gathered here to dedicate this church (*or* building) to God's glory. Let us now stand together and join in the act of dedication.

To the glory of God, the Creator, Maker of heaven and earth;

To the glory of Christ, the Savior of the world;

To the glory of the Holy Spirit, the divine presence in the world;

We dedicate this church.

For the worship of God;

For the reading and proclamation of God's word;

For the celebration of the sacraments (*or* ordinances) of the gospel;

We dedicate this church.

For the celebration of marriage and the strengthening of family life;

For the dedication, teaching, and guidance of children;

For the strengthening of all believers and their training as Christ's ministers in the world;

For services of memorial and bringing comfort to those who mourn;

For the work of evangelism in this community and through-
out the world:
We dedicate this church.
To the memory of all whose life and love have in times past
been given to the mission and work of this congregation.
We dedicate this church.
(*The above litany may be adapted to reflect the type of
building being dedicated.*)

The minister says:
Let us pray: Eternal God, be present with us as we dedicate
this church (*or* building) to your honor and glory. Grant
that what we offer in this place may be worthy of your
great love and that the words of our mouths and the
meditations of our hearts will be acceptable to you, our
strength and our redeemer. Grant that all who come to
this place, whether it be in joy or sorrow, life or death,
victory or defeat, doubt or faith, may find here your
grace and your love; a sign of hope. To this ministry we
dedicate your house and we dedicate ourselves. **Amen.**

The congregation shall stand and say:
**We now declare this house to be consecrated to the wor-
ship and service of God, to whom be honor, glory, and
majesty, today and forever. Amen.**

*The Lord's Supper may be shared, after which a hymn of
celebration may be sung. The minister then says:*
Go forth from this place into the world, there to minister in
the name of Jesus Christ. Return to this place to receive
food for life and to give glory to God.

The grace of Jesus Christ, the love of God, and the abiding presence of the Holy Spirit go with you this day and all days. **Amen.**

Church Anniversary

Some congregations observe their anniversary annually; others only in landmark years (25, 100, 150, etc.). No matter when an anniversary is observed, it is a joyous occasion for celebrating the life, history, and future of the church.

Scriptures

O God, we love the house in which you dwell, and the place where your glory abides. Our feet stand on level ground; in the great congregation we will bless the name of God.

—Psalm 26:8, 12

We ponder your steadfast love, O God, in the midst of your temple. Your name, O God, like your praise, reaches to the ends of the earth. Walk around Zion, go all around it, count its towers, consider well its ramparts; go through its citadels, that you may tell the next generation that this is God, our God forever and ever.   —Psalm 48:9-10, 12-14

Jesus said: "Where two or three are gathered in my name, I am there among them."   —Matthew 18:20

No one can lay any foundation other than the one that has been laid; that foundation is Jesus Christ. Do you not know that you are God's temple and that God's Spirit dwells in you?   —1 Corinthians 3:11, 16

Come to Jesus Christ, a living stone, though rejected by mortals yet chosen and precious in God's sight, and like living stones, let yourselves be built into a spiritual house, to be a holy priesthood, to offer spiritual sacrifices acceptable to God through Jesus Christ.   —1 Peter 2:4-5

O God, you are our God; we seek you.
  We have looked upon you in the sanctuary,
  beholding your power and glory.
Because your steadfast love is better than life,
  our lips will praise you.
We will bless you as long as we live;
  we will lift up our hands and call on your name.
Our souls are satisfied as with a rich feast,
  and our mouths praise you with joyful lips.
                          —Psalm 63:1, 3-5

Additional Scriptures

Psalm 100; 111; 118:19-29; 122; 133
Jeremiah 31:31-34
Matthew 7:24-27
John 15:1-17
Acts 2:1-21
1 Corinthians 12
Ephesians 2:19-22; 4:1-16
Philippians 1:3-6
Colossians 3:1-17

Prayers

Almighty God, who set in Christ the one foundation of every church, renew our human temple, that through us it continues to serve you. Be with us in our tasks of decision making and program planning, that we will reflect the light of your Spirit. Have mercy on us as we go boldly into the world preaching and teaching your word and bringing the love of Jesus to all. This we ask in the name of Christ, our Cornerstone. **Amen.**

To you, O God, who has built your church upon the one sure foundation, Jesus Christ, we lift up our hearts this day in gratitude. We thank you for the word preached in this church, and for the symbols of our membership in the Body of Christ. We thank you for the good fellowship of your people; and for the eternal blessing of grace which you have given us through Jesus. We thank you for this church building, this whole congregation, and each of its members and friends. We bless your holy name for those who have established this community and built this house of prayer. To you, O God, be praise and glory in the church throughout all ages; through Jesus Christ. **Amen.**

O God, make the door of this house wide enough to receive
   all who need human love and fellowship; narrow enough
   to shut out all envy, pride, and strife.
For you, O God, are the foundation of our days.
Make its threshold smooth enough to prove no stumbling-
   block to those seeking shelter, but rugged and strong
   enough to turn back temptation.
For you, O God, are the foundation of our days.
God, make the door of this house the gateway
   to your eternal kingdom.
For you, O God, are the foundation of our days. Amen.

—On St. Stephen's Walbrook, London, adapted

Come, you thankful people,
   gather here within these sheltered walls.
Harnessed by the Spirit's tether,
   here the voice of Christ now calls:
"Come, you wounded and you weary,
   Come and I will give you rest."
Then refreshed, take up your journey
   in the fellowship of the blest.

Here release all ancient angers,
   here let hate and bias go,
here give welcome to the strangers;
   we are one in life's great flow.
We are all God's sons and daughters,
   sanctified by love divine,
passing through baptismal waters
   to become the Spirit's sign.

Come, Almighty God, deliver
   every soul from pain's distress.
Let your justice like a river,
   flow to all the world's oppressed.
Free the prisoners, lift the lowly
   by your never-ending grace.
Help us see all things as holy,
   all united in love's embrace.

—Rodney R. Romney © 1990 AmaDeus Group
Sing to the tune AUSTRIAN HYMN

SUGGESTED HYMNS AND SONGS
For Church Dedications or Church Anniversaries
(see hymnary.org or other sources as noted)

All Are Welcome (Marty Haugen)
Built on a Rock, the Church Doth Stand (Nicholas F. S. Grundtvig)
Called to Gather as God's People (Carl P. Daw Jr.)
Come Celebrate the Journey (John Dalles)
Come, Great God of All the Ages (Mary Jackson Cathey)
God Among Us, Sense of Life (Fred Kaan, *The Only Earth We Know*, Hope Publishing Company and Hope Hymns Online)
Great Is Thy Faithfulness (Thomas O. Chisholm)
In Harmony We Join to Sing (Jacque B. Jones, *Songs Unchanged Yet Ever-Changing*, GIA Publications, Inc.)
Living Stones (Mary Louise Bringle)
O God, in Whom All Life Begins (Carl P. Daw)
Our Church Is Like a Tree of Faith (Mary Bitner)
You Are Called to Tell the Story (Ruth Duck)

Farewell to a Place of Ministry

In current times, churches may be decommissioning sanctuaries or buildings for the congregation's use, or may be turning them over for another purpose in the community. A service of farewell is a recognition of that sacred place in the church's history and ministry.

Litany of Farewell

Praise God, from whom all blessings flow! We have come to the moment when it is time to close one chapter and begin another.

May we now depart in peace, according to God's word.

We leave with hearts full of gratitude for the spaces we have called holy, and for all that has happened here, shaping us and growing us into the people and the church we are today.

May we now depart in peace, giving praise to God's Spirit.

As we close the doors to this worship home, we recall and cherish the shelter we found within these walls, the proclamation of the scriptures, fellowship through prayer and singing, life beginnings and life endings, and joyful partnerships with one another and with Christ.

May we now depart in peace, giving thanks to Christ Jesus.

May others find this a place for becoming the people God created them to be.

May all who gather here know God's promise of hope.

And now, for our own church family, as we go from this place to new adventures and new mission, let us bless the journey:

May the love of God, which is broader than the measure of our minds,

The grace of Jesus the Christ, which is sufficient for all our needs,

(*All:*) And our communion with the Holy Spirit, which will lead us forward in faith, go with us this day and all our days. Amen. —N. H.

Farewell to a Church Member or Family

Life is much more mobile now than in the past, with individuals and families coming and going from membership more often. It is a true blessing to recognize someone for their time spent in the congregation and send them on their way with gratitude and prayer.

Responsive Farewell

Gracious God, we lift up your servants and our friends, (*Names*), as they complete their seasons of life and ministry here at this church. We thank you for their years of faithful friendship and service. We thank you for their desire to be fruitful for you and to be fully given to you. We lift up these further thanksgivings and blessings:

(*The congregation offers their spoken prayers.*)

Holy One, we remember that when Abram and Sarai went out from Haran,

You were with them.

When the Israelites left Egypt,

You were with them.

When Naomi and Ruth left Moab,

You were with them.

When the twelve disciples left their families and homes,

You were with them.

When Barnabas and Saul were sent out by the church in Antioch,

You were with them.

And when the time came for Jesus to leave this earth and prepare a place for us, he said,

"I am with you always, even to the end of the age."

And now we ask your care and blessing on these our friends. O God, lead them into new settings where they will thrive and bear good fruit that will last. As we miss each other's presence, renew our hope of eternity together. Then open our hearts to welcome the many others you want us to receive in fellowship here. We pray in the name of Jesus. **Amen.**   —Russell Yee

Blest be the tie that binds our hearts in Christian love;
The fellowship of kindred minds is like to that above.
When we are called to part, it gives us inward pain;
But we shall still be joined in heart, and hope to meet
again.   —John Fawcett (1739–1817)

God be with you till we meet again,
By his counsels guide, uphold you,
With his sheep securely fold you,
God be with you till we meet again.
                              —Jeremiah E. Rankin (1828–1903)

PART 7

Other Times for Services and Blessings in Ministry

For this service you perform
not only meets the needs of God's people,
but also produces an outpouring of gratitude to God.

—2 Corinthians 9:12 (GNT)

THE CHURCH'S WORSHIP extends beyond the Sabbath services. Through the pastor, deacons, and lay members, the church reaches out to homes, hospitals, and other places where members of the congregation share their joys and concerns. Whether it be the addition of a new family member, a critical or chronic illness, or the dedication of a new home, the church should stand beside its members and enter into their joy or pain.

As with previous parts of this manual, the materials in this section are intended to provide a suggested pattern or order for the occasions shown. Ministers and lay leaders alike are encouraged to create services and blessings that fit the unique circumstances of each situation.

Blessing or Dedication of a Home

This service can be a part of a housewarming party in which members of the congregation and others gather with the family to celebrate their new home. As part of the blessing, the threshold may be anointed. Or, each room of the house may receive prayer or a blessing by a light sprinkling of water (using a bowl of water and one's fingertips or a small branch).

As the dedication begins, the minister or a lay leader says:
We are gathered here to share with this family (*or* with this friend, *in the case of a single person*) the joy of a new home, and to dedicate this home to God. May it become a place where God's love is made known.

The Hebrew Scriptures declare, in Deuteronomy 6: "Hear, O Israel: The Lord is our God, the Lord alone. You shall love God with all your heart, and with all your soul, and with all your might. Keep these words that I am commanding you today in your heart. Recite them to your children and talk about them when you are at home and when you are away, when you lie down and when you rise."

And in Psalm 133 we hear: "How very good and pleasant it is when kindred live together in unity."

In the Gospel of Matthew, chapter 7, Jesus told this parable: "Everyone then who hears these words of mine and acts on them will be like a wise person who built a house on rock. The rain fell, the floods came, and the winds blew and beat on that house, but it did not fall, because it had been founded on rock. And everyone who hears these words of mine and does not act on them will be like the foolish person who built a house on sand. The rain fell, and the floods came, and the winds blew and beat against that house, and it fell."

The leader says:

Peace be to this house, and to those who live within these walls.

A hymn or song may be sung by those assembled, or by a soloist.

The leader or a member of the household may then read one or more of the following passages of scripture, or selections chosen by the household.

1 Chronicles 17:23-27
Isaiah 32:16-18
Philippians 4:4-8
Colossians 3:12-21

The scripture reading may be followed by a few brief words of reflection from the minister or another person, after which a leader says:

Let us ask God's blessing upon this home: O God, may your blessing come to this house and household. Grant that Jesus Christ may ever be present among those who dwell within its walls. Make this home a place with an open door and a warm hearth, always giving welcome to all who need hospitality and the loving embrace of a friend. Give to *each/this* member of the *family/household* a sense of being linked to every other member of our congregation and to you, O God, that this home may be a sign of the unity you have given to all persons in Jesus Christ, who taught us to pray:

Our Father (Creator God), who art in heaven . . .

The leader may give a closing blessing:
May God bless you and keep you. May God's face shine upon you and be gracious to you. May God look upon you with love and give you peace. **Amen.**

Suggested Hymns and Songs
(see hymnary.org or other sources as noted)

All Are Welcome, stanzas 1, 2, and 5 (Marty Haugen)
Come and Find the Quiet Center (Shirley Erena Murray)
Come Away from Rush and Hurry (Marva J. Dawn)
Happy the Home When God Is There (Henry Ware)
Jesus Come, for We Invite You (Christopher Idle)
Lord of All Leisure Time (Bryan Jeffrey Leech)
My Hope Is Built on Nothing Less (Edward Mote)
O, Blest the House, Whate'er Befall (Christoph von Pfiel)
O Give Us Homes Built Firm upon the Savior (Barbara B. Hart)
When Love Is Found and Hope Comes Home (Brian A. Wren)
Would You Bless Our Homes and Families (Walter H. Farquharson)

Blessing or Thanksgiving for the Birth of a Child

This service is intended primarily for the immediate family of the child but may be used with others present as well. It can be carried out in the hospital or in the home. With adaptation, this service could also be used for a newly placed foster or adopted child, or any child who is coming to join the family.

The minister or lay leader says the following:

As we offer thanks to God for the birth of (*Name*) and welcome *him/her* into this family, let us hear these words of scripture, from Psalm 127: "Children are a blessing and a gift from God."

And from the Gospel of Mark: "People were bringing little children to him in order that he might touch them; and the disciples spoke sternly to them. But when Jesus saw this, he was indignant and said to them, 'Let the little children come to me; do not stop them; for it is to such as these that the kingdom of God belongs. Truly I tell you, whoever does not receive the kingdom of God as a little child will never enter it.' And he took them up in his arms, laid his hands on them, and blessed them."

(*Other scripture passages may be read, such as Psalm 103:17-18, Psalm 139, or Luke 9:46-48, or as chosen by the family.*)

An extemporaneous prayer may then be offered, or this simple litany as follows, with those gathered responding, "We thank you, O God."

Let us pray: For the world which you have created and sustained, for its vastness and wonders:

We thank you, O God.

For this little child, (*Name*), your new creation:

We thank you, O God.

For the safety of *his/her* birth and the promise of a healthy and vital life:

We thank you, O God.

For the skill of doctors and nurses and caregivers:

We thank you, O God.

Grant your blessing upon (*Name*) and upon this family, that *his/her* coming may deepen the bonds of love that brought this child into the world. May that love sustain and nurture (*Name*) and bring *him/her* into the fullness of maturity. These blessings we ask in the name of Jesus, who said, "Let the children come to me," and who taught us to say when we pray:

Our Father (Creator God), who art in heaven . . .

A closing blessing may be given:
May God bless you and keep you. May God's face shine upon you and be gracious to you. May God look upon you with love and give you peace. **Amen.**

Suggested Hymns and Songs
(see hymnary.org or other sources as noted)

Children of the Heavenly Father (Carolina Sandell)
He's Got the Whole World in His Hands (African American spiritual)
Jesus Loves Me, This I Know (Ann B. Warner)
Little Children, Welcome! (Fred Pratt Green)
Savior, Like a Shepherd Lead Us (Dorothy A. Thrupp)
These Treasured Children (Jacque B. Jones)

Prayer Service for Healing

Many congregations regularly include prayers for healing in their worship. A practice less familiar in some church traditions is holding an ancient ritual for a particular person in need of healing. This may take place in a home or hospital as well as in a church, with the person surrounded by the congregation. Although the word *minister* is used below, a layperson can also lead a service for healing.

If a prayer service for healing is not a common part of your church life, it is important to give those in attendance some background on what is intended. The healing of body, mind, or spirit is an act of God who is both Creator and Redeemer. As sacred communities we are called to offer comfort and hope to those in need, asking in the spirit of Christ, who prayed, "Not my will but yours be done." These are prayers *for* healing, not a healing in and of itself.

As part of scheduled worship, the service for healing can come at the time of congregational prayer (prayers of the people, pastoral prayer, altar prayer), or it can be a special service held at any time or place, for an adult or for a child.

The service begins as the minister reads from these or other suitable scripture passages:

Psalms
Psalm 23; 91; 103; 145

Healing stories
Matthew 4:23-25; 8:1-17, 28-34; 9:2-8, 18-34
Mark 3:1-6; 8:22-26; 10:46-52
Luke 4:31-37; 7:11-17; 17:11-19
John 4:46-54; 5:2-15; 9:1-12
Acts 3:1-10

On prayer
Romans 12:9-12
Ephesians 6:13-18
Philippians 4:4-9
1 Thessalonians 1:2-5
1 Timothy 2:1-6
James 5:13-16
1 John 5:13-15

The minister may then offer a few brief words concerning health and healing. If the service is included in a scheduled time of worship, the minister invites any who desire prayers for healing to come forward and kneel or stand with the minister, and to indicate the need for which they desire prayer.

The minister then offers an extemporaneous prayer for that person's special need, or as follows:

We praise you, merciful God, for the loving care that you have given to (*Name*). We now come before you with *his/her* special need. If it be your will, may *he/she* be restored to fullness of health. This we pray in the name of Jesus Christ, who brought healing and wholeness to those who came to him with outstretched arms and open hearts. **Amen.**

If it is the custom of the congregation, the minister may anoint with oil each person requesting prayers, saying:

I anoint you in the name of our loving God, and of Jesus Christ, the great healer.

After the anointing, or in place of the anointing, the minister may place a hand on the person's head, or pray over the group, saying:

Let us pray: Eternal God, who sent Jesus Christ into the world to bring health and wellness to all, let your same power of healing now rest upon (*Name or Names*). Grant deliverance from illness and a return to health. Guide all physicians and other helpers who will care for your beloved child. We ask this in the mighty name of your blessed son, Jesus. **Amen.**

After a time of silence the minister gives a blessing:
May the God of peace be with you. And may your spirit,
mind, and body be made whole through the healing power
of God's love. **Amen.**

Suggested Hymns and Songs
(see hymnary.org or other sources as noted)

Bless the Lord, My Soul (Taizé Community)

Come, in Our Dark Time (Shirley Erena Murray, *A Place at
  the Table*, Hope Publishing Company and Hope Hymns
  Online)

God, Help Your Church to Learn (Sharon Allen, *My
  Child Is a Flower*, Hope Publishing Company and Hope
  Hymns Online)

Heal Me, Hands of Jesus (Michael Perry)

In Every Changing State of Mind (Daniel C. Damon)

Lord, in Our Lonely Hours (Fred Pratt Green)

O Lord, Hear My Prayer (Taizé Community)

There Is a Balm in Gilead (African American spiritual)

When My Life Feels Stripped of Meaning (Barbara Hamm,
  Hope Publishing Company and Hope Hymns Online)

Blessing for Those in a Chronic or Terminal Health Condition

As members of our congregations age, and as people live
longer in general, we will find ever more occasions for
giving spiritual care to those who are fragile, confined to
home, or enduring dementia or other conditions. More-
over, illness or accident can strike at any age. Many of
these are situations in which physical healing or return to
full health is not the expected outcome.

As ministers, whether ordained or lay, we will be asked to visit those who are dealing with these conditions, at home, in hospice care, or in a health facility. Often, the blessings and prayers we bring will benefit not only the one who is ill, but that person's family and caregivers as well.

Prayers

Loving God, who is beside us in all times and circumstances of our life, we pray today for (*Name*), that your constant presence will be fully evident through the hands and hearts of all who provide medical and spiritual care. Ease any pain or fear; calm and comfort body, mind, and spirit for (*Name*) and those who are anxious. Bring healing if it be your will. May this dear one rest in the assurance of your grace and mercy, and that you are near to all who call upon you in the time of trouble. Remind us all of the promise Christ made, who said, "Lo, I am with you always." We offer this prayer in the peace and hope that pass all understanding. **Amen.**

God of all suffering, healing, grace, and mercy:
During this time of prayer our hearts and minds are directed toward Jesus. As we remember the sacrifice and suffering he endured, we hold in thought and prayer those in our community (*or give the name or names*) who suffer daily from chronic, debilitating, or terminal conditions. Give (*them/him/her*) the strength and the willingness to bear this illness, Gracious God, but also the courage to continue to fight the good fight. Give the medical teams the wisdom and knowledge to care for them and to treat them with compassion and dignity. Guide also the family and

caregivers at this time of concern. We ask you, Heavenly Healer, to intercede on behalf of all who are ill so that they may feel your constant and loving presence. In the name of Jesus, the Great Physician, we pray. Amen.

—Karen Lee Deweese

All may pray together the Lord's Prayer:
Our Father (Creator) who art in heaven . . .

If desired, the one being prayed for may be anointed for peace and grace, or a hand may be laid upon the person's head while offering this blessing:
May the God of love be with you, calming your spirit and bringing you peace. Amen.

Blessing for Times of Trouble

Along with issues of physical health, our people may face serious concerns for mental health, addiction, relationship, finances, and other matters. Offering a ritual for these times of trouble can be quite powerful in the life of the one affected, and for their families as well. Giving time and the ministry of presence to listen actively, empathize, and console may offer a lifeline to someone in great need of respite from turmoil.

Anyone showing such pastoral care and concern may pray for the specific situation, followed by the Lord's Prayer, and then offer words of hope and blessing:
May the God of love be with you, calming your spirit and bringing you peace. Amen.

An Order for Taking the Lord's Supper to Those at Home or in the Hospital

After the regular observance of the Lord's Supper in worship, some churches follow the custom of taking the remaining bread and cup and sharing the elements with those who were unable to be present at that day's services. Similarly, a minister or lay team may schedule regular visits with those who are confined to home or a care facility, bringing the communion elements to share.

The minister or lay leader begins the worship with words similar to the following:
We bring you this bread and cup that have been set apart for remembrance and thanksgiving. As we eat and drink together, let us recall with gratitude our Savior Jesus Christ and pray that his presence will be made real to us here.

Let us pray: Gracious God, as we eat of this broken bread and drink of this cup, may Jesus Christ be made known to us. Through him may we receive that food and drink which is nourishment for our life today and for life eternal. **Amen.**

One or more of scripture selections may be read:
O taste and see the goodness of God;
    happy are those who dwell in the Holy One.
Hold God in awe, you faithful ones,
    for those who worship God will want for nothing.

—Psalm 34:8-9

O send out your light and your truth; let them lead me; let them bring me to your holy hill and to your dwelling. Then I will go to your altar, O God, to God my exceeding joy; and I will praise you. —Psalm 43:3-4

The cup of blessing that we bless, is it not a sharing in the blood of Christ? Because there is one bread, we who are many are one body, for we all partake of the one bread. —1 Corinthians 10:16-17

Other suitable scriptures include:
Psalm 116:12-14
Mark 14:17, 22-25
Luke 24:13-35
John 6:35, 51; 20:19-23
2 Corinthians 5:14-21

If desired, the readings may be followed by a few words from the minister or one of those participating.

The minister or deacon concludes with the words of the institution of the Lord's Supper:
On the night when he was betrayed, Jesus took a loaf of bread, and when he had given thanks, he broke it and said, "This is my body given for you. Do this in remembrance of me." In the same way he took the cup also, after supper, saying, "This cup is the new covenant in my blood. Do this, as often as you drink it, in remembrance of me." —1 Corinthians 11:23-25

Then the minister or lay leader gives an extemporaneous prayer of thanks or one of the prayers of remembrance and thanksgiving from Part 2, Gathering at Christ's Table.

Following the prayers, the minister or lay leader offers the bread to each person and says:

Take and eat the bread of life, giving thanks in remembrance of Jesus Christ.

After the bread has been eaten and there has been a moment of silence, the minister or lay leader hands the cup to each person and says:

Take this cup and drink, for it is the sign of the new covenant in Christ Jesus. Give thanks in remembrance of him.

After the cup has been shared and there has been a moment of silence, the minister or lay leader concludes the service with the Lord's Prayer and extemporaneous prayer, or as follows:

We thank you, loving God, for bringing us together here. In your presence, help us to remember not only Jesus Christ but also our fellow church members who have eaten of this bread and shared in this cup. Be gracious to them and to us, as we leave this time of communion. May each of us be witnesses to your love, and be strengthened in our faith as we journey forward with you. **Amen.**

The minister or lay leader may give a benediction:

And now may the blessing of God the Creator, Christ the Redeemer, and the living presence that is the Holy Spirit be with you this day and remain with you always. **Amen.**

PART 8

The Art of Worship Planning

Then let us all do what is right,
strive with all our might toward the unattainable,
develop as fully as we can the gifts God has given us,
and never stop learning.

—attributed to Ludwig van Beethoven

S A COLLECTION of resources for worship planners, a manual such as this is designed to be consulted both for regular Sabbath worship and for special occasions in the life of the congregation and church family members. I hope that the preceding chapters have helped guide you through these seasons and times and added to your repertoire of worship materials and ideas.

But beyond this book, how does one choose from the mass of materials available from a variety of sources? How do we create cohesive services that praise God and maintain "the unity of the Spirit in the bond of peace" (Ephesians 4:3)? Is worship planning an art? I believe it is. Here are a few personal reflections on learning and teaching this art.

When I was starting out in ministry while still a college student, almost my entire focus was on music in worship, particularly the music of the choir. Later, as a seminary student preparing for pastoral ministry, my theological studies on the history of worship and sacred music broadened that focus. My music ministry evolved, then, as I came to understand and embrace the centrality of congregational song in the hearts of the people.

I've loved hymns all my life, claiming the dual blessing of an upbringing in the Lutheran chorale tradition and an introduction to gospel, folk, and other hymn styles while in my twenties. Congregational song continues to expand its wealth of expression through the revival of chant and through praise music and other contemporary forms. The availability of hymns and songs via the Internet and such sites as hymnary.org, OneLicense.net, CCLI, and Hope Hymns Online brings an abundance of congregational song, both old and new, to worship planners, musicians, and pastors. Major hymnals are published every year, along with a multitude of smaller collections of sacred music for the people of God.

A wealth of resources exists not only for music but for a wide range of other worship and liturgical materials, both in online form and in print. Yet I find that relatively few pastors, musicians, and worship planners are aware of these tools. The students I teach are often astonished to find that such extensive resources are easily available for the task of creating worship services that speak to twenty-first-century Christians. Many of us still tend to rely on the tried and true—prayers, songs, and hymns of decades or centuries past. This is not to say that these historic materials don't have meaning and value for us today; many of them are timeless and deserve to be a continuing part of our worship. But the canon on hymnody and liturgy has never closed: words and music are constantly and thoughtfully being created, revised, and shared every day—if we'll just pay attention.

I invite you to consider a typical Sabbath worship service at your church. How long is it? One hour? Two? During those minutes—perhaps the only time that the majority of your church family is in one place together during a given week—what percentage of the service is given to the sound of just one or two voices: those of the pastor, the preacher, the worship leader? How often does the congregation speak with one voice, through unison prayer or responsive reading and scripture? How many songs and hymns are included in the service? Are the selections truly singable, or is your congregation playing a passive role while the musicians up front stand in as singers of the people's song? Does your worship embody spoken word and music that lifts up and reinforces a clear and challenging word from God to do justice, love mercy, and walk humbly? How often are other types of creative or embodied arts included, such as movement and dance, sign language, drama, and visual arts?

Throughout my life as a teacher, pastor, musician, and worship planner, I've become convinced that if the people trust and respect their leaders; if the congregation is given the chance to understand, participate in, and embrace change; and if that change is introduced in a thoughtful and well-timed manner, the community's worship can be gradually but steadily transformed—with the community's blessing. I'm talking not about the outward trappings but the heart of worship: God's word, the teachings of Jesus, and the continuing revelation of walking the Christian path while navigating an increasingly challenging world.

Here, then, is a method for worship planning, week by week and season by season, that can both enhance and deepen your congregation's experience as the Body of Christ.

Plan ahead. The *arc* or continuity of worship is significant. This means that the majority of what takes place in a given service has been planned ahead: what takes place is not a series of incidental episodes, but a sequence harmonized around a theme or idea. Nor does "planned ahead" imply that the arc of the service is specified to the last detail in advance; at its best such planning is intentional *and* open: attentive to the theme while leaving scope for the workings of the Spirit. Mindful planning brings freedom rather than confinement.

Start with the scriptures. Identify the passages that will be shared in the service, and which ones relate directly with the central message of the preached word. For those congregations that use a lectionary, these scriptures are available months, even years, ahead of time. The psalm of the day, the Hebrew Scripture reading, the Epistle, and the Gospel do not all have to be used in each service; we of the less-liturgical church traditions have abundant freedom in how we make use of a lectionary. Some churches, for instance, prefer to use the appointed readings only during certain seasons, such as Advent or Lent.

Many pastors wish to preach and focus upon their own choice of scripture each Sunday. Some choose a book of the Bible and preach through it, by chapter or passage. Others create a topic for several weeks, such as "The Good Shepherd," and draw on scriptures that speak to that theme. There are myriad choices for worship and preaching themes. The main point is this: allow the scriptural theme to be woven throughout the service, through the prayers and the music.

Collaborate on the music. Once you have your theme for a single Sunday, or for a series of Sundays, make a list of possible hymns and songs for the congregation to sing. Keep in mind that the people's song has been integral to Christian worship for hundreds of years, and with good reason. The word heard from scripture and pulpit can inform, challenge, edify, and be a primary source of spiritual formation. But it is the words we take into our own mouths, and lift up to God in the singing voice, that express our faith, hope, and love most fully. What your congregation will sing cannot be an afterthought! Work with the minister of music or choir director. Think together about other service music as well: solos, choral anthems, ensemble, and organ or other instrumental music. Not every piece has to express the theme of the day or season, but the more harmony you can bring to the arc of worship, the better. Get into the habit of working several weeks ahead.

Use a variety of resources. Scour the indices of the hymnal your congregation has in the pew. (Do you need to consider updating that hymnal? Quite possibly!) Look through any books of worship materials you own, as pastor or worship planner. Visit a website such as textweek. com, where you can search not only by the Sunday in the lectionary cycle but also by scripture passages. These will lead you to a wealth of commentaries, scripture studies, sermons, liturgies and prayers, hymn and song suggestions, materials for children, artwork on your theme, and more.

Frame the sermon. Since the worship in most of our free church traditions gives the preached word central focus, consider, in particular, how the sermon will be framed by the other elements of the service. Consider having the gospel lesson (or other sermon text) read and then followed by a hymn or song, anthem, or solo that retells the story or relates directly to the meaning of that scripture passage. Following the sermon, plan a congregational hymn that strongly underlines the message, highlighting the theme and calling the people to commitment.

Consider how the service will begin and end. How will you call the people to worship? What is the first music they will sing together? Will you include a psalm, read or sung? (I include one of the psalms in worship almost every Sunday of the year at some point in the service, but most often toward the beginning.) What is the mood or frame of mind that you would like to craft for your people when they first come together as a worshiping body and then as they depart? The final words of worship, both sung and spoken, should bring the service to an inspiring and hope-filled conclusion.

How does it flow? Finally, put it all together and then pay special attention to the flow, the most important consideration for the arc of worship. Do all things work together for the good, for your theme? Are your transitions from element to element graceful and clear? Are you avoiding the emcee syndrome: "Now we'll hear the scripture. Now we'll sing a hymn. Now we'll pray"? Over time you can train your congregation to be on their toes, liturgically speaking, and no longer needing someone to tell them what comes next at every point. Having a fairly consistent order of worship helps, but you also want to be able at times to move things within the basic structure—not to mention leaving room for the Holy Spirit. This is why, in Part 1, I advocate for the arc that flows episodically, but also thematically, from Opening Our Hearts for Worship, to Hearing and Proclaiming God's Story, to Offering Our Joys, Laments, and Thanks, to Going Out Praising God. Within that overall structure are plenty of possibilities for variation.

The connective tissue and nuance of a worship service can be provided in several ways: a printed order is, in my experience, the best way to show the entire service in a form the people can follow, so that all can know what to expect. In the interest of saving expense and being more eco-friendly, however, many churches now use screens at the front of the church to display the elements of worship. This can work well for announcements, biblical texts, sermon titles, and other items; it does not work well, however, in providing an overall sense of how worship will unfold. You might consider still providing a simple, one-page bulletin that is merely an order of worship, which illustrates the arc of the service and which may also be useful in orienting visitors and guests to your congregation's unique flow in worship.

Electronic devices are useful tools, certainly, but sometimes these technologies come with unintended consequences. Let us not allow the tools to eclipse the heart of worship, which is a human heart. For example, the ever more common practice of displaying on screen *only the texts* of hymns and songs, with no music available to the congregation, has two consequences. First, it may hinder worshipers in their ability to join in gathered singing, if a tune is unfamiliar or difficult to follow. Second, it may deny church members a historic gift that many of us received from the church—learning how to read music! If technologies are not supporting our people in learning to use their own voices in praise of God, then we also deprive our people and ourselves of an extraordinary joy.

My best advice, then, is this: Research and explore the current and ever-unfolding riches available, in print and online, for worship and music planning. Collaborate, bringing ministry staff and lay people together to learn more about the breadth and depth of possibilities for vital worship; go beyond your own practices and find out what other churches are doing. Borrow from neighbors, books, and websites and try new things, not as gimmicks but as opportunities to enliven and deepen your congregation's worship life. But always return to center, which is God's word—no Christian church ever went wrong by continual exploration and celebration of the word in worship, whether by song, proclamation, or prayer. Finally, be sure that you are always helping your people find their own voice, as worshipers and children of God.

This is our vocation, our sacred calling, and our joy, not only for the Sabbath but for every day of our lives. As Clement of Alexandria wrote in the second century,

All our life is like a day of celebration for us;
we are convinced, in fact, that God is always everywhere.
We work while singing, we sail while reciting hymns,
we accomplish all other occupations of life while praying.

May it be so!

Selected Resources for Worship Planning

textweek.com

Lectionary, scripture study, and worship links. Even if you don't follow a lectionary you can search by hundreds of scripture readings to find materials that relate to a chosen passage.

worship.calvin.edu

The Calvin Institute of Christian Worship website. The institute promotes the scholarly study of the theology, history, and practice of Christian worship and the renewal of worship in worshiping communities across North America and beyond.

hymnary.org
A comprehensive index of hymns and hymnals. In partnership with The Hymn Society (www.thehymnsociety.org), hymnary.org is one of the most complete databases of hymnody on the planet.

hopepublishing.com/hymnody
Hope Hymns Online, Hope Publishing Company. A resource that helps find many recently written congregational hymns and songs according to theme, scripture reading, and other search categories.

Music Licensing and Copyright Permissions

Observing copyright when using published music for worship is extremely important for the local church's integrity in the world. Usage licenses are generally available with affordable fees based on your church membership. Details about two companies that provide permissions and licenses for worship music can be found at:

onelicense.net

us.ccli.com (Christian Copyright Licensing International)